A Guidebook for Teaching
BIOLOGY

Harold J. McKenna
City College of New York

Marge Hand
Brentwood Public School System

Allyn and Bacon, Inc.   **Boston • London • Sydney • Toronto**

This book is part of A GUIDEBOOK FOR TEACHING Series

Library of Congress Cataloging in Publication Data

McKenna, Harold J.
  A guidebook for teaching biology.

  (A Guidebook for teaching series)
  Includes bibliographies.
  1. Biology—Study and teaching (Secondary) I. Hand,
Marge. II. Title. III. Series.
QH315.M45 1985   574′.07′12   84-14521
ISBN 0–205–08302–1

Printed in the United States of America

10 9 8 7 6 5 4 3 2 1 89 88 87 86 85 84

About the Authors

Harold J. McKenna is currently an associate professor of science/environmental education at the City College of the City University of New York. He has taught at the secondary school level in biology and general science, developed an environmental studies program for in-service teacher training, authored numerous articles and several books, and conducted in-service teacher training institutes sponsored by the National Science Foundation. He received the Ed.D. from Columbia University.

Marge Hand is currently a high school biology teacher in the Brentwood Public School System, Long Island, New York. She has taught at the middle and high school levels, in both traditional and alternative education programs, has been instrumental in developing an experimental program in appropriate technology for the environment, and has conducted in-service workshops at the City College of New York, where she is an adjunct instructor. She has written several articles in the field of science education and has developed and conducted workshops in sex education. She received the M.A. from the City University of New York.

Gene Standford, *Consulting Editor for the Guidebook for Teaching Series*, received his Ph.D. and his M.A. from the University of Colorado. Dr. Stanford has served as Associate Professor of Education and Director of Teacher Education Programs at Utica College of Syracuse University and is a member of the National Council of Teachers of English and the International Council on Education for Teaching. Dr. Standford is the author and co-author of several books, among them, *A Guidebook for Teaching Composition, A Guidebook for Teaching Creative Writing, A Guidebook for Teaching about the English Language,* and *Human Interaction in Education,* all published by Allyn and Bacon, Inc.

Contents

Preface

A Guidebook for Teaching Biology is designed to provide lessons that demonstrate the application of biological principles and concepts. Included are relevant content background and resources for developing student understanding of these significant biologic concepts and processes. The hundreds of classroom experiences, containing independent as well as group and class activities, are intended to reflect a variety of teaching strategies. It is impossible for biology teachers to use all of them, but a selective choice of strategies can add interest and effectiveness in their teaching of biology.

The activities include suggestions and Reproduction Pages for developing a basic understanding of the science of life. They contain laboratory and field skills, ideas for oral and visual projects, experiential exercises, role playing, small group activities, discussion questions, individual student investigations and research ideas, class assignments, information for teachers on how to teach particular concepts, and evaluation activities for assessing student achievements.

There are many so-called methods books on how to teach, this book is not meant to be one of them. It does not suggest rigid adherence to a specific instructional approach or the use of particular instructional materials. Teachers can select those activities and materials that best suit their own curriculum and teaching strategy. We hope the variety of activities, many innovative and others classic, presented in this book will tempt teachers to test them and encourage them to try new techniques as well.

The selections in each chapter of this *Guidebook* unavoidably reflect our own preference regarding the teaching of biology to secondary school students. We believe, for example, that students learn most effectively when they actively participate in the learning experience. There is a time and a need for individual, small group, and entire class work; for example, group activities facilitate the exchange of ideas and provide meaningful socializing experiences. Finally, we believe that in order for students to understand their world, they need to see, feel, smell, and taste aspects of the environment. Emphasis, therefore, has been placed on laboratory and field trip exposure so that each student can be immersed in the process of science.

In addition, keep in mind that the *Guidebook* is meant to supplement a basic text in biology. The authors, therefore, have attempted not to duplicate activities and materials commonly found in such texts.

The book discusses the evolutionary development of the external environment, as well as that of the internal environment and structure of life-forms. The central concept of this book, and, we believe, biology, is that of homeostasis: the maintenance of an organism's internal environment, which is different from the external environment. Both concepts are discussed separately, as well as interphased, in order to develop the trends in evolution from simple to complex. Each of the ten chapters includes:

1. An Introduction, which provides an overview of important themes and ideas for instruction.

2. A list of Performance Objectives for measuring students' achievements based on the methods and materials in the chapter, saving teachers the tedious job of writing objectives for lesson plans.

3. A brief Content Overview, which presents concepts not commonly found in a basic biology text. (This includes important issues current in biology, as well as conceptual models that reinforce the basic concepts students need to grasp in order to understand the working of nature.)

4. The body of the chapter, the Learning Experiences, which deals with the ideas and materials for student activities. Designed to stimulate interest and develop insight, they may be modified to fit almost any curriculum. An added feature is that they include Reproduction Pages that can be duplicated for student use. Located in the back of this book, these perforated pages will save teachers hours of preparation time.

5. A list of suggestions or additional activities for assessing student learning experiences. These include traditional teacher evaluation methods, such as writing an essay, as well as direct observation of laboratory and field skills, and the use of the Reproduction Page questions and diagrams.

6. An annotated list of resources, books, filmstrips, films, and other resources that can help the teacher. Appendix A lists the addresses of the producers of these resources.

Please note that in this book, in keeping with guidelines for nontechnical publications, names of organisms, unless stated in binomial nomenclature, are not capitalized.

Although much of the material in this book is derived from our own experience, we wish to acknowledge the contributions of Robert A. Bosco, biology teacher at the Deer Park public school system, Deer Park, New York, for his interest in this project and for offering recommendations and activities that he uses and finds meaningful, especially in the chapter on genetics.

A guiding force in the preparation of this book is a classic source book, *A Sourcebook for the Biological Sciences*, prepared several decades ago under the able leadership of three great science educators, Evelyn Morholt, Paul Brandwein, and

Alexander Joseph. This book is still available and highly recommended for the "bread and butter" activities needed to prepare solutions, slides, and students to learn biology.

Our thanks also to Maria Gross for her devoted service in typing the manuscript from hand-written pieces of paper and the time and interest she gave to the project. In addition, special thanks go to Bob Roen, former managing editor of the *Guidebook* Series, for his recommendations and interest in initiating our undertaking of this project.

Finally, for permission to reprint materials previously published, we wish to thank National Science Products, Inc., National Kidney Foundation of Southern California, and Millipore Corporation for excerpts from several of their important publications.

Harold J. McKenna
Marge Hand

1

Teaching Biology:
Let's Start at the Beginning

INTRODUCTION AND OUTLINE

A newborn infant, faced with the task of recognizing and understanding the innumerable variety of entities and experiences present in the world he or she has just entered, begins by separating what is internal from what is external. "What is me?" "What is not me?" This is evidenced as the child constantly touches and sucks toes and fingers, repeatedly confirming the double sensation. The basis of learning is found in this ability to separate and categorize: What is food? What is not food? What is a person? What is not a person?

Similarly, students, faced with the tremendous challenge of comprehending the infinite varieties and functions of life, find it beneficial to return to this basic pattern of learning, starting at the beginning. What is life, with its unique internal composition? What is not life—all the abiotic elements and qualities in the external environment. It is important to view each organism as a unique creature, moving, growing, interacting with everything about it external to itself, taking from these surroundings what is useful and rejecting or eliminating what is not—and all with the purpose of surviving, of preserving its own unique characteristics.

Such is the approach of this book: to present biology within the context of a large conceptual model, that of life-forms maintaining and reproducing a relatively stable, select internal environment within a larger and generally dissimilar external environment that is constantly undergoing change. This is the central concept of this book and a key concept in all of biology; it is termed *homeostasis*. Scientists believe that the steadier an organism's internal system, the more independent it is of the external environment and therefore the more highly evolved it is.

In order to maintain a certain internal environment, an organism constantly needs nutritional, gaseous, and liquid substances to replace those it has metabolized. It must have a system for ingesting these materials, as well as one for eliminating the waste

1

by-products. In multicellular organisms, there must be an internal transport system reaching each cell to bring in these essential nutrients while carrying out the waste products. The ingested substances may have to be broken down to a size and form suitable for cellular ingestion, and, in the case of higher life-forms, certain sense and motor organs may be required in order to obtain essential nutrients.

Besides maintaining the composition of the internal environment, organisms—in varying degrees—must maintain the physical and chemical characteristics of the internal environment: a certain temperature range, pressure, pH concentration, salinity, and so forth.

Chapters 2 to 5 of this *Guidebook* have been organized around the key concept of homeostasis, logically building on this principle to incorporate the evolution of the organ systems of higher forms of life. Chapter 2 focuses on the evolution of the external environment of earth compared to the internal environment of life-forms and discusses the essential needs of life-forms in order to maintain their internal environment, and thereby survive.

Chapter 3 presents the principles of ecology that maintain the external environment, and Chapters 4 and 5 discuss the systems developed by different organisms in order to obtain nutrients from their external surroundings and to process these raw materials into a form suitable for the maintenance of their internal milieu.

Chapter 6 discusses the different sensory systems present in organisms enabling them to function effectively in their environment.

The *Guidebook* then goes on (in Chapters 7 and 8) to discuss the survival of the species and how a species passes on a particular internal environment and structure to each of its offspring.

Since one way of understanding how a system functions is to watch it under adverse conditions, Chapter 9 discusses how life-forms function in extremely different abiotic environments: the ocean and outer space. It also describes how systems operate or fail to operate under adverse biotic conditions: diseases.

Chapter 10 concludes with controversial issues in biology that are affecting our present life-styles for good and ill and promise to revolutionize the future.

BIOLOGY: A WEB OF OVERLAPPING CONCEPTS

As with any other science, biology should develop objective thought processes through observation and reasoning. Some texts and teachers, however, present the course in such a way that it is a series of somewhat sequential facts, so disassociated from the everyday activities and functions of living organisms that students may feel that biology is uninteresting or not relevant. How absurd that the study of one's own body and how it functions could be irrelevant! That the study of life itself could be anything but fascinating! Yet some courses promote this feeling by failing to present factual information—such as parts of sensory organs or reproductive systems—within the context that makes them interesting and relevant: the adaptations of sense organs in different species to suit various environments or the courtship and mating behavior that blends with given reproductive systems.

For this reason, the *Guidebook* has attempted to present the science of life as a web of overlapping concepts and to show that the functioning of living things is based on a series of principles that determine how a particular organism will react in a given environment and whether it will survive. In this attempt, we have included numerous interesting examples that illustrate this conceptual model and have stressed another important theme that permeates this book: the evolutionary development of species in adjusting to their external environment. Individual organelles, organs, systems, and processes are all adaptations that evolved in a certain species because, under the dominion of the laws of the physical world, this particular adaptation was required for the species to live in a given environment for a given period of time. A simple example illustrating such an adaptation is that of the semipermeable membrane surrounding cells.

Living cells must take in oxygen and nutritional particles and expel carbon dioxide and other waste products produced during aerobic metabolism. If, however, the cell membrane allowed for a free flow of liquids, gases, salts, and other substances between the cell and its external environment, following the laws of diffusion, these substances would continue to move in or out of the cell until they were equally concentrated on both sides of the membrane. Since living cells need to maintain a relatively stable internal environment in order to survive, a semipermeable membrane evolved, allowing for a limited exchange of substances with the external environment, thereby meeting the transport needs of the cell without losing its distinct composition.

The presentation of conceptual illustrations such as this serves to awaken students' admiration and awe for the complexity of life and gives them a comprehensive understanding of biology within the context of the physical and chemical laws of nature. The depth of this understanding will be determined by the degree to which students relate the various principles demonstrated by different activities. For example, the link between a tick's affinity for butyric acid and its need for warm-blooded prey (Chapter 4) should be associated with the positive and negative taxes of lower animals that lead them to essential nutrients or away from toxic substances; the fact that starch does not pass through a semipermeable membrane in osmosis experiments (Chapter 2) should relate to the need for starch digestion by the enzyme amylase in order for it to be broken down into simpler molecules and absorbed by the body (Chapter 5). Encourage your students to make such connections as they undertake the many activities in this book.

DIVERSIFYING ACTIVITIES

Another way to make biology more personal is to involve your students in activities in which they can actually see biological principles at work. Many of the Learning Experiences are classroom experiments or demonstrations; some involve outdoor investigations and field trips. Even group or individual research projects on a topic of the students' own choice require a personal involvement that a lecture does not always elicit. By alternating hands-on activities with lectures, readings, and films, you can give your students a more interesting and comprehensive understanding of biology. Some activities contain technical material, and others are relatively simple. Choose activities that are appropriate for a given class or individual student.

The following pages contain some suggestions that we found helpful in carrying out specific types of activities.

Organizing a Field Trip

Except for the weather, the greatest factor in determining the success of a field trip is the degree of organization prior to the trip.

After personally checking out locations and choosing the one most suitable for studying a particular aspect of biology, begin by obtaining the proper permissions from school administrators and finding out which mode of transportation offers the greatest convenience at the lowest cost. In some school districts, applications for field trips must be submitted weeks or even months in advance. Allot enough time to prepare your students intellectually for the topics to be covered and to have them—and you—obtain the equipment and permissions necessary.

Prior to the trip, distribute and discuss information pertinent to the trip. This information should include such items as the goals of the study; the exact location, date, meeting, and return time and rain date for the trip; detailed travel directions; the total cost, including meals or a suggested lunch if food is not available; and required equipment—both personal, such as old shoes or rubber boots, and special equipment, such as plankton nets and first aid kits. It is wise to include a map of the area.

Other handouts should include directions, questions, and charts that facilitate the recording of data during the investigation. Assign different groups of students to perform various tasks, and be sure students know what is required of them—data, samples, diagrams—on their return. Although such organization is time-consuming on your part, it usually makes the day less emotionally draining, much more pleasant, and ensures some unique and memorable learning experiences for your students.

Laboratory Experiments

Whenever we approach the philosophy behind laboratory experiments, we are reminded of a lecture at a science conference in which the speaker gave a somewhat simplistic description of a typical experiment found in a traditional lab manual. A student is given five different-sized keys and a lock. The purpose of the experiment is to find out which key fits the lock. Although the student can see the answer immediately, he is told he must follow a scientific approach, trying each of the keys, writing the results, and finishing with a general conclusion. Although the illustration may contain a slight dose of cynicism, it succinctly embodies the redundance and closed-mindedness that turns students off. While a format for writing up an experiment is helpful, the format should be limited to information required to achieve the goal.

If students understand that the purpose of an experiment is not just to collect data but to find answers to specific questions, they are more likely to approach the experiment with a determined, enthusiastic attitude. You can help by suggesting questions and charts to record the information, but true learning takes place only if students can come to valid conclusions on their own.

One of the best ways to achieve this goal is to have students work in groups of four to six after the experiment is completed. (During the experiment, if equipment allows, it is best to have students work in groups of two to three.) Have students write their results in charts on the chalkboard, and ask them to make conclusions based on these results. Allow the different groups to state the logic of their conclusions, debate contradictory interpretations, and arrive at the set of conclusions the class deems most logical. If their conclusions are incorrect, ask questions that would reveal incongruities; if their data are inconclusive, you might encourage them to repeat the experiment or seek new information to clarify results. At all costs, do not just tell them their conclusions are wrong and offer the "correct" answers—even if they ask (and they will!). To do so would negate the value of doing the experiment and would serve only to lessen your students' confidence in their ability to make judgments.

During the analysis of data, encourage students to use mathematical tools such as graphs and histograms to arrive at conclusions. For example, in Activity 11 of Chapter 8—arriving at the genetic ratio that shows the dominance of purple color in corn kernels—students could graph each group's results of the number of purple kernels versus the number of white ones. Such a graph should not only result in an approximate linear relationship showing a 3:1 proportion but should also indicate if one or two groups obtained results inconsistent with the general findings of the class.

Responsibility for equipment used during experiments should be delegated to students as much as possible. You might appoint individuals to hand out very fragile or expensive equipment and to place other equipment in a location readily available to students. Individuals may be given extra credit for making sure chemicals, glassware, thermometers, and other materials are properly replaced, cleaned, and accounted for. The more you delegate such tasks, the more responsibility students develop and the more it frees you to observe and guide students in developing proper techniques and attitudes in a safe, enjoyable way.

Small Group Activities

The group setup and delegation of authority described in laboratory experiments may be expanded to facilitate overall classroom management and to develop independence, judgment, and healthy social interaction in your students. Some educators advocate setting up the classroom so that the class is divided into several groups of four or five who act as a unit in completing activities. Once instructions are given, individuals are encouraged to seek help from other group members rather than the teacher. Students work on the project, reading or investigating together, and arrive at joint conclusions. The teacher may decide to have each student make a copy of the results or to have one paper submitted from the entire group. Some teachers even assign a group member to keep records in a group folder of homework, tests, and other materials so that each member is aware of how she or he is doing and any work that is missing. Group points for completing projects, taking care of equipment, bringing in required materials, and so forth are usually used as a motivational technique. Such points may be used in assessing class participation marks.

Although the system has some dubious effects, such as heightening an atmosphere of competition and at times frustrating studious pupils who are working with some less studious, the idea has been tried and effected some very positive results. Students became much more productive and independent, asking less questions dealing with obvious answers or instructions already stated. They were encouraged to evaluate their own interaction and eventually changed many negative patterns of interacting and worked more effectively as group. Problem students were often encouraged through group pressure to be more productive, and discipline-type problems were lessened. Although such a system initially requires a great deal of organizing by the teacher, once implemented, it frees the teacher from many of the more mundane tasks related to teaching and offers students an opportunity to grow emotionally as well as academically.

Controversial Issues

True education is the development of the whole child, and although schools have emphasized academic development, educators have long realized the need to affect students' attitudinal development. While we feel it is important for educators not to impose their own value systems on their students, we do think it is important for students to look at new trends in biology and to see how these fit into their own values and philosophy system. Too often adolescents—and adults—allow society and "fate" to make decisions for them. What this often comes down to is an individual not making a decision or taking action until events occur that eliminate most choices. Such trends in modern society as teenage pregnancy and suicide often stem from individuals' not evaluating their own actions and attitudes and taking more control of their own lives. Other trends, such as genetic engineering, although they are not within the realm of the average person's power, will affect each individual and so must be studied and evaluated as beneficial or destructive within the student's own framework of values. Individuals may then use their own political power to encourage or discourage such trends.

Although these controversial issues have been grouped together in Chapter 10 for treatment purposes, we advise interspersing them when studying related topics; for example, genetic engineering may follow an activity on DNA.

For most teachers, the questions of community involvement and curricular decision making are of less immediate concern than problems of teaching strategies. The prospect of approaching students with controversial material can be almost frightening. The teacher may ask, "How can I be sure to offer my students the pros and cons of an issue in a balanced presentation? How can I keep students, whose emotions may become overwhelming, on a reasonable, and logical train of thought? How should I respond to questions about my own values?"

To answer these questions, teachers can use a teaching technique of small group learning circles. (You may want to use this discussion technique initially to motivate the students to research more information, or you may want to use the technique to ascertain results after an activity.) Divide students into four to six pupils per group to promote interaction. The traditional seating structure in the classroom needs to be altered so that students can sit in a circle and interact facing one another to discuss the issue at hand. Be sure that all students in each circle have an opportunity to express their ideas and feelings.

Once these groups are in operation, it is important that you remain neutral. You may be tempted to point out to the groups the "right way to think out the issue," but such an approach cannot promote intellectual growth of students. To stimulate discussion and thinking on an issue, you need to offer unbiased, carefully-thought-out questions that will encourage students to examine critically all views that are presented in the discussion of the issue. Avoid offering comments indicating either approval or disapproval. If students are willing to contribute their ideas and concerns about the issue, they should be honored with comments such as "thanks for that idea" or "I never thought of it that way."

Enthusiasm is often contagious, so it is helpful if teachers display some enthusiasm and personal familiarity with the issue. Avoid giving information that students can obtain from written material or from each other. During the discussion, try to be more of a group member than an authority figure. After the initial discussion, direct the students to sources of information, such as the library, making sure that both sides of the issue are researched, or have copies of relevant articles on hand. In a follow-up discussion, ask students if they have any new ideas or have changed any opinions. They may wish to debate the issue again.

In preparing to discuss a controversial issue, we have found it helpful to list various aspects of the issue on a piece of paper, making two columns: the pros of the issue and the cons. If the pros greatly outweigh the cons, or vice-versa, ask students to research opposing views from updated textbooks, journal articles, and other materials. Once they have searched out all the possible pros and cons of the issue available, have them evaluate each in terms of their own biases. In this way, they can gain a clearer understanding of the topic.

After the various aspects of an issue are brought forth in a discussion, allow individuals to form their own conclusions, if there are any to be made. If students exhibit a great deal of conviction about certain controversies, you might encourage them to discuss what actions can be taken based on their conclusions.

RESOURCES FOR TEACHING

Following is a selected list of materials and resources for teaching biology. These materials and those in other chapters are meant to update and supplement the extensive bibliographies that exist in most teachers' guides. Addresses of publishers and supply houses for films and filmstrips can be found in Appendix A at the end of this book.

Books, Articles, and Pamphlets

BSCS, *Feeling Fit,* Human Sciences Program, National Science Programs. A curriculum study produced for use at the junior high school level on human health issues.

Doran, Rodney L., *Measurement and Evaluation,* NSTA. An excellent account on assessing the cognitive, psychomotor, and affective outcomes in science instruction.

Geswein, Karen G., and Frederick J. Geswein, *Health Education Puzzles and Puzzlers,* J. Weston Walch. Contains numerous crossword puzzles, word searches, and similar material in the areas of health and biology.

Guyton, Arthur C., *Physiology of the Human Body,* Saunders. An excellent resource textbook which, although written at the college level, explains basic biological principles and concepts in a clear, logical manner.

Harms, Norris C., and Robert E. Yager, eds., *What Research Says to the Science Teacher,* NSTA. An excellent compilation of articles from leading researchers on the trends in science education in the 1980s.

Hickman, Cleveland, et al., *Integrated Principles of Zoology,* Mosby. A comprehensive, updated text on the principles of zoology in a well-developed, conceptual presentation that contains numerous interesting illustrations.

Hickman, F. ed., *New Directions in Biology Teaching,* NABT. A compilation of articles on issues in biology and science education from the writings of leading science educators.

Kahle, Jane, *Teaching Science in Secondary School,* D. Van Nostrand. An excellent methodology text discussing the latest trends in science curricula, as well as various teaching strategies.

Morholt, Brandwein, Joseph, *A Sourcebook for the Biological Sciences,* Harcourt Brace Jovanovich. A unique compilation of techniques for biological demonstrations and laboratory lessons.

Nickelsburg, Janet, *Fieldtrips: Ecology for Youth Leaders,* Burgess. A brief but comprehensive guide for teachers wishing to conduct nature field trips.

2

Beginnings

INTRODUCTION

This chapter examines the evolution of the external environment and how the internal environment of living creatures evolved, how it remains distinct from the external environment in higher animals, and how, amid the constant flux caused by body metabolism, organisms use substances from their surroundings to maintain the equilibrium of this internal milieu. These considerations are all encompassed in the key concept of *homeostasis.*

It is advisable to discuss the "big bang" and protoplanet theories prior to introducing theories on the inception of life on earth. This content does not readily lend itself to classroom demonstrations; however, the readings and field trips included in the Learning Activities, might elucidate or relate to the concepts.

In presenting the evolution of the internal environment of higher animals, we strongly recommend that you view and show in your class the film *Hemo the Magnificent,* a Bell Telephone Production. Although an old film, it remains one of the best on the topic.

In order to comprehend the regulatory strategies that ensure the stable internal environment of life-forms, students must have a thorough understanding of the concepts of diffusion and osmosis. While Learning Activities are distinct and may be arbitrarily chosen, the activities on diffusion and osmosis form a basis for many of the succeeding activities. We suggest you do at least one or two of these initially. In explaining to students the function of sophisticated regulatory systems, it is convenient to begin, as evolution did, with marine life and move on to terrestrial organisms.

The activities following those on osmosis have been divided into chemical and physical changes in the environment—the former involving changes in salinity, water balance, and pH and the latter dealing with changes in pressure and temperature.

An important aspect of homeostasis is the selectivity of life-forms in choosing which materials from the external environment are to be ingested in order to replace those metabolized. Are essential nutrients the same for all organisms? A discussion of the basic food nutrients essential to humans follows naturally at this point. An abundance of information and experiments on the topic can be found in all introductory biology texts. Stress that the nutritional value of food is greatly affected by the way in which it is processed, stored, and prepared.

After completing Chapter 2, students should understand that homeostasis is dynamic rather than static. Through it, constancy of composition is maintained despite the continuous shifting of components within the system. Once students understand the concept, mention that homeostasis is maintained by the coordinated activities of numerous body systems, such as nervous and endocrine systems, and especially by the organs that serve as sites of exchange with the external environment, among them the lungs or gills, kidneys, alimentary canal, and skin. The specific functions and structures of these systems are covered in Chapter 5.

PERFORMANCE OBJECTIVES

As a result of the Learning Experiences in this chapter, students should be able to:

1. Describe the heterotroph hypothesis on the beginning of living things.

2. Define and give several examples of homeostasis.

3. Describe and illustrate some problems in maintaining the salt and water balance in plants and animals.

4. Describe and illustrate the effects of pressure and temperature changes in the environment on plants and animals.

5. Identify six adaptive mechanisms found in plants and animals that are involved in homeostasis.

6. Describe and illustrate the effects of acidic or alkaline environments on plants and animals.

7. Demonstrate the pH parameters of an organism by placing it in environments varying in degrees of acidity and alkalinity.

8. Identify and describe a nutritionally sound balanced diet.

CONTENT OVERVIEW

External Evolution

Proposed explanations of how life arose occur in the mythology and religious literature of most of the world's populations, as well as in scientific papers. Some of these theories include the following:

1. Life on earth was supernaturally created.

2. Life on earth is of extraterrestrial origin.

3. Complex living things can arise from nonliving material, referred to as spontaneous generation.

4. Primordial life could have arisen spontaneously, under favorable conditions, from the abiotic materials of the primeval earth and its atmosphere. This is the modern theory of abiogenesis, or the heterotroph hypothesis.

A review of the accepted hypothesis can be undertaken by referring to A. I. Oparin's work, found in textbooks and articles on evolution.

Homeostasis

After the external environment had begun to achieve a balance whereby autotrophic life-forms replenished oxygen and produced food needed by heterotrophic forms, while the latter produced needed carbon dioxide, it remained for these simple life-forms, and later more complex species, to achieve a stable internal environment. This dynamic internal equilibrium, termed *homeostasis,* is a key factor in understanding the purpose or function of every life activity, every organ, and every organ system of each species.

Homeostasis may be likened to an organism's having a certain carrying capacity for specific substances in its internal environment. Different species have different amounts of varying substances. When a given molecule is broken down and eliminated from a cell, a new molecule of the substance is absorbed through the membrane. For example, if the blood of a vertebrate has too much water or salt, the kidney removes the substance from the blood and excretes it in the urine. Very sophisticated systems are at work in each organism to help that organism maintain a relatively stable internal environment, chemically and physically. In order to replace metabolized substances, animals must have a way of ingesting and assimilating new materials present in their surroundings while eliminating waste products from their bodies. During this constant exchange of materials, how does the organism withstand the continuous fluctuations in temperature, pH, pressure, chemical composition, and other factors found in the external environment?

Animals survive in the sea by adopting one of two strategies: either they allow free exchange between the environment in which they live and their blood and body fluids, or they evolve mechanisms such as impervious shells or coverings to insulate their special internal chemical composition from their environment. Lower animal groups from protists to starfish usually adopt the former, while higher groups, such as lobsters, worms, and marine vertebrates, evolved mechanisms for preserving a stable internal chemical composition different from seawater. Certain internal physical characteristics, such as a specific body pressure, also must be maintained by these higher animals, and some—such as marine mammals—must preserve a stable body temperature as well.

Since students might assume that lower organisms have a wide tolerance for variables because they permit a free exchange with their environments, point out that most of these organisms live in surroundings that have very stable chemical and physical components (such as the ocean) and that if there was a drastic change, many of these organisms would die. While these organisms do not possess the mechanisms of higher organisms to preserve a stable internal environment, the stability of the external environment ensures this preservation.

Chemical Changes in the Environment: Maintaining Salt and Water Balance

Animals, especially those living in a water medium, must maintain a stable salt concentration in their body fluids. All vertebrates, whether aquatic, terrestrial, or aerial, maintain salt concentrations of body fluids at about one-third that of seawater. Some coastal invertebrates and all freshwater fish are, therefore, hyperosmotic regulators; marine fish, on the other hand, are osmotic regulators. Most marine invertebrates are osmotic conformers.

In higher animals, the balance of salt and water is maintained by means of such structures as glomeruli in the kidneys, special salt-excreting or salt-absorbing cells in gill membranes and skin, and salt-excreting glands located between the eyes of marine birds and reptiles. This last structure accounts for the clear fluid often seen dripping from the beak of marine birds and the copious "tears" shed by female turtles while laying eggs.

Marine mammals are able to drink seawater because their kidneys produce urine that is more concentrated than the surrounding seawater. Humans lack this ability since the human kidney produces urine of a lower concentration of salt than seawater.

The concentrating ability of the kidneys of some desert animals, such as the kangaroo rat, is so high that they can live indefinitely on a diet of dry cereal grains without ever drinking water. They live on the water liberated during metabolism of their foodstuffs.

Physical Changes in the Environment: Pressure Stabilization

Whales are able to withstand drastic changes in pressure without experiencing the negative effects encountered by scuba divers because these marine mammals have evolved several marvelously suited adaptations.

First, they do not breathe compressed air. Whales submerge with only the nitrogen contained in one deep breath, and it is dissolved in the body fluids at only a fairly low pressure. As the whale descends, the increasing pressure on its body flattens the thorax and squeezes the lungs. As the lungs collapse, air is forced out of them into the thick-walled windpipe and bronchial tubes where it cannot be absorbed. This process reduces the nitrogen absorption until, at 100 meters depth, the lungs are completely collapsed and absorption is eliminated. Scientists believe that some of the nitrogen is also absorbed by the oily foam in the complex air sacs and may be released during exhalation.

A whale can survive a long dive—a maximum of over 1 hour for sperm whales—on only one deep breath for several reasons. The whale's lungs are surprisingly small for the mammal's size; however, they carry only about one-tenth of the oxygen stored for use in a dive. In a human diver without apparatus, one-third of the oxygen is stored in the lungs. In whales, most of the oxygen is stored in the muscles where it is bound to myoglobin, a substance related to hemoglobin. (This myoglobin accounts for the almost black meat found in diving animals.) To offset the limited supply, the whale's use of oxygen during the dive is conserved by the almost complete shutdown of inessential body activities. The heartbeat slows down (from 60 to 30 beats per minute in the killer whale), and the blood circulation supplies only the vital functions of the heart and nervous system. The swimming muscles function without oxygen, receiving energy from anaerobic respiration. The resulting lactic acid is stored until the whale surfaces. The whale immediately inhales fresh oxygen, breaking down the lactic acid to form water and carbon dioxide that is exhaled through the spout.

LEARNING EXPERIENCES

External Environment

1. In discussing with students the beginnings of life, there are many good articles that should be read in class and followed with discussions. Passages from A. Oparin's *Life: Its Nature, Origin and Development* (Academic Press) are especially good in this regard.

2. There are many good filmstrips and films available to introduce students to the evolution of the earth and life. Some we recommend are:

   a. *Journey into Time* (14 min.), Sterling.

   b. *Life, Time and Change* (set of 12 films, 28 min. each), AIBS Film Series in Modern Biology.

   c. *Our Changing Earth* (13 min.), Film Associates.

   d. *The World Is Born* (20 min.), Disney.

   e. *Story in the Rocks* (18 min.), Shell Oil Company.

3. Another interesting way of explaining the beginnings of life is to visit a museum with natural history exhibits. Seeing many prehistoric organisms may add to the visual education of the students. Discussion of the size of these organisms and reasons for their extinction are interesting topics.

4. A good demonstration that elicits class interest is showing students how a simple autotroph, such as green algae, might have arisen from a heterotroph. By means of such an activity, students can see that organic substances introduced into a sterile culture of algae will be assimilated directly. Place in separate sterile test tubes a culture of nostoc (a blue-green algae) and a culture of spirogyra (a green algae). Add organic compounds (any containing carbon, hydrogen, or nitrogen oxide) and place both test tubes in a dark place for several days or weeks. Observe growth and other visible factors. Compare the cultures. You should note that both will assimilate the organic material and that spirogyra survives without sunlight. You may wish to set up an experiment to compare this set with another set placed in sunlight.

5. A demonstration showing anaerobic metabolism in a heterotroph is to place a blue-green algae, such as nostoc, in a test tube with sterilized organic compounds. One way to obtain this condition is to add a few drops of a vegetable oil to the test tube containing the nostoc and organic compounds submerged in water. The purpose of using the oil is to prevent additional oxygen from entering the setup. Observe over several days or weeks that the plant is able to survive without additional oxygen.

6. Primitive environments can be seen in the field, such as a marsh or swamp. Take the class on a trip to such a community. If you observe a "pond" within these communities, you can probably collect organisms that are primitive in nature, and you should be able to smell hydrogen sulfide being generated by the blue-green algae and anaerobic bacteria. This might have been the start of the early earth in its movement toward evolving higher forms of life. Collect samples and study them under the microscope in the lab.

7. You may wish to visit a local sewage treatment plant in which anaerobic organisms are used to decompose sludge. Discussion of this process can be brought into focus with the start of life on earth.

8. A visit to a nearby planetarium might afford the opportunity to see a show on the "big bang" theory of how the earth was created from a gaseous cloud. This visual demonstration is one that has interested students for many years.

9. For more able students, discuss a classic paper by M. Calvin, "Chemical Evolution and the Origin of Life," *American Scientist* 44 (July 1956): 248–251.

10. Have students plan a short debate on the theories of evolution versus creationism. This should spark good discussion and come to grips with the reality of what science is all about. (See Chapter 10 on controversial issues.)

Chemical Changes: Diffusion and Osmosis

11. In order to elicit the interest of students in the concept of osmosis, discuss with them the following questions: Do all animals obtain needed water by means of drinking through their mouths? What do sponges do in this regard? How do roots in plants take in water? If water can be absorbed through membranes, why don't animals lose all their body fluids through their skin? How do plants and lower animals prevent unwanted substances, such as dirt, germs, and toxic materials, from entering their bodies? Discuss the advantages of a semipermeable membrane and the principle of osmosis.

    The following demonstrations are excellent visual presentations of diffusion and osmosis through a semipermeable membrane.

12. Prepare Lugol's iodine solution by dissolving 10 g of potassium iodide in 100 ml of distilled water; then add 5 g of iodine. Pour diluted Lugol's solution into a large test tube, cover the test tube with a wet goldbeater's membrane, and secure the membrane with a rubber band. Now invert the test tube into a beaker containing a 1 percent starch paste, as shown in Fig. 2.1. Prepare a second setup in the same manner, but this time place the starch paste in the

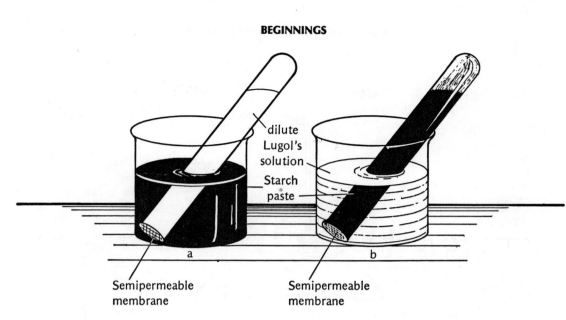

dilute
Lugol's
solution

Starch
paste

a   b

Semipermeable   Semipermeable
membrane   membrane

Figure 2.1.   Diffusion setup.
Molecules of iodine solution (Lugol's) pass through the semipermeable
membrane, while the starch does not. The black color appears in the starch
solution but not in the iodine solution.

test tube and the iodine solution in the beaker. Have students note that molecules of the iodine solution pass through the membrane, while starch does
not, as shown by the characteristic blue-black color that appears in the starch
solution and not in the Lugol's solution in the beaker in (a) and in the test
tube in (b). The starch is insoluble and therefore needs to be digested to
diffuse through a membrane.

13. A similar demonstration to show the diffusion of salt through a membrane
may be performed using copper sulfate solution (blue) and distilled water.

14. The following setup demonstrates the principle of osmosis: Pour heavy
molasses into the bulb of a thistle tube while covering the tube opening with
your finger. Then cover the bulb with a wet semipermeable membrane (goldbeater's) and invert it into a beaker of water. Clamp the tube, as shown in Fig.
2.2, to hold it in place. Water in the beaker will diffuse rapidly through the
membrane, causing the level of molasses in the thistle tube to rise. The water
is moving from a higher concentration through a membrane to a lower concentration, a process called *osmosis*.

15. A similar setup using a raw potato may be used to show the passage of water
through the semipermeable membranes surrounding the living cells of the
potato. Using an apple corer, remove a center cylinder of a raw white potato.
Leave about a ½ in. thickness at the bottom of the potato. Fill the cavity with a
concentrated sucrose solution and cover the opening with a one-hole rubber
stopper through which a piece of glass tubing has been inserted. (See Fig. 2.3.)
Place the potato in a beaker of water, as shown in Fig. 2.3, using a clamp to
hold the tube upright. Melted paraffin may be used to seal the stopper. Water
will diffuse through the membranes of the cells in the potato to the cavity and
rise in the tube, carrying some of the sucrose with it.

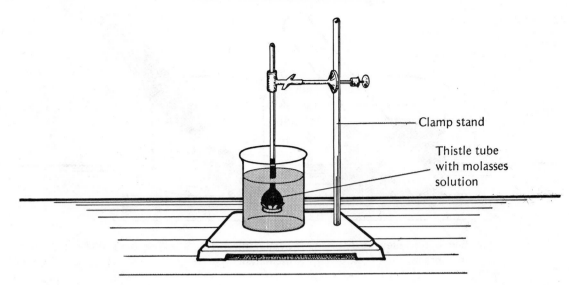

Figure 2.2. Osmosis demonstration.
Water in the beaker diffuses through the goldbeater membrane attached to
the end of the thistle tube, causing the level of molasses in the tube to rise.

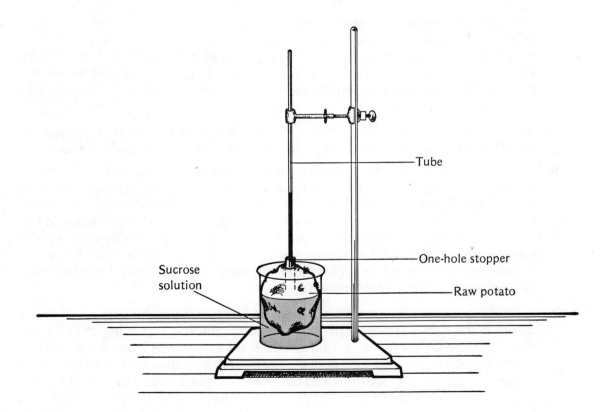

Figure 2.3. Raw potato diffusion setup.
The cavity in the potato is filled with sucrose solution. The water diffuses
through the cell membranes of the potato to the cavity and rises in the tube,
carrying some of the sucrose solution.

Salt and Water Balance

16. After demonstrating the principles of diffusion and osmosis through a semi-permeable membrane, discuss how plants and animals effectively use these principles in obtaining water through root hairs or outer membranes. Discuss some of the problems that plants and animals might encounter because of these principles; examples are loss of needed water in a medium of high salt concentration or the absorption of too much water in a dilute medium.

    Have students prepare a wet slide of onion or elodea cells. Instruct students to observe the cells under the microscope, blot the water surrounding the cells, and replace the liquid with a few drops of highly concentrated salt solution. Then they can watch the cells react. Ask why the cells shriveled or dehydrated.

17. To show how differing concentrations of salt affect osmosis in plant cells, have students cut three slices from a small potato and place one slice in each of three labeled beakers. Use cross-section slices about 0.5 cm thick. Beaker 1 should contain 100 ml of distilled water, Beaker 2 100 ml of a 1% salt solution, and Beaker 3 100 ml of a 5% salt solution. Instruct the students to soak the slices for about 10 minutes and then feel each slice. Note how the slices in Beakers 2 and 3 feel spongier and more flexible than the slice in Beaker 1. Ask why the control slice is more rigid. Relate this result to plants wilting when they are not watered.

18. How do animals survive in media of differing salt concentrations? To introduce the lesson, explain to students that shipwrecked survivors sitting in a lifeboat surrounded by seawater can die of thirst if freshwater is not available. Then ask why marine vertebrates—most of which have salt concentrations in their body fluids similar to humans—can drink seawater and live. What are the varying mechanisms that animals have evolved in order to maintain a stable water and salt concentration internally in the face of differing amounts of water and salt present in the external environment? Discuss the different problems faced by freshwater animals, marine animals, and shore invertebrates. Use the diagram on Reproduction Page 1 to contrast the problems and adaptations found in freshwater and marine fish. Mention the specialized glands or cells present in turtles, marine birds, and amphibians. Since the ability of the kangaroo rat, a desert rodent, to go without drinking water is so unique, students usually find the table on Reproduction Page 1 fascinating. After discussing the various methods animals have of maintaining salt and water balance, have students fill in the answers in Column B. (Answers: (1) salt gland between eyes; (2) smaller glomeruli and special salt-excreting cells in gills; (3) smaller glomeruli and solid urine; (4) active transport through gills; (5) salt gland between eyes; (6) active transport through skin.)

pH Tolerance

19. Review the pH scale as a measurement of hydrogen ion concentration and discuss the differences between acids and bases. Explain how homeostasis also involves maintaining a stable pH concentration within the cells of an organism.

Have students prepare a microscope slide of plant cells from the tip of an elodea leaf. After they observe the cyclosis in the cells using a compound microscope, add several drops of vinegar or acetic acid. Use a piece of towel at the other end of the cover slip to act as a wick drawing the acid through the cells. Note the effect on the cells. When the cells die, cyclosis ceases.

Repeat the experiment, this time adding several drops of dilute ammonium hydroxide. Again observe what happens in the cells.

20. Yeast cells can tolerate a pH range of about 4.5 to 8.5. The following demonstration is an excellent way of showing the effects on yeast if the limitations of this range are exceeded. Discuss the ability of yeast to produce alcohol through the fermentation of sugar. Mention that carbon dioxide gas is a by-product of this process. Set up three 250 ml Erlenmeyer flasks. In one, pour 200 ml of vinegar (about 3.4 pH); in another, 200 ml of distilled water (about 7.0 pH); and in the third, 200 ml of ammonia water (about 11.1 pH, purchased in a supermarket). To each flask add 20 g of glucose and 2 g of yeast. Cover each flask with a one-hole stopper containing a glass bend, and connect rubber tubing to each. The other end of each tubing should be placed in separate test tubes containing limewater. Place the flasks on a hot plate, and gently heat them for several minutes. As fermentation takes place, carbon dioxide will bubble into the limewater and turn it milky. Note that yeast functions best in the water since a pH of 7.0 is within its tolerance range. For more colorful results, you can use a bromthymol blue indicator in each test tube and note which setup shows the greatest color change. The rate of bubbling is also in direct proportion to the amount of fermentation taking place. Be sure the amount of glucose, yeast, and heat is the same in each setup to ensure valid results.

21. Using Reproduction Page 2, have students determine the pH tolerance of an ameba. Ask students first to view the amebas under a microscope, noting the action of cyclosis and their method of mobility. Be sure you have a viable sample of amebas; sometimes samples from supply houses do not survive shipment. Elicit from students the fact that cyclosis is evidence of living amebas. If students have not done Activity 20, explain that each organism has a specific tolerance range for pH and that they will find the ameba's range by placing samples in solutions of differing pH values. (See Reproduction Page 2 for possible solutions to use.) Encourage students to determine what tests or controls are needed in order to obtain valid results. Explain the use of a universal indicator, and be sure the pH values of solutions have been checked before use. Have students record their data on Reproduction Page 2 and begin testing the samples in the various solutions. Students should place a small sample of the amebas on a slide and blot the excess water before adding several drops of the solution. Note that there will be a small amount of dilution. Again observe the ameba under the microscope to see the effect. After students have recorded all the data on the Reproduction Page, they should discuss their results. By figuring the average pH values on both ends of the range, students can determine the most valid approximation of the ameba's pH tolerance. Students should find the ameba able to tolerate a pH range of about 4.2 to 8.2.

22. Once students have learned that organisms have specific parameters for different variables, the role of tropisms and taxes in directing an organism toward a suitable environment or away from a toxic one is a natural progression. This enables students to understand how separate systems work for the good of the whole organism and provides background and an excellent connection to animal responses covered in Chapter 6.

   The following is a simple experiment showing a positive and negative taxis in the paramecium. In the first part of the experiment, demonstrating a positive chemotaxis, food materials diffuse through a culture medium; paramecium respond by swimming toward the food. Mount a drop of culture fluid containing some debris, and examine it under the microscope. Students will find the protists clustered around the food materials. To show a negative chemotaxis, soak a bit of thread in dilute hydrochloric acid. Then place the thread across a drop of thick culture of paramecia mounted on a slide. View the slide under the microscope, or hold it against a dark background. You will see a cleared area around the thread, showing that the paramecia have moved away from the acid. Discuss with students how these responses are necessary to the survival of the paramecium.

   Ask students to find out what happens when they bring a cotton applicator dipped in ammonium hydroxide near an earthworm. Have them interpret their results.

Physical Changes

PRESSURE

23. The following activity may take two class periods, the first dealing with the inability of a human diver to adapt to pressure differences in the ocean and the second showing how a whale is adapted to move through vast differences in pressure in minutes without harmful effects. Begin by asking students what can happen to a scuba diver who dives too deeply or surfaces too quickly. Most students have only a vague idea of why a person gets the bends, nitrogen narcosis, or other diving-related problems. To simplify the explanation, draw a diagram on the blackboard indicating the increase in pressure—14.7 lbs. per sq. in. or 1 atmosphere of pressure for every 33 ft. of descent. Discuss what the pressure would be at a depth of 100 or 200 ft. Ask how that compares with the normal air pressure in a person's lungs. Then discuss how the diver's air regulator equalizes the internal pressure with that of the ocean. Finally, pose the problem of the diver's surfacing too quickly, with body fluid and air in the lungs still at relatively high pressures. Suddenly, he or she is surrounded by water at a much lower pressure, causing the air in his or her lungs to expand and releasing the gases—especially nitrogen—that were dissolved in body fluids under high pressures. You might compare this to bubbles of carbon dioxide rising from a bottle of soda when the cap is removed. Discuss the possible dangers that these pockets of nitrogen can cause.

   On the second day, review the dangers that scuba divers face, and ask how marine mammals, such as the sperm whale, can dive hundreds of feet and surface in a matter of minutes without risking the bends. Allow students to hypothesize their own ideas. Then discuss the various adaptations whales have evolved to produce such a unique diving ability. Students will be fascinated by the sperm whale, which has been found to reach depths of over 3,000 ft. and remain submerged for over an hour. Remind students of the pressure at that depth and the fact that the whale does not breathe while submerged. Then describe how the whale conserves and stores oxygen during dives. You might conclude the lesson by encouraging students to find out if dolphins, porpoises, and other sea mammals have the same adaptations.

TEMPERATURE

24. Another internal physical characteristic that some animals must maintain is a certain body temperature. Introduce the lesson by reviewing the concepts of warm-blooded and cold-blooded animals and asking students how warm-blooded animals sustain a warm internal temperature (such as 98.6° F in humans) amid a cold environment. Since students often think only of insulation—such as clothing in humans or fur in animals—as a means of maintaining body temperature, clarify the problem by presenting a similar situation with a nonliving substance. For example, ask students how they could keep a quart of soup hot in a cold environment without using external heat. Is there any insulation that would totally prevent heat loss? Yet warm-blooded animals constantly maintain a certain body temperature; therefore, there must also be an internal source of heat. This source is cellular respiration.

   The following demonstration is a simple way of proving that heat is constantly being generated through respiration. Have students set up two pint vacuum bottles in the following manner. Fill one bottle four-fifths full with either germinating beans, corn grains, oats, or pea seeds on a bed of moist absorbent cotton (about one-fifth of the bottle). Cover the bottle with a one-hole rubber stopper, insert a thermometer, and seal the space around the stopper with modeling clay to make it airtight. In the second bottle, set up a control using seedlings killed in formalin. Be sure the seeds have been properly disinfected before germinating them by soaking them in the formalin for at least 20 minutes. To germinate the seeds, soak them overnight in sterile gauze soaked in distilled water in a disinfected petri dish. This precaution must be taken; otherwise, there may be evidence of a temperature change in the control due to heat generated through bacterial decay. After the control seeds have been germinated, they can be killed by resoaking them in formalin or chlorine solution for another 20 minutes. If you do not have access to vacuum bottles, use two regular pint-size bottles and pack the seeds in glass-wool insulation or excelsior. The germinating seeds should show a temperature rise within 24 hours.

25. Now that students understand the relationship between body heat and cellular respiration, introduce the necessity of cellular respiration for musclar movements and the resulting production of heat. This would explain the instinctive and involuntary activities of animals when they are cold—running or jumping around, shivering, teeth chattering, and so forth. On the other hand, heat production, being a natural consequence of bodily movement, poses the problem of an overproduction of heat in a warm environment. After asking students what natural mechanisms lower body temperature, perform some simple demonstrations showing how evaporation of fluids from the body

surface will lower the temperature. One demonstration would be to have students, working in pairs, place some room-temperature water on their partner's right palm and alcohol on the left. Since alcohol evaporates more rapidly than water, the left palm will feel much cooler in seconds. A second demonstration would be to set up a thermometer as a psychrometer by wrapping the bulb with a wet gauze (the water should be at room temperature) and attaching a strong string through the hole on the top of the thermometer. Carefully whirl the thermometer through a small circle and note the cooling effect on the temperature reading. A dry bulb thermometer might also be whirled as a control for comparison.

General Activities

26. Have students set up several long-term experiments involving changes in water balance, salinity, temperature, and pH that show the limitations in tolerance levels of various plants. Reproduction Page 3 gives some examples. Have students write their data and findings on the chart. Instruct them to be sure that everything but the variable they are testing remains unchanged. For example, if they are testing the effect of acid pH, be sure both the control and the test plant receive the same amount of water, light, heat, soil composition, and other variables, with the acid fertilizer being added only to the test plant.

    After observing the effects of the different variables, discuss with students why one species can survive in a certain environment as opposed to a different species. Mention some adaptations that plants have developed to survive in a particular environment—for example, the surface roots and lack of typical leaves in a cactus to obtain and conserve water.

27. Ask students if there are some life-forms that have such wide parameters they can survive almost anywhere on earth. Have them research tolerance ranges of various types of bacteria or insects. An excellent example of the amazing survival ability of some insect pests can be seen in the common American cockroach, which can live on paper or wiring if no food is available and can go for three months on water alone and one month on nothing at all. The cockroach's waterproof cuticle or body wall is an excellent adaptation for aiding the prevention of dehydration. A suggested reading is "The Indomitable Cockroach," *National Geographic* (January 1981).

28. Have students research the termite, with its unique ability to live on a diet of wood. After students read about the part protozoa play in helping the termite to digest cellulose, discuss briefly symbiotic relationships and their role in the survival of certain organisms. Be sure to mention the various microorganisms that live in humans and are essential to their survival. This lesson is a good lead-in, not only to the following activities on food, but also to the chapter on ecology, which follows.

FOOD

29. Have students bring in articles on diet and nutrition from current magazines such as *Prevention*, *Science Digest*, and *Discover*, as well as news reports that

deal with the relationship between diet and disease. You may want students to write reports or hold discussions or debates on the topics.

30. There are many tapes available on diet from various health food or food supplement companies; indeed most companies are happy to lend out their tapes. But since these materials may contain statements biased toward the company's products, try to give a balanced presentation on such controversial issues. Teach students to be critical listeners and to try, after reviewing various sides of an issue, to arrive at their own conclusions.

31. There are also numerous films and filmstrips on diet and the effect of various food substances on health. An excellent filmstrip that discusses processed versus natural foods in comparing vitamin and protein content is *Food: The Choice Is Yours* (Encore Filmstrips).

    During these lessons, be sure to stress that the nutritional value of foods is greatly affected by the way in which they are prepared. (Obviously their taste and one's appetite are also greatly affected.) You might want to inject some pragmatism—and probably humor—by having class members relate their own experiences in beginning the culinary arts. Encourage students to read the informative pages of some highly recommended cookbooks that discuss the best ways of storing and preparing foods in order to preserve their nutrients.

32. After discussing the nutritional value of various types of food and the importance of a balanced diet, have students evaluate the nutritional content of a typical lunch or dinner they consume. It has been found that students are motivated if the meal they are to evaluate is one cooked in the school kitchen. This allows them to interview other students and to receive their feedback on the same meal. It also allows them to express some valid complaints they might have about the lunch program. Obviously this activity is a delicate situation and requires tact and objectivity in collecting data and formulating conclusions. However, we have found that for that reason alone, it is a good learning experience and often engenders an understanding of the problems of those in charge of school lunches, as well as those eating them.

    In initiating this activity, you may have to help students obtain any necessary permissions and set up interviews with the cafeteria cooks and supervisors, remembering, however, that the more responsibility students take on themselves, the more they will learn. Students can work in groups of about five each. After each group has prepared questions for interviewing the cafeteria cook and supervisors, the class as a whole can formulate a list of questions for each interview. Be sure they have included questions on how menus are prepared and who does the preparation, as well as the special training required for this job. Remind students that economics as well as nutrition is also an important factor. Review the basic food groups—dairy products, meats and high protein foods, vegetables and fruits, and bread and cereals—listing specific foods found in each group and discussing the effects of each group on the body. Have students explain to the cook that they would like to evaluate two or three meals according to these food groups and that they will be interviewing students during lunch. Reproduction Page 4 may be used for interviewing students, or your class may devise its own worksheet for this purpose. We advise that one member from each group form a representative body to meet with the cook and supervisor and that each group evaluate only one meal. Perhaps the first two groups could hold student interviews on Monday, the second two on Tuesday, and so on. Each group should list the date of the meal and the food group to which the various foods belong; for example:

Date	Food	Food Group
April 4	Chicken	Meat
	French fries	Vegetables and fruit
	Bread	Bread and cereal
	Celery and carrots	Vegetables and fruit
	Apple cobbler	Vegetables and fruit
	Milk	Milk and dairy products

Then, using Reproduction Page 4, have three students in the group interview ten students each. After all the interviews are completed, students can collate their results for each meal. Then discuss which food groups were not represented, which foods seemed to be most liked, which were most often wasted, and so forth. Ask students to evaluate the meal on the basis of a balanced diet and whether most students actually ate a balanced meal. If the answer to either of these questions is no, determine ways in which students might work to improve the situation. Ask the cafeteria staff if they would like to see the results of the study. Obviously there are elements of nutritional value that students will not be investigating in this study—vitamin content, the amount of salt, sugar or fat content, and caloric content, for example. But this activity should plant the seed of critical awareness in discerning what is nutritionally sound and will introduce the realization that what goes into the body now is one of the greatest factors in determining future health.

ASSESSING ACHIEVEMENT OF OBJECTIVES

Ongoing Evaluation

The extent to which students have learned about the chemical changes and water balance can be measured by having students submit for evaluation the final products of the activities in this chapter.

Final Evaluation

For an overall evaluation of students' ability to recognize the theories of evolution and the mechanisms involved in homeostasis, assign an in-class essay developed from the facts found in the recommended films and readings, as well as the activities in this chapter.

Several of the activities in this chapter can be used for evaluating students achievement. You may also use the Reproduction Pages 1–4 for evaluation purposes.

RESOURCES FOR TEACHING

Following is a selected list of materials and resources for teaching about the evolution of the external environment and homeostasis. These materials—and those in other chapters—are meant to update and supplement the extensive bibliographies that exist in most teachers' guides. We have listed materials and resources that meet our criteria of being especially useful to teachers.

Books, Pamphlets, and Articles

Alexander, Richard, *Darwinism and Human Affairs,* University of Washington Press. Explains the concepts of Darwinism as it pertains to human affairs, both politically and economically.

Bergman, Jerry, *Teaching about the Creation-Evolution Controversy,* Phi Delta Kappa. Illustrates basic issues of both sides of the picture. An excellent source for teachers since both sides are presented logically.

Calvin, M., "Chemical Evolution and the Origin of Life," *American Scientist* 44 (July 1956). A classic article on the theories of evolution based on biochemical analysis.

Ehrlich, Paul, *The Process of Evolution,* McGraw-Hill. A clearly organized book on the slow but meaningful processes involved in natural selection.

Oparin, A., *Life: Its Nature, Origin and Development,* Academic Press. A comprehensive study of Oparin's theory of evolution, which changed the way we view the origin of life.

Other Resources

Hemo the Magnificent (30 min.), Bell Telephone. Clearly depicts how simple life-forms could have originated only in the sea and how internal circulatory systems developed as organisms became more complex.

Life, Time and Change (set of 12 films, 28 min. each), AIBS Film Series in Modern Biology. Explores the evolution of the earth and life and the various adaptations of natural selection.

The World Is Born (20 min.), Walt Disney Studios. A fine film that explains clearly how the universe was developed.

Story in the Rocks (18 min.), Shell Oil Co. Illustrates how fossils play a vital role in developing theories of evolution. Free of charge.

Food: The Choice Is Yours (15 min.), Encore. This filmstrip illustrates the importance of a balanced diet and the role nutrients play in developing a healthy body.

Journey into Time (14 min.), Sterling Movies. A good introduction to the evolution of the earth.

Our Changing Earth (13 min.), Film Associates. Shows the continuous evolution of our planet.

3

Our Present Environment

INTRODUCTION

A good way to introduce students to the study of life is through its environments. By introducing students to ecology, they see the interrelationships that exist between living things and the nonliving environment. Through various activities, students can readily relate their experiences to their present environment and see the interconnections.

The best approach to teaching biology is to relate the science of life to something that students can see, feel, touch, and smell. From the study of ecology, you can expand the study of life to include many other facets needed to understand how living things function and survive. For this reason, this chapter appears early in the book. If you wish to use this as a building block, you can see how the study of life emerges (Fig. 3.1).

Many activities in this chapter illustrate concept building such as understanding ecosystems, cycling, energy principles, and succession. Field studies use the outdoors to investigate living things in various environmental settings, while the laboratory studies bring the out-of-doors inside for careful experimentation and observation.

One of the best types of activities you can undertake at the start of studying environments is to take the students on a field trip. If your geographic proximity permits, you could bring the students to a salt marsh or swamp, to a deciduous forest or a pine forest, or to a seashore environment. Through such exposure, you can begin to relate to the class the interrelationships of climatic conditions to the effects on the survival of living things. In the field, you can point out various living populations and how these populations interact with each other, creating an ecological community, and how these communities interact to form ecosystems. Before planning a field trip, see Chapter 1 for tips on field trip organization.

This chapter has been divided into several main segments—population and community, abiotic and biotic, field studies, and ecosystems—for clarity. Since the content area of ecology is usually covered in most biology textbooks, we have decided not to

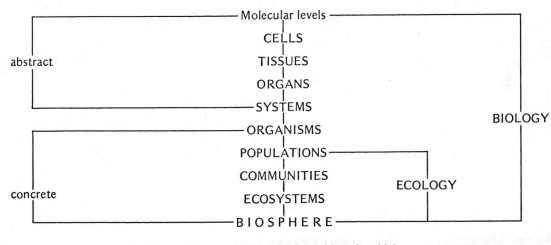

Figure 3.1.   Organizational levels of life.

discuss these concepts in the Content Overview. A quick review of any chapter on ecology found in a text will prove most helpful. We have, however, chosen to discuss the principles of energy flow and some topics which might not be included so readily in a basic textbook.

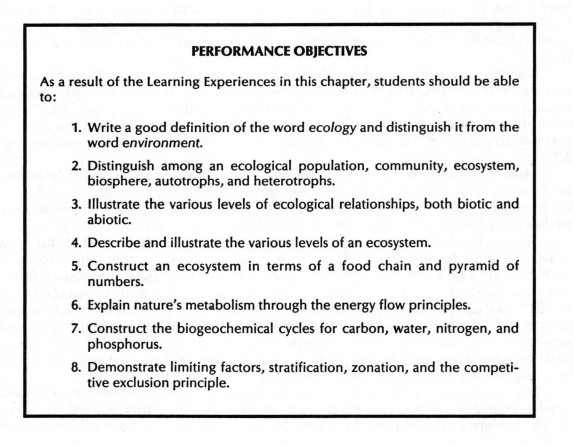

PERFORMANCE OBJECTIVES

As a result of the Learning Experiences in this chapter, students should be able to:

1. Write a good definition of the word *ecology* and distinguish it from the word *environment*.

2. Distinguish among an ecological population, community, ecosystem, biosphere, autotrophs, and heterotrophs.

3. Illustrate the various levels of ecological relationships, both biotic and abiotic.

4. Describe and illustrate the various levels of an ecosystem.

5. Construct an ecosystem in terms of a food chain and pyramid of numbers.

6. Explain nature's metabolism through the energy flow principles.

7. Construct the biogeochemical cycles for carbon, water, nitrogen, and phosphorus.

8. Demonstrate limiting factors, stratification, zonation, and the competitive exclusion principle.

CONTENT OVERVIEW

The basic principles describing the transfer of energy are called the first and second laws of thermodynamics. It is sufficient for our purposes to say that the first law indicates that energy is neither created nor destroyed. The second law states that no process is entirely efficient in converting potential energy to work; in other words, some of the original energy is always lost as heat. The energy that an organism uses for its work comes from the breaking down of organic molecules, usually food within its cells.

Let us follow the flow of energy through an individual animal. The food that it eats contains a certain amount of stored energy; it may be called the animal's gross energy intake. Since the processes of digestion and assimilation are not totally efficient, some of the energy is lost in feces. Also, some of the energy stored in compounds that are digested and absorbed is later given off in various excretions, such as urine and sweat. The undigested, unassimilated, and excretory reactions are often called *excretory energy*. The energy remaining is essentially the energy that the animal has to perform its work. Some of the energy is used simply to maintain existence in such activities as repairing and replacing cells, pumping fluids, and obtaining and digesting foods. The other portion is required for growth and behavioral activities, such as mating and nest building.

The importance of an energy balance within populations and communities adds up to an energy-efficient ecosystem. In studying the energy in ecosystems, you study the trophic structure of communities based on food chains and food webs.

About 30 percent of the sunlight reaching the earth's atmosphere is reflected back into space, about 50 percent is absorbed by the ground, vegetation, or water, and about 20 percent is absorbed by the atmosphere, which does not seem to leave much for photosynthesis. In fact, only about 0.02 percent of the sunlight reaching the earth's atmosphere is used in food making by green plants. Nevertheless, all organisms in the ecosystem depend on this small percentage for their survival. (See Reproduction Page 11 for a simplified energy flow diagram of an ecosystem.)

Elements in organic compounds move from the abiotic to the biotic portion of the ecosystem through producers and consumers and are returned to the abiotic portion of the ecosystem through excretory processes of producers, consumers, and decomposers.

Energy flow is a one-way process. Energy enters the ecosystem as sunlight and leaves as heat, which is dissipated in the universe. However, materials move in more or less complete circular systems known as *biogeochemical cycles*. (See Reproduction Page 13.)

Within ecosystems we also see at work various factors that limit the growth of organisms. These limiting factors enable the system to remain stable and not become overcrowded or less diverse. In many instances, certain populations and communities can take over and succeed, and others are limited in their growth and survival requirements. One can readily see the processes of succession taking place in forests, open meadows, and lakes. In order for one population to replace another, both abiotic and biotic aspects must be met. In this way, ecosystems are in a dynamic pattern of change, which ensures their survival. All of the ecosystems of the earth combined form the delicate and beautiful biosphere, the living layer of our planet.

LEARNING EXPERIENCES

Populations and Communities

1. Take several pint jars and place about twelve fruit flies (*Drosophila melanogaster*) in each jar. Put the jars with the flies in places where temperatures vary; you might place one jar in a refrigerator and another in a steam bath, for example. Observe how the flies interact with each other. This exercise shows the effect that temperature has on a population of fruit flies. At this point you could define an ecological population to your students. You may also do the same demonstration using a population of plants, such as elodea, or a population of animals, such as guppies.

2. For an activity illustrating the biotic environment that may be spread over several weeks, insert in a bowl a goldfish, three or four guppies, and several strands of elodea or freshwater seaweed. Students can observe the relationships between populations in this aquarium model by seeing the guppies feeding on the elodea and the goldfish feeding on the guppies, thus establishing a food chain. Such relationships form an *ecological community*.

3. Bring a pond community into the classroom for the study of the interrelationships that exist among various populations. These populations relate to various abiotic factors needed for their survival. From a nearby pond or lake, collect samples of water, fish, and plant life. Place all in a cleaned 10 gal. aquarium tank, and over the next few months observe the relationships that exist in this pond community, right in your own classroom. Students should be able to observe species diversification on both macroscopic and microscopic levels and food chains, cycling, and various limiting factors involved with species. Secure another 5 gal. of pond water for replacement in your aquarium over the months of activity.

4. Another activity students can do to illustrate the interrelationships between the abiotic and biotic environments is to use a pH scale. Bring in several house plants, and make their soils acidic by using commercial acid-loving fertilizers, such as Hollytone or Hyponex. In several days the plants should react to this "acid" feeding. Students should be able to recognize that some plants are doing very well and others are not. You can expand the activity by using lime on other plants to see the effects of alkalinity. (*Hint:* Remember that evergreens are acid-loving plants; bulbs, such as tulips, are alkaline loving.)

   From such an activity, students can explore and discuss such environmental issues as acid rain. You can discuss why in pine forests you rarely see tulips growing. Try to give practical applications to each of the activities.

Field Activities

5. In the field, you may wish to undertake some estimations of population size. There are several mathematical methods you may employ. See Reproduction Page 5 for one such method. You may modify this method to meet your own community needs.

6. Another day, you could analyze a community in the field using a quadrat method to estimate the density of a population. This can be done by using Reproduction Page 6.

7. Reproduction Page 7 is a guide for an organized field trip to a marine environment. It details the preparation that is needed in terms of knowing the site and offering students specific activities while in the field. It is important to remember that the most successful field trips are those in which the students are actively involved in doing something while learning. Having a field trip in which students walk around with the teacher and listen to a lot of talking will not be successful. One reason nature walks are usually not successful with secondary school students is that they are not given a chance to be active learners and cannot appreciate the walk unless there is something meaningful for them to do. This Reproduction Page illustrates thought-provoking questions that can be answered at the site and specific activities that the students can complete while at the site.

8. Have students take photographs of various ecological populations found within a community located in your geographic area. These population photographs can be brought back to the classroom and made into a community collage in which students place the photograph of the proper population into the created community in which they fit. This can be an ongoing project. You may wish to use magazine photographs as well as your own. This is a good technique for having students identify populations and understand which populations belong with what other populations, thus forming an ecological community.

9. Have students develop a community map using their school neighborhood. A group of students should walk a square block around the school (500 m × 500 m) and on a pad note various biotic and abiotic factors found there: temperature, shade, pH of the soil, types of trees and weeds, and animal life present, for example. These data may be brought back to the classroom and grouped on a community map, enabling the students to see the ecological relationships that exist around their own school community. You can include on such a map the social, political, and economic factors of the neighborhood, such as number of fire hydrants, whether there are litter baskets on corners, where a mailbox is located, and so forth. These factors can then be discussed in terms of their importance in a human community.

10. Take field trips around the school lawns, along a beach at low tide, in an open field, in a forest, or in a vacant lot. Students are certain to find some kinds of biota living together dependent on one another. A discussion of this interdependence can be undertaken.

11. Study a pond by having students list the different kinds of animals and plants they find in or around the pond community. They can begin to group organisms according to whether they are attached to the bottom of the pond; free swimmers; surface skimmers; vertebrates or invertebrates; and so forth. With a dip net made from an old nylon stocking, students can collect living specimens from the pond. Have the students spread out the contents from the net collection on a white surface and note the variety of living things found in the

pond. The students should be able to realize that many different species (populations) make up this pond community.

12. City dwellers can develop a pond environment on a flat roof of a building—even the school building. By blocking off the drains on the roof so that water will accumulate rather than drain off, you can create a pond community. After a heavy rain, water can accumulate on the roof, creating a pond-like environment. A few days after the rain has stopped, remove samples of water from the "pond." Observe the water samples under the compound microscope. Students should begin to see organisms surviving. Periodically take water samples and observe. In a few days you should notice the diversity of micro-populations. A good discussion on how these organisms got into the "pond" can be generated. As the pond dries up, you will note stages in succession taking place. Through these stages, there will be changes in the populations originally observed.

Abiotic Activities

13. In order to have students grasp the concept of light as an abiotic factor in an environment, use a photographic exposure meter to measure light found within various environments. Through this technique, students can grasp the idea that certain organisms require great amounts of light, while others do not require such amounts of light to survive. Students can record various light intensities using this meter in different environments and record those plants and animals seen in such conditions. Students should be able to develop a list of organisms that require high amounts, medium amounts, and low amounts of light in various types of environments, such as a forest, an open field, a beach, and so on.

14. Temperature is another abiotic factor that students can measure by doing the same activity as in Activity 13, except this time they can record various temperatures using a calibrated mercury thermometer. Students should be able to make relationships between the amounts of light and the changes in temperature.

15. Students can simply determine the "current factor" of a stream by placing a lightweight object in a stream and recording the time it takes to travel a given distance. Through this technique, students can see which organisms can survive in strong and weak currents within a stream community. A list of various organisms found in both types of currents will enable students to determine the population adaptiveness to this mode of living.

16. Evaporation is another important abiotic factor. Students can determine the rate of evaporation from a community, such as a lake or forest by using a Livingston atmometer. Instructions usually accompany this device and will prove important for its operation.

17. By using either a sling or a cog psychrometer, students can determine the relative humidity of an environment. These devices are simple to use and can be obtained from a scientific supply house.

18. If your budget permits, you may wish to purchase Hach or Lamotte environmental test kits from a scientific supply house. These kits enable students to test water and soil in various communities for salinity, pH, soil texture, biological oxygen demand (BOD), and many chemical compounds, such as carbon dioxide, phosphates, and nitrates. The kits are easy to use and rather quickly supply data about various environments. They offer students an opportunity to do an actual test on site and become involved in observational skills.

Biotic Activities

19. Before students begin working with living things, they should know something about a biological key so that they can easily classify organisms they find. Reproduction Page 8 offers a simplified biological key to major plants and animals for use in both the field and laboratory. You may use these keys on a regular basis as you investigate various living things.

20. In studying living things, students should understand various organisms' niches within their surroundings. Have students go to a given environment, such as a beach, forest, pond, or lake, and observe different organisms within their niches. A simple niche to observe is the feeding level of the organism. It may be a specific plant that an organism is eating or a specific insect or seed. For example, insects you observe may have different niches; therefore, they are not competitive with one another. This is an important concept to develop. In general, no two populations can exist in the same surroundings for a given period of time and have identical niches. Thus, students should begin to develop this competitive exclusion principle through their careful observations in both the field and in the lab. You may wish to make a simple chart for students so they can easily keep a record.

Organism	Environment Found	Abiotic Factor	Niche
1. Rainbow trout	Lake	Freshwater, cold temperature, well oxygenated	Carnivore
2.			
3.			
4.			
5.			

21. A good activity for use when studying living things in a soil community is to collect about a 1 ft. block of soil (12 in. × 12 in. × 5 in.) from a garden, meadow, woods, or a vacant lot. Divide the class into about four groups so each group can bring back a soil sample from a different area. These samples should be placed in a large plastic bag and labeled as to their geographic location and the abiotic factors of the area from which the soil was taken (such as temperature, pH, and moisture). When the soil samples are in the classroom, students can compare the four samples as to texture, color, and other physical characteristics. Students also should examine the soil for living things, such as earthworms, dandelions, insect larvae, plant seeds, millipedes, and other forms of life. Have some students sieve out the soil into a white pan and examine

closely for organisms. Collect the organisms in small jars and identify using the biological keys found on Reproduction Page 8. Students should be able to identify the various organisms from each sample of soil and also how many of each organism was found. A data sheet can be kept on each soil sample, so students can begin seeing relationships that exist between abiotic and biotic factors.

22. Students may transfer small portions of the soil samples to dishes containing a little sterile water. Set these dishes aside for about 1 week to 10 days and then examine each dish with a hand lens. Observe plant seedlings, molds, and other forms of life. You may also find small worms and insects in the dishes. Use a binocular microscope for close examination of the organisms present.

23. Place a small amount of soil on a glass slide with water and examine it under the microscope. Identify and classify living organisms. You may also wish to streak a sterile needle dipped into a sample of soil across the surface of nutrient agar in a petri dish. Incubate and examine it under a microscope after about 3 days. See if there are any bacteria you can identify.

    In addition to studying the biotic aspects of the soil environment, you may wish students to study the abiotic aspects of the soil samples. A simple abiotic factor that can be tested in soil is pH. Use litmus paper as an indicator. Acid turns blue litmus red; alkaline turns red litmus blue. Each student can test several samples of soil. Lay moistened strips of litmus paper (both red and blue) side by side in several flat dishes. Put about ½ teaspoon of a sample soil on the strips and, using a medicine dropper, moisten the soil with a drop or two of distilled water. Turn the dish and inspect the litmus paper.

Ecosystems

24. To understand the relationships of the various components of an ecosystem, have the students begin with the study of a sealed aquarium. The aquarium can be very simple, consisting of a large jar containing sand, water, several aquatic plants, and a small, herbivorous fish. In this simple ecosystem, the plants are the producers. The fish, a primary consumer in this instance, feeds on small bits of the plant. Its wastes, in turn, provide the plant with the nutrients and carbon dioxide necessary for future growth. If you wish to make a simpler mini-aquarium instead and still see the relationships that exist between organisms, place in one test tube a snail with pond water or aquarium water; in another test tube, place a snail and a plant together.* Seal both tubes. The best way to seal such a tube is to take the test tube with only a small amount of water in it, and flame it around its center, then twist the tube until the glass softens and eventually forms its own seal. Students can compare the results of each tube and see the relationships that exist. See Fig. 3.2.

---

*Aquarium water refers to tap water that has been exposed to the open air so the chlorine can be partially evaporated from the tap water.

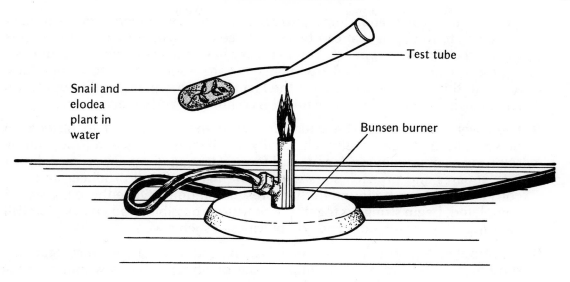

Figure 3.2. A simple mini-aquarium.

25. To develop the concept of ecosystem further, you may use an activity similar to Activity 24 but with a terrarium instead. Use a jar containing soil and have various land plants and simple animals live together in balance. The plants and animals can be secured from a local woodland community. Students can seal the jar with paraffin and observe any changes in the system. The chances are that it will not be in balance, and death will occur. A discussion of why organisms are dying enables students to see the delicate balance needed if all life is to survive.

26. You can expand the terrarium activity by discussing various types of ecosystems found on the earth. One group of students may develop a desert terrarium, another a marsh terrarium, and so on. In this way students can compare various ecosystems in terms of their biotic and abiotic requirements.

27. Use Reproduction Page 9 to illustrate a model ecosystem. Have students identify several producers from various types of communities. Do the same for the consumers—herbivores, carnivores, and the decomposers. Once students have a clear understanding of specific examples of each trophic level, discuss with the class the reasons why the producer and decomposer boxes are the largest. Ask the class to explain why each consumer box is decreasing in size in the illustration on Reproduction Page 9. This page will demonstrate to the class the two basic laws of thermodynamics.

Ecosystem Principles

28. You are now ready to develop with students the many ecological principles involved in keeping ecosystems operating and balanced. These include energy flow, biogeochemical cycles, limiting factors, stratification, zonation, competitive exclusion, and succession. Let us start with energy flow. Have students

examine the sealed aquariums and/or terrariums developed previously. Observe any food chains that can be readily seen in each. Have students discuss the food chains they observe. You may now have students involved in discussing food chains in natural environments that are readily observed in their local areas. In this way, you can discuss the fact that each organism and population has its own habitat and niche within the community and/or ecosystem.

29. Food web activities can be interesting even though difficult to observe in nature. Students can develop an activity in which they create a food web by selecting a community, such as a local forest. Have students cut up cards into 1 inch squares and on each square write the name of one producer and one consumer that can be found in that forest community. Once these names are completed, begin stringing together the various possible food chains. You will note the many possibilities and complexities of such a web.

30. Autotrophic demonstrations are enlightening and fairly easy to show. Students should become aware of the importance of photosynthesis within an ecosystem. One activity that shows that simple sugar is made as an end product of photosynthesis in green plants is to keep some sprouted onion bulbs in the light for several days. Cut about 1 in. lengths of the green shoots and place them into a Pyrex test tube. Add about an inch of Benedict's solution, and boil the contents in the tube. Students will note the color changes from blue to shades of green to a reddish-orange color, indicating the presence of simple sugars.

31. You can demonstrate the role that light plays in the process of photosynthesis by placing a healthy geranium plant in a sunny window with a strip of black construction paper placed across both sides of the center of one leaf. (See Fig. 3.3.) Keep the plant in the sun for several days. After about 3 days, remove the test leaf, peel off the paper, and boil the leaf in water for a few minutes to soften the leaf. This process breaks down the cellulose of the walls of the leaf. Next, place the softened leaf in a beaker half full of ethyl alcohol and warm on a hot plate. (Do not heat over open flame.) Since chlorophyll is soluble in alcohol, the green pigmentation should be extracted. Next, wash the leaf with water, spread it out flat in a petri dish, and cover with Lugol's solution. After about 5 minutes, rinse off the excess iodine solution and hold the leaf up to the light to show the blackish area on the leaf indicating the presence of starch. Students should see all the exposed green part of the leaf blackish in color. The only part that should not contain starch is the covered area.

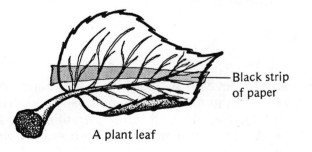

Black strip of paper

A plant leaf

Figure 3.3.   Role of light in photosynthesis demonstration.

32. Another important part of the photosynthesis process is the absorption of carbon dioxide by plants. This can be shown simply by using an elodea plant and the indicator bromthymol blue. This chemical is blue in alkaline solutions and yellow in acid solutions. Thus, a slight increase in acidity, as when carbon dioxide is added to the solution, will change the blue color to yellow. When carbon dioxide is absorbed, as in photosynthesis, the yellow color is changed back to blue. In a beaker, dilute 0.1% bromthymol blue solution with aquarium water in which elodea has been growing. Be sure the solution is a deep blue color. If it is not, you may add a trace (1 drop per liter) of ammonium hydroxide to turn the solution a deep blue. Have a student breathe through a straw into the indicator solution until the solution turns yellow. Now have the students pour this yellow solution into three large test tubes, as follows:

    a. A tube with no plants but exposed to light.

    b. A tube with a sprig of elodea having an end bud, exposed to light.

    c. A tube like b but covered with aluminum foil.

    Now place all these tubes in sunlight. Within 30 minutes, tubes containing plants exposed to sunlight will show a color change from yellow to blue, indicating absorption of carbon dioxide. Most students enjoy this activity since it tests their ability to remember the color code.

33. You may do a similar test for carbon dioxide on land plants by setting up an apparatus, such as a bell jar containing a geranium plant, and a beaker of sodium hydroxide pellets. The pellets remove the carbon dioxide from the bell jar environment, thus not allowing the plant to absorb the gas. To test this, do the starch test on a leaf of the plant after it has been placed in the sun. You will find a negative starch test, indicating that starch was not produced because no carbon dioxide was available to the plant.

34. Another activity is to show the importance of the stomates on the underside of leaves in allowing carbon dioxide to enter the plant. You can easily demonstrate this point by keeping a geranium plant in the dark for several days. Check to make sure starch is not being made. Coat one leaf of the plant (underside) with vaseline, thus clogging the stomates. Place the plant in the sun for several days, and then check to see if photosynthesis has been carried out by testing for starch in a leaf not coated and in the leaf that was coated with vaseline.

35. A final activity on photosynthesis is to show the role of oxygen in the process. This can easily be demonstrated by using a freshly cut sprig of elodea that has been placed in bright sunlight. Students can notice the bubbles of a gas escaping from the freshly cut stem of the plant. One easy way to show this escaping gas is to place the freshly cut sprig of elodea in a test tube containing water. Add 2 ml of 1.25% solution of sodium bicarbonate. The bicarbonate will provide a source of carbon dioxide for the plant and will help the process. To check which gas is bubbling from the stem of the elodea, place the sprig in an inverted funnel and place the funnel setup in a test tube containing water. Place all in a beaker of water and set in the sunlight. After a short period of time, the gas bubbling from the plant will replace about ½ in. of water. This gas may now be checked for oxygen. See Fig. 3.4.

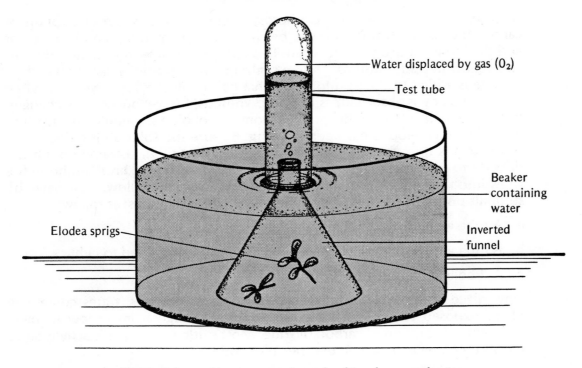

Figure 3.4.   How oxygen is evolved in photosynthesis.

36. It is easy to demonstrate to a class various heterotrophs. Have students examine saprophytes in the classroom. Various molds are readily available in wooded areas or may be purchased from a biological supply company. Or students can grow their own mold, such as the blue-green mold found on stale bread, in a petri dish that is kept moist and placed in the dark. Students can observe, using a compound microscope, how these organisms grow and obtain nourishment.

37. Have students obtain samples of water from a quiet pond. By examining the samples under a microscope, they can begin to see what is being eaten and what is doing the eating. By dredging the bottom of the pond, they might be able to collect various decomposers and examine them under the microscope.

38. Examine a lichen under the microscope and see the relationship between the algae and the fungi. Students can readily identify the two types of plant. They can then examine lichens growing on trees and rocks. These pioneer plants can be discussed as an important part of the process of succession.

39. Parasites are interesting to study in the laboratory. From microscopic observations, students can readily note how parasites are adapted to their mode of life. Have students dissect a freshly killed frog. Check for parasites by opening up the main organs, such as urinary bladder, liver, and lungs. You may note various flatworms. The best way to observe the parasites is to cut open one of the frog's organs. Using Ringer's solution, wash the organ, remove the solution with a medicine dropper, place the solution hopefully containing parasites on a microscopic slide, and view. See if the students can identify the various

parasites and guess how they obtain their nourishment. You may have to refer to a parasitology text for picture identification. This activity requires patience, but the reward is worth the undertaking.

40. Use Reproduction Pages 10 and 11 to illustrate energy flow. This diagram shows on an annual basis the incoming energy and how it changes form and decreases at the various trophic levels. Several problems are posed for students to solve as a result of their understanding of the laws of thermodynamics and energy flow.

41. A good activity on energy flow is to have students read an article on aquaculture or fish farming. Much has been written on these topics from studies done in China and the United States. Students can read and discuss the energy efficiency of using fish as a food source. Students should be aware that there is very little energy being lost as heat since fish are cold-blooded animals.

42. Another way of showing students energy flow is through a biotic pyramid. You may wish to refer to the laws of thermodynamics given in the Content Overview. Reproduction Page 12 shows such a pyramid and offers several problems for students to try to solve and discuss.

43. In addition to energy flow within an ecosystem, all living things require some forty chemicals that are passed through the various trophic levels. Ecologists speak of this cycling of chemicals as biogeochemical cycles. Reproduction Page 13 illustrates various cycles, which may be used for review and for discussion.

44. The following activity demonstrates the oxygen–carbon dioxide cycle. Have students set up a simple jar aquarium with a sprig of elodea plant placed in a sealed jar with aquarium water. Be sure to add some bromthymol blue indicator to the solution. The experiment works best if you have the students change the bromthymol blue indicator to yellow by exhaling from a straw into the solution. (See Activity 32 for details.) Then place the sprig of elodea in the yellow solution and seal the jar. Place the setup in bright sun, where the solution should turn blue. Why? At nighttime, the solution should turn yellow again. Why?

45. Another simple activity will show students the importance of the nitrogen cycle. In your discussion of this cycle, mention the nitrogen-fixing bacteria needed in the cycle. Students can view these bacteria by collecting plants, such as beans, alfalfa, or clover, and checking their roots for tiny nodules (swellings). Wash the roots, add a drop of sterile water, and observe the roots under the microscope. You may wish to use methylene blue stain for a clearer view.

46. Now that the students have seen the actual bacteria and where they are found in the cycle, you can demonstrate the effects these bacteria have on plant growth. Have students sterilize four small flowerpots containing soil in an autoclave or oven. Then add nitrogen-fixing bacteria to the soil in only two of the flowerpots. These bacteria may be purchased from a biological supply company. Add an equal quantity of white clover seed to each of the four flowerpots. Let students observe which pots have the best growth of clover plants.

47. In order to show students factors in their environment that limit growth due to having either too much or too little of something they require, you might wish to do the following activity.

    In a jar, place a male and female guppy with aquarium water. Observe the fish for several days and note their behavior. On the third day, begin feeding the fish with dry fish food, which may be purchased at a local tropical fish store. Start by giving only a very small amount of food. Observe the fish. Continue giving the guppies only a fraction of the amount suggested for several days. Observe any changes in their behavior. As the days progress, keep giving them more and more food until you exceed the amount suggested. Note any changes in their behavior. You may ask your students to hypothesize as to what they think might happen. Students may keep a daily log of observed activities.

48. Another good activity showing limiting factors is to use a freshwater fish, such as a guppy or trout, and show the effect with salt water. Each day add ½ teaspoon of table salt to a gallon jar containing freshwater and a fish. Record the amounts of salt used each day and any changes in the fish's behavior. You might need to use ⅛ teaspoon daily rather than ½ teaspoon if the fish is overreacting too soon. Observe the limits of the fish's salinity by the change in its behavior before death occurs.

49. Discuss with the class the various limiting factors found in lakes, ponds, deserts, and other environments. In this way, they can better grasp the importance of changes within their environment. You might even begin a list of limiting factors for human beings.

50. One of the most important concepts in ecology is that of ecological succession. Explain to students that it is through this process that diversity increases, and populations change in order to adapt to new conditions. You can demonstrate this process by the following activity.

    Using a vacant lot, have a group of students do a survey of the different types of plants and animals found in the lot. Over several months and even years, the survey should be updated by other students who can add or delete biota from the original list. In this way, students can see biotic changes, if any, that are taking place over time in the lot.

51. Another demonstration might be to develop a plot of ground in your own school yard. Dig up a 10 ft. × 10 ft. × 1 ft. plot and level it so that bare soil is exposed. After several days or weeks, students should observe which organisms are the first to invade the plot. Discuss possible reasons for this. As weeks go on, students can observe the various stages of succession.

52. There are many good filmstrips and films on succession. A particularly good one is *Succession: From Sand Dune to Forest* (Encyclopedia Britannica).

ASSESSING LEARNING EXPERIENCES

Several of the activities in this chapter can be used for evaluating students' achievement. By using Reproduction Pages 5 and 6, you can assess students' understanding of population ecology. Using Reproduction Page 7, students can be assessed in terms of biotic and abiotic factors involved in community ecology. Using Reproduction Page 9, have students complete the problems to assess their understanding of ecosystems.

In assessing students' achievement of energy flow, food chains, and food webs, have students answer the problem/questions at the end of Reproduction Pages 10, 11, and 12.

For an overall evaluation of students' ability to recognize biogeochemical cycling, assign an in-class essay describing three of the cycles found on Reproduction Page 13.

RESOURCES FOR TEACHING

Following is a selected list of materials and resources for teaching about ecology and environmental factors. These materials, and those in other chapters, are meant to update and supplement the extensive bibliographies that exist in most teachers' guides. We have listed materials and resources that meet our criteria of being especially useful to teachers.

Books, Pamphlets, and Articles

Asimov, Isaac, *Photosynthesis*, Basic Books. A classic treatment of this important ecological process.

Benton, Allen H., *Biology and Ecology*, McGraw-Hill. Illustrates the various ecological principles that may be used in theory or in practice.

Buchsbaum, Ralph, *Basic Ecology*, Boxwood Press. A concise, clear text on ecological principles.

Clapham, W. B., *Natural Ecosystems*, Macmillan. A concise overview of world ecosystems described in meaningful terms.

Emmel, Thomas, *An Introduction to Ecology*, Norton. An excellent book on population ecology.

Gleason, H. A., *Plants of the Vicinity of New York*, New York Botanical Gardens. A biological key used for field study in the greater New York area.

Meunschner, W. C., *Key to Woody Plants*, Cornell University Press. A technical biological key used for identifying woody plants in the United States.

Whittaker, Robert, *Communities and Ecosystems*, Macmillan. A concise analysis of community ecology and its relationship to global ecosystems.

Other Resources

Succession: From Sand Dune to Forest (20 min.) Encyclopedia Britannica. A film illustrating the concept of ecological succession.

4

Processing Part I:
Breaking Down Nutrients
Obtained From the Environment

INTRODUCTION

In keeping with the basic idea that has permeated the previous chapters of this guidebook—the need for living organisms to maintain a relatively stable internal environment—we have introduced this chapter on processing using a problematic approach: How are organisms suited to obtain, process, and assimilate needed materials from their external environment to replace those used during metabolism? To concretize the problem, we begin the Learning Experiences with two activities reviewing diffusion and osmosis. These are followed by activities that investigate various physical and chemical means that might be used in breaking down different substances and one activity that asks which of these means are used by living organisms in processing raw materials from the environment.

If your students have a strong background in chemistry, you may want to cover only one or two activities from this sequence, but it is advised that you use at least Activity 3 and Activity 9 to present a logical basis for the rest of the chapter.

In both chapters on processing, we have included only cursory material on such traditional activities as dissections of laboratory animals, blood tests, diagrammatic studies of digestive systems, and similar materials since they can be found in most biology texts.

The material on enzymes is especially important not only because enzymes are clearly essential to the overall homeostasis of organisms but also because of the influence of such variables as pH, temperature, and inhibitory substances on enzymatic reactions. The total integration and specific parameters of physical and chemical variables within organisms cannot be stressed enough if students are to achieve a comprehensive understanding and appreciation of the wonder and complexity of life.

Included on Reproduction Page 16 are tables on pH values of several substances, including body fluids. These tables may prove to be an invaluable resource during enzyme activities, as well as other experiments, both in finding common liquids of varying pH to use in activities and in illustrating the precision and complexity of the chemistry of living organisms.

The elimination of solid waste is an important topic to cover. Doctors and nutritionists are becoming more aware of the relationship between improper digestive and eliminative functioning and major health problems in the gastrointestinal tract such as colo-rectal cancer, which is fast becoming the leading type of cancer in Americans. In the light of promoting this awareness, Chapter 4 includes material on this topic. Initially students often find the topic awkward and humorous, but experience shows that after discussion, they become much more concerned about their diets and begin to recognize symptoms that indicate an improperly functioning gastrointestinal system.

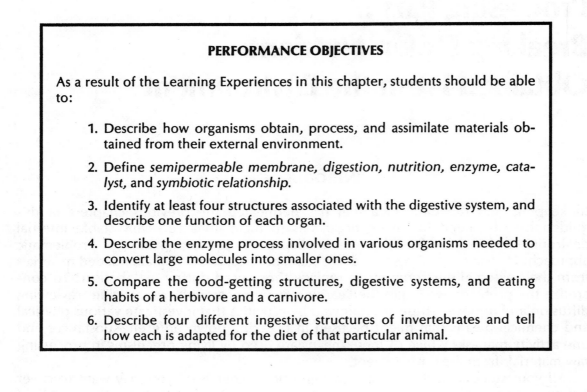

PERFORMANCE OBJECTIVES

As a result of the Learning Experiences in this chapter, students should be able to:

1. Describe how organisms obtain, process, and assimilate materials obtained from their external environment.

2. Define *semipermeable membrane, digestion, nutrition, enzyme, catalyst,* and *symbiotic relationship.*

3. Identify at least four structures associated with the digestive system, and describe one function of each organ.

4. Describe the enzyme process involved in various organisms needed to convert large molecules into smaller ones.

5. Compare the food-getting structures, digestive systems, and eating habits of a herbivore and a carnivore.

6. Describe four different ingestive structures of invertebrates and tell how each is adapted for the diet of that particular animal.

CONTENT OVERVIEW

Digestion and Ingestion

Heterotrophic organisms must obtain food from the external environment and therefore require a digestive process that will change the raw food available to a form that can be transported and absorbed at the cellular level. Some organisms, such as blood parasites, obtain nutrients in a form suitable for direct absorption, but most heterotrophs process food through either intracellular or extracellular digestion.

Intracellular digestion is a primitive process typical of lower invertebrates. The obvious limitation to this type of digestion is that only small particles of food can be handled. Nevertheless, it is practiced by many multicellular invertebrates such as cnidarians and flatworms and is typical of filter-feeding marine animals such as brachiopods, rotifers, bivalves, and cephalochordates.

Vertebrates and higher invertebrates digest their food extracellularly by secreting digestive enzymes in the intestinal lumen. Extracellular digestion is advantageous because bulky foods may be ingested, the digestive tract can be more specialized and therefore more efficient, and food wastes are more easily discarded. Without extracellular digestion, the enormous variation in feeding methods of higher animals could not have evolved.

Such a variety in feeding methods also presupposes a wide diversity in ingestive adaptations whereby the food-getting apparatus of a species is related to its diet.

Herbivore versus Carnivore

The adaptations of ingestive organs and more specialized digestive tracts account for the great diversity in feeding habits. This diversity can be seen in an overall comparison of these organs in herbivorous and carnivorous vertebrates.

In the teeth of herbivores, the canines are suppressed while broad molars are high-crowned and have enamel ridges for grinding. Rodents have incisors with enamel only on the anterior surface so that the softer dentin behind wears away more rapidly. This accounts for their chisel-shaped teeth, well adapted for cutting plant fibers. In contrast, carnivores often have low-crowned molars and strong, sharp canines for tearing and piercing. They also have powerful, clawed limbs for killing.

In general, herbivores have large and long digestive tracts and must eat a large amount daily to survive. Carnivores have shorter digestive tracts, eat separate meals, and have more time to hunt and explore.

The plant food that a herbivore must consume, while potentially nutritious, contains a great deal of cellulose. Few enzymes can attack the strong chemical bonds found in cellulose and, as far as is known, no vertebrate is able to synthesize a cellulose-splitting enzyme. Only a few herbivorous invertebrates—such as shipworms, certain crustaceans, silverfish, and some wood-boring beetles—can produce cellulase, the enzyme that splits the bonds of cellulose. Other herbivores must use symbiotic intestinal microorganisms to digest the cellulose ground up by molars or other specialized mouth parts. This microflora of anaerobic bacteria is usually harbored in huge fermentation chambers in the gut.

Since protein is more easily digested than many plant food products, the digestive tract of carnivores is shorter, the cecum is usually small or absent, and the carnivore obtains more nutrition and energy from a smaller amount of food. However, since a carnivore must find and conquer its prey, it may expend a great deal of energy in obtaining one meal.

The symbiotic relationship necessary for cellulose digestion in most herbivores is not unique. Microflora exist in the digestive tract—as well as other systems—of all higher animals, including humans, and are essential in various processes of digestion and elimination of wastes.

Chemistry of Digestion

Thousands of biochemical reactions are constantly taking place in all living organisms. Although these or comparable reactions would still occur in the absence of catalytic enzymes, they would proceed at too slow a rate to support life or would require unphysiologic conditions.

A certain amount of energy, called the *activation energy,* is required for any biochemical reaction to occur. This may be achieved by heating molecules to their activation level, during which state molecules may react with each other to form a larger molecule, or a molecule may break apart to form smaller units. Unfortunately, moderate heat denatures (that is, destroys) the activity of many body proteins. The role of an enzyme is to decrease the amount of energy needed to start the reaction. Since the whole process of attachment, reaction, and detachment that takes place in enzymatic reactions occurs very quickly, some enzymes are capable of interacting with up to 5 million substrate molecules per minute at 0° C and, within limits, about double that for every 10° C increase in temperature.

Most enzymes are denatured irreversibly at a temperature between 50° C and 80° C. Others are very resistant to high temperatures; crystalline trypsin, for example, is reversibly denatured at 100° C, and Taka-diastase is irreversible only above 140° C. *Reversibly denatured* means that it is inactive as a catalyst at the high temperature limit but resumes catalytic activity when cooled.

Enzymes are also inactivated by salts of heavy metals, such as copper or mercury, and may be affected by the presence of other substances such as drugs. Also, each enzyme is catalytically active within a limited range of pH; for example, the optimal pH range for the activity of salivary amylase is between 6.7 and 6.8. (See Reproduction Page 16 for the optimal range of various enzymes.) In the case of each enzyme, activity gradually declines on either side of the optimum. The pH sensitivity of enzymes is thought to result from the necessity of a particular charge distribution about the active center for optimal activity. Since different enzymes are composed of amino acids in different proportions, the optimal pH of an enzyme is likely to be a characteristic property dependent on its composition.

LEARNING EXPERIENCES

1. You can initiate the chapter on processing by reviewing the basic parts of a cell and the function of the semipermeable membrane. One student can construct a model of a cell by preparing a gelatin block using Knox clear gelatin, to which a small amount of phenolphthalein solution had been added. Enclose the block in a membrane (dialyzing tubing). Suspend the model over or bring it close to an exposed pan containing a solution of ammonium hydroxide. Ask students to account for the reddish color in the gelatin. Review the experiments on diffusion in Chapter 2, and initiate a discussion on the nature of exchange of materials through a membrane. Which materials diffuse readily into or out of the cell? How does concentration affect this diffusion? How must nutritional materials be prepared by an organism so that they might

be able to pass through a semipermeable membrane? This discussion leads to the following unit of activities on mechanical and chemical principles of processing.

2. The following activity also reviews the process of osmosis and the need for food particles to be broken down in order to pass through a selective membrane.

   Soak three 4 in. lengths of dialysis tubing in water for several minutes until it separates when rubbed between your fingers. Tightly tie off one end of each tubing and label each end A, B, and C. Fill each tube to within 1 in. of the top with the following solution: Tube A, water; Tube B, 50% glucose; Tube C, 50% starch. Tie the tops tightly with nylon thread. Carefully rinse Tubes B and C under cold running water and check for leaks. Lay a glass rod or pencil across the top of a beaker and suspend the three tubes from the rod. The beaker should be approximately three-fourths filled with tap water. Be sure the tubes are not touching one another and that the water in the beaker is at least as high as the level of the solutions in the tubing. Allow the setup to remain undisturbed for 24 hours.

   On the following day, using the nutrient tests for starch (Lugol's solution) and sugar (Benedict's solution), check the water in the beaker for the presence of these nutrients. What results were obtained? How do students account for the difference between the diffusion of sugar and starch through a membrane? Bring up the need for starch to be broken down to smaller molecules to pass through the membrane. Test the contents of Tube A for starch and sugar. What accounts for the diffusion of glucose into the tube? Discuss your results in terms of the movement of nutrients through the intestinal wall and into the blood vessel or from blood vessels into cells.

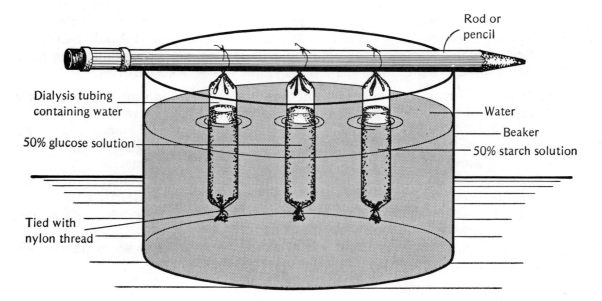

Figure 4.1.   Osmosis demonstration

Mechanical and Chemical Principles Involved in Processing

3. After reviewing the need for nutrients to be in a simple form in order to pass through various membranes into cells, present students with several common food items, such as a slice of bread, a piece of raw meat, and a piece of hard candy. Elicit from the class the different methods they would use to break down the food items into particles small enough to pass through a membrane. At this point in the unit, do not accept responses such as eating it or using an enzyme. Write all acceptable answers on the chalkboard. Through questioning, direct the discussion to include all the various chemical as well as physical means of breaking down food until you have arrived at a comprehensive list, such as the following:

Mechanical:　　Cutting, tearing, grinding, mashing.
Chemical:　　Use of an acid or base or an effective solvent.
Physical:　　Melting or burning through the application of heat.

You might present students with a mixture such as fruit juice to bring in methods of filtering used by organisms. If your students lack an adequate background in chemistry, you may want to concretize the concepts of decomposition, solubility, melting, and so forth by using the following activities.

ACID (CHEMICAL)
4. Demonstrate the decomposition of sugar by pouring a small amount of concentrated sulfuric acid over a volume of about 100 cm³ of sugar contained in a 600 ml beaker. Be sure to perform this demonstration yourself since it requires concentrated acid. (Note the volume changes as the new substance is formed.)

5. Suspend various substances, such as pieces of wood, plants, metals, and food items, in dilute acids or bases to see if they can be broken down by this means. Be sure to measure such items as metal by mass before and after immersing for a given period to verify the results. Students should not handle items directly after removing from the acid; items to be measured should be rinsed. Record which items reacted with the acid or base, and approximate the rates of reaction. Are the resulting particles visible to the naked eye?

6. Have students test various substances in different solvents and describe their rate, if discernible, of solubility in each solvent using the terms "Very Soluble," "Soluble," "Slightly Soluble," or "Not Soluble." Only small amounts of solute and solvent are required. Test for solubility in a watch glass or petri dish, stirring with a glass rod. Use inorganic as well as organic substances in common solvents (such as water, alcohol, oil, and carbon tetrachloride) that demonstrate varying properties. Samples might include sugar, citric acid, starch, wood shavings, iron filings or small bits of magnesium ribbon, bits of cooked egg white, fatty substances, and moth flakes.

You might have students mix two solvents together to see which liquids mix or dissolve readily.

HEAT (PHYSICAL)
7. Demonstrate the effects of varying amounts of heat on different substances to see if melting or decomposition takes place. Use such items as butter, sugar,

raw egg, raw meat, or celery sticks. Note the difference between the effect of a direct flame and varying degrees of heat on the substances. Which substances melted? Which underwent decomposition? Have students note how a gas was produced in some of the reactions, and relate this occurrence to decomposition and boiling of water present in foods.

8. You can verify the decomposition of a substance by catching the gas given off and testing it. For this experiment, 5 g of sodium chlorate could be strongly heated in a test tube and the resulting gas tested with a glowing splint to identify it as oxygen. Catch the gas by placing a one-hole stopper containing bent glass tubing in the mouth of the test tube containing the sodium chlorate. Attach a rubber hose to the glass tubing, and insert the other end of the hose in a test tube filled with water inverted in a beaker of water. Two such test tubes will be needed to hold all the gas produced. After corking the test tube of gas with a stopper, remove the tube from the water, invert it, remove the stopper, and test for oxygen using a glowing splint.

9. After demonstrating the various physical and chemical means of breaking down food, ask students which of these methods are used by the human body. Which are used by all living organisms (such as dissolving)? Which specific methods are used by certain organisms, such as filter feeding by some marine invertebrates, herring, and baleen whales? The following activities illustrate various methods used by organisms to break down food. While some foods are referred to as "melting in our mouths" and some enzymes are active only in the higher temperatures of warm-blooded animals, it would be wise to stress that usually you use heating methods before ingesting food. Many foods, such as fatty meats, are easier to digest because the heat has melted out much of the fat and weakened the tissue, making it easier to digest.

Mechanical Process of Digestion in Organisms

10. Elicit from students the various adaptations in predatory mammals used in the mechanical breakdown of food (for example, claws and teeth). Show a diagram or model of a set of teeth found in an adult human. Which teeth are used for cutting, tearing, grinding, and so on? Compare these teeth with the teeth of other carnivorous mammals. Show an illustration of the teeth of a ruminant or other herbivore. Have students research the mouthparts present in various vertebrates. Be sure to include filter-feeding whales and animals with distensible jaws, such as the snake.

11. Compare the food-getting apparatus and behavior of several different animals: (grasshopper, worm, fish and snail, and daphnia). This activity may be carried out over several days, or you may want different groups of students studying different animals and have a follow-up discussion, with each group tabulating and comparing their results.

    a. *Grasshoppers:* Have students determine which foods make up the grasshopper's diet and which organs are used to obtain and ingest the food by setting up the following experiment. Obtain four or five grasshoppers (or crickets), and place each in a separate glass or clear plastic jar. Be sure there is a piece of moist paper towel in the bottom of each jar and that the jar is covered securely with a piece of stocking, cotton gauze, or fine wire. Have various foods ready for testing: orange rind, apple, cracker, lettuce, sausage, and hamburger. Distribute a jar to each student. Have them lower the test foods one by one into the jar and observe the insect's responses for about 3 minutes. The results should be recorded in their notebooks. Did all the grasshoppers prefer the same types of food? If some did not eat at all, repeat the experiment the following day. Where is the mouth located? Were other appendages used in obtaining the food?

b. *Worm:* Have students place several earthworms on moist paper toweling, observing their method of motion and determining if they have front and back ends. Place a small amount of powdered yeast in the path of each worm and observe its reactions. Students may also place the worms in a piece of glass tubing slightly longer and wider than the worms. Instruct students to close one end with clay and loosely fill the tube with moist soil. After placing another piece of clay over the open end, watch the earthworm closely to see how and where it takes in food particles. The earthworm is known as nature's version of the vacuum sweeper; have students suggest a reason for this designation.

c. *Fish and snails:* If you have access to a classroom aquarium or can set up a homemade one, have students study the eating habits of fish and snails. After placing several different types of fish in the tank (some good freshwater fish samples are catfish, goldfish, guppies, and angelfish), note the location of the mouths of different types of fish. Are any fish eating the plants you placed in the tank? Then drop a pinch of dry fish food into the tank. Note which fish swim to the surface to obtain the food and which catch the food on the way down or off the bottom. Next, drop tiny bits of uncooked liver into the tank. Have students note if any fish prefer the liver to the dry food. Place several specimens of snails in the tank, and instruct pupils to observe the snails' behavior. Did they eat any of the fish food or liver as it descended or after it settled on the bottom? If the glass of the tank is coated with any green algae, watch what happens to it as the snail crawls along. Place a snail on a watch glass or beaker containing a small amount of the aquarium water. After adding a few grains of dry plant food, tell students to hold the watch glass or beaker above their heads and watch the snail as it glides along the bottom, noting how it ingests the food.

d. *Daphnia:* Place several drops of daphnia culture on a glass slide. Do *not* add a cover slip. Have students locate the mouth or other food-getting structures under low power. On a separate slide, mix a small amount of dry yeast with a drop of neutral red indicator. Place a drop of water on the daphnia slide, and mix in a small amount of the yeast. Observe each under low power, and then combine the mixture with the daphnia culture and watch the daphnia's behavior. Students can repeat the experiment using dry plant food, crumbled egg yolk, or protozoa if they are available.

Have students compare the various food-getting structures and the diets of each animal studied. Did students find any relationship between structures and diet in each case? Did land animals possess similar food-getting structures when compared with aquatic animals, or were these structures more related to diet? How do human food-getting structures compare with those of these animals?

Ingestion Activities

12. A good activity for students to undertake to see a clear-cut process of ingestion is to use a wet mount technique of a paramecium with a unicellular green algae, chlorella. By having these two living things together on the same slide, students will note the paramecium ingesting the chlorella with its cilia. Then the students can actually see the "green" algae passing into the food vacuole of the paramecium from the oral groove.

13. Another good ingestion activity is to have students prepare a wet mount of hydra and a daphnia. Students can readily see the hydra catch the daphnia using the nematocysts on its tentacles. Students can see the stunning action of these cells and how the daphnia moves toward the hypostome of the hydra.

14. The process of ingestion can be studied using insectivorous plants, such as the venus fly trap. You may wish to grow these plants in your classroom. The tubers are available from any biological supply house. You can set up a rather interesting experiment in which you place one plant in soil rich in nitrogen, such as regular house plant soil. In another container, place soil deficient in nitrogen (such soil can be obtained from a bog area). You will note that the plants growing in the soil rich in nitrogen will not catch their prey, since the nitrogen requirement is already met. In the soil that lacks nitrogen, you will observe the plant trapping flies or other insects in order to secure the needed nitrogen from these animals. Many variations can be used to illustrate the same point.

15. A demonstration to show whether a paramecium can determine a food product from a nonfood product can be undertaken. To a wet mount containing a paramecium, add some carmine red particles, and observe the organism "ingesting" this red dye. You can actually see the red color in the food vacuole of the paramecium. Now observe how long it takes for the organism to realize this is not a food product. See if the organism rejects the dye or accepts it. Observe whether the paramecium will look for a food source after accepting the dye. There are many types of activities that you can associate with this demonstration.

16. If you prefer to use a large organism to demonstrate food preferences, you may use a frog *(Rana pipiens)*. Many students do not realize that frogs starve themselves to death in a laboratory setting due to the lack of moving food available to them. You can experiment using live mealworms (beetle larvae) in a container with a frog compared to offering the frog a piece of chopped meat (not moving). You can also fool the frog by moving a lure in front of it and observing its ingestion action. Students should be able to conclude that a frog will strike and ingest only a moving object. Why? What does this tell you about the diet of a frog? Is it mainly a carnivore or a herbivore? Is its internal environment maintained by nutrients from plants or animals? Be innovative, and try other ideas.

17. A good demonstration showing how effective a mosquito is at food getting is to fill a thin white balloon with animal blood (secured at a meat market). Insert this balloon into a cage containing mosquitoes. Students can readily see the mouthpart of the insect and how it obtains the blood from the balloon. (A surgical glove works even better because of its thin wall.)

18. Using Activity 17, you can undertake a more scientific investigation in which you measure the amount of blood an adult mosquito ingests over a given period of time and how frequently food getting is required. This activity can then be compared to other insects that ingest leaves of plants. A good discussion of food chains can follow.

19. Have students observe prepared microscope slides of insect mouthparts. (Slides can be purchased at any biological supply house.) Be sure to include a chewing type, sucking type, and lapping type and the long proboscis of the butterfly for nectar gathering. Each mouthpart can be drawn by the student. See how each has been modified for the mode of living and survival of the insect being studied. By referring to Reproduction Page 14, students can see the various types for comparison. This is a good activity to show how insects became specialized food gatherers and how adaptations of their mouthparts facilitate their survival in a given environment.

Symbiotic Relationships

20. A dramatic activity is to show the importance of microorganisms in the guts of animals to aid in digestion. Such a relationship can be studied using the common wood termite. Secure live specimens of the termites either from a local forest (in a rotting log) or a biological supply house, and observe how these insects are able to digest wood. Most animals are unable to digest cellulose unless there is some symbiotic relationship that exists within their digestive system, such as in the termite. Once you have established a small termite population, by placing these insects in an aquarium of rotting food and wood chips, you will note eggs being laid. Isolate several of these eggs, and allow them to hatch away from the termite population. You will note after several weeks that these new hatchlings die since they are unable to secure the tiny flagellate, *trichonympha,* which are usually secured by ingesting the fecal pellets ejected by the adults. If you now separate several of these young termites and offer them a pellet containing the flagellate, in time they will be able to digest wood shavings as food. Be sure to have the students observe *trichonympha* through the microscope. A slide can be prepared by tearing the pellets with dissecting needles and distilled water. You can mention that *trichonympha* are present in other herbivores to aid in cellulose digestion. Your students might not be aware that such symbiotic relationships exist in all higher animals; for example, in the human body, there are numerous microorganisms such as lacto-bacilli and e. *coli* that aid in digestion, absorption, and elimination of nutrients.

21. Have students research animals that illustrate the various methods of food getting and ingestion such as filter feeding, sucking mouthparts, poisonous

tentacles, bioluminescent lures, and electrical shocks. Note that toothless animals such as birds swallow stones to help break down food internally.

Herbivores versus Carnivores

22. A good way to show how an animal's organs have adapted to suit its feeding habits is to compare the systems of a herbivore and a carnivore. Reproduction Page 15 outlines the differences and can be used in conjunction with this lesson. More detailed information may be found in the Content Overview.

    Begin the lesson by asking your class to guess how many times a day a deer eats vegetation or a cow eats grass. More than likely—at least with the cow—students will respond that it eats all through the day. Then ask how often an animal such as a cat, dog, lion, or fox probably eats. If some students have pet snakes, ask about the reptile's feeding habits. Show that, in general, herbivores eat continuously, while carnivores eat separate meals—usually only a couple of times a day and in some cases, as with the snake, not even every day. Discuss the fact that since it is more difficult to digest plant food, herbivores must eat a great deal of it in order to obtain a sufficient amount of nutrition to survive. Give specific examples; for example, a 6-ton elephant must eat about 400 lbs. of fodder each day. After going over the comparison on Reproduction Page 15, stress that since carnivores must find and catch their prey, there is a premium placed on intelligence, while prey must possess keen senses and agility in order to escape carnivores. In discussing the keen senses of prey, you may want to use Activity 37 in Chapter 6, which compares the eyes of a predatory animal with those of its prey.

Chemistry of Digestion

ENZYMES, pH, AND TEMPERATURE
23. Introduce the role of enzymes in digestion by discussing their structure, function, and the factors that influence their effectiveness. (See Content Overview.) It might be helpful to have students refer to Reproduction Page 16 in explaining the catalytic action of enzymes. Mention that the activity of enzymes is affected by various factors. At this point, you may want to give students a comprehensive presentation of these factors and use the related activities in subsequent classes to reinforce their understanding of the principles involved. You can use inductive reasoning by eliciting from students possible variables that affect enzymatic activity and having students carry out several Learning Experiences that demonstrate optimum pH and temperature levels for certain enzymes. Then, through a discussion of the results, have your class formulate various principles involved in enzyme reactions.

24. While enzymes are involved in all phases of chemical digestion and the use of acid alone in breaking down food does not exist in biological reactions, you may want to perform the following activity to illustrate the utilization of hydrochloric acid's decomposition properties in digestion, as well as the relationship

between a strong acid medium and the effectiveness of the enzyme pepsin. In this experiment, students will construct an artificial stomach and two control setups to study the effect of gastric juices on various food samples. First, using a large container and a hot plate, set up a water bath, maintaining the temperature of the water at about 37° C (body temperature). Place a plastic sandwich bag inside a 250 ml beaker, rolling the top of the bag back over the surrounding lip of the beaker and securing the plastic bag in place by wrapping a rubber band around the top of the beaker. Set up two other beakers in the same manner. In the first beaker, thoroughly mix 1 g of pepsin in 200 ml of water and label the outside "pepsin." In the second beaker, pour about 150 ml of dilute hydrochloric acid (4 ml of concentrated hydrochloric acid to 250 ml of distilled water) and label it. Be sure to caution your students about handling acid, and review procedures to follow in the event of a spill. The third beaker, labeled "artificial stomach," should contain a mixture of about 40 ml of pepsin from the original 200 ml and 40 ml of hydrochloric acid. Place the three beakers in the water bath, and maintain the temperature at about 37° C. Now have students prepare the food samples. Tell them to tie bite-sized pieces of hard-boiled egg white, beef jerky, hard bread, and fresh fruit or raw vegetable to pieces of nylon thread (one sample of each for each of the beakers). Be sure each piece is tied securely and each piece of thread is long enough to suspend the food in the beakers. Suspend the five samples of food in each of the three beakers at the same time. Instruct your students to shake the beakers gently about every 10 minutes. Have them observe the condition of the suspended food after 15 minutes, 30 minutes, 1 hour, 2 hours, and, if possible, 24 hours. Tell them to record their findings using the data chart on Reproduction Page 17, and discuss the results. What chemical actually digested some of the foods? Which factors affected its potency? Note that the foods digested here were proteins.

Have students test new samples in the artificial stomach using a much higher or lower temperature. Try changing the pH concentration considerably (using a sodium carbonate solution) and note the results. Ask students why the body could not utilize a much stronger acid concentration than is already present. You might wish to discuss the relationship between stress and ulcers here. You could also have students test the acidity of the artificial stomach and then test the effect of adding 10 g of sodium bicarbonate. This would be a good introduction to the body's buffer system.

25. You might want to tell your students about the first direct observation of the stomach's digestion conducted by Dr. William Beaumont on a young patient, Alex St. Martin, whose bullet wound healed leaving a 10 cm² wide opening directly into his stomach. Accounts of his study can be found in his *Experiments and Observation on the Gastric Juice and the Physiology of Digestion* (Pittsburgh, 1833).

26. This activity shows how amylase in saliva breaks down starches and complex sugars to simple sugars. You may use either saliva or amylase from a biological supply house. If saliva is to be used, instruct your students to chew a piece of paraffin or a rubber band to stimulate the flow of saliva and collect the saliva in a small jar or beaker. In the first part of the activity, you will use 5 test tubes set up in the following manner:

Tube A: A piece of crumbled cracker in 5 ml of water.
Tube B: A pinch of flour in 5 ml of water.
Tube C: A piece of chopped and mashed gumdrop in 5 ml of water.
Tube D: A pinch of glucose in 5 ml of water.
Tube E: 2 or 3 ml of saliva or a solution of 0.5 g of amylase in 3 ml of water.

Test each tube for sugar by adding 5 ml of Benedict's solution and heating the test tube slowly for about 5 minutes. Record which tubes gave the characteristic red color indicating the presence of a simple sugar.

Again set up Test Tubes A, B, C, and D as in the first part; this time add 3 ml of saliva or a solution of amylase to each test tube. After about 5 minutes, test for sugar. Have students record the results and compare them with the findings in the first part of this activity. What do these results show? Ask what effect the enzyme in saliva has on starches and sugars. Question students about the use of Test Tube E in the first part. Stress the need for controls in lab activities. Note also how the complex sugar in the gumdrop had to be broken down to a simple sugar to give a positive reaction with Benedict's solution. Why is this breakdown necessary?

27. This activity demonstrates how fats are broken down in a similar manner through the action of the enzyme lipase. Explain that as starches are composed of small units of sugar, fats are made up of a combination of units of glycerol and fatty acids. We can tell when fats are broken down by testing the end products for the presence of acid.

First prepare two test tubes: one containing 3 ml phenol red and 3 ml fresh cream or oil, labeled Tube A, and the other containing 3 ml phenol red, 3 ml cream, or oil, and 2 ml lipase, labeled Tube B. Place these tubes in a hot water bath (35° C to 40° C) for approximately 10 minutes. Ask students why the water bath is set at this temperature in this activity.

During the waiting period, prepare the following test tubes:

Tube C: 3 ml phenol red and 3 ml dilute acid.
Tube D: 3 ml phenol red and 3 ml dilute base, such as sodium hydroxide.
Tube E: 3 ml phenol red and 2 ml lipase.

Place these tubes in the hot water bath.

Have students record the results for all the test tubes. Ask them what color phenol red is in the presence of an acid. Which color in the presence of a base? Which test tubes gave a positive result for acid? Ask why Tube B tested positive for acid, and why it was necessary to test the cream or oil and lipase separately with phenol red. Again stress the importance of controls in reaching valid conclusions.

28. In order to investigate the effect of temperature on the enzyme lipase, have students prepare three setups of Test Tube B from Activity 27 (phenol red, cream, and lipase), placing each one in water at different temperatures. For example, one could be placed in an ice bath, the second in water just under the boiling temperature, and the third in a water bath somewhere between these two extremes. (You may want to set up more than three tubes and check out the digestive action of lipase at equal intervals between 0° C and 100° C.) After determining in which test tubes digestion takes place most rapidly, students could prepare a data table and graph their results.

29. To show the specificity of enzymes, have students test some sugars and starches, with lipase and phenol red determining if the lipase will break down nutrients other than fats. For the same purpose, they could test fats with Benedict's solution and saliva. This type of activity stimulates students to experiment on their own and aids in giving them a total picture of a research endeavor.

30. Have students follow the directions on Reproduction Page 18 to test for ascorbic acid in juices. This exercise will enable students to do an experimental test, work with indicators, and measure the quantity of substances in various foods. It can also serve to reinforce the idea that the way in which foods are prepared and served affects their nutritional value.

ELIMINATION
31. Discuss the importance of the proper elimination of solid wastes. Ask students how long it takes to digest a meal properly and eliminate the waste products. It should take about 24 hours; many Americans require 48 or even 72 hours to digest and eliminate the food they have eaten.

Discuss the problems caused by constipation or diarrhea, and ask students if they are aware of the efficiency or inefficiency of their own systems. If students are not aware of how to tell the time interval it takes for food to pass through their alimentary canal, mention items such as corn, which have indigestible parts and are easiy visible when they pass out of the body. If students find that their systems are slow in processing food, encourage them to eat roughage or bran, exercise more frequently, and drink water. You can relate this activity to those on symbiotic relationships by mentioning that some people eat foods, such as yogurt, or food supplements, such as acidophilus, that contain bacteria that aid in digestion, thereby replenishing naturally occurring microflora that have been destroyed—for example, by antibiotics.

Mention that just as doctors can detect certain diseases or dysfunctions by the composition of the urine, they can also receive indication of such problems as liver diseases by the color of the feces.

You may wish to bring out the fact that solid waste contains many nutrients that could not be utilized by that particular animal but might be utilized by other organisms. This is why manure is used to replenish nutrients in the soil.

ASSESSING ACHIEVEMENT OF OBJECTIVES

The extent to which students have learned about food getting, ingestion, and assimilation of materials can be measured by having them submit for evaluation the final products of activities in this chapter.

For an overall evaluation of students' ability to recognize how insects secure food parts, and the differences between herbivores and carnivores, assign an in-class essay asking students to describe each, using Reproduction Pages 14 and 15. To assess students' understanding of enzyme action, assign an in-class essay in which students explain the material on Reproduction Page 16.

Several of the activities can be used for evaluating students' achievements. Among the Reproduction Pages that can be used for evaluation purposes are 17 and 18.

RESOURCES FOR TEACHING

Following is a selected list of materials and resources for teaching about the processing of food and nutrition. These materials and those in other chapters are meant to update and supplement the extensive bibliographies that exist in most teachers' guides. We have listed materials and resources that meet our criteria of being especially useful to the teacher.

Books, Pamphlets, and Articles

Beaumont, W., *Experiments and Observations on the Gastric Juice and the Physiology of Digestion*, Allen Press, (1833). A classic book depicting the experimentation of one of the first digestive demonstrations on gastric digestion. Worth looking at for its details and anecdotes.

DeCoursey, Russell, *The Human Organism*, McGraw-Hill. An excellent text on the various systems in the human body.

Fleck, Henrietta, *Introduction to Nutrition*, Macmillan. Offers teachers a sound look at the basic underlying principles of nutrition.

Giese, Arthur, *Cell Physiology*, W. B. Saunders Co. A detailed textbook on modern concepts of the functions and structures of cells. Technical language used.

Green, J. H., *An Introduction to Human Physiology*, Oxford University Press. A concise, factual, and highly scientific account of the functioning of all organs and systems found in the human body.

Lloyd, L. E., *Fundamentals of Nutrition*, W. H. Freeman. A scientific review of the basic facts needed for a sound understanding of the principles of nutrition.

Shank, J., et al., *Guide to Modern Meals*, McGraw-Hill. Nutritional advice is offered in planning a balanced diet. For high school students.

Other Resources

BSCS, *Human Sciences Program: Feeling Fit*, National Science Programs. An excellent health curriculum with hands-on experiences and guides for secondary school students.

Nutrition on the Run, Guidance Associate. Filmstrip showing the hidden facts of fast foods and snacks. Great for teenagers.

Hold the Ketchup (20 min.), Churchill Films. A film that explores the important facts of sound nutritional practices.

Exploding Nutrition Myths, Bergwall Productions. A high-school-level filmstrip with cassettes exploring the facts and fictions of eating.

Good Sense about Your Stomach (15 min.), Time-Life. A video-recording developed by the American Medical Association exploring important facts about gastric digestion.

5

Processing Part II: Metabolism, Excretion, and Regulation of Body Systems

INTRODUCTION

Since one of the purposes of eating and digesting food is to obtain a ready source of energy for vital functions, organisms must be able to release and utilize the energy available in nutrients. This is accomplished by metabolism, which for most organisms is generally an aerobic process. This chapter examines aerobic metabolism—its requirements (fuel foods, oxygen, and enzymes) and by-products (carbon dioxide, water, and so forth) and how these enter and leave the body of the organism. The discussion includes the respiratory, excretory, and transport systems and concludes with the endocrine system, which regulates all aspects of processing and functions in conjunction with the nervous system that is discussed in Chapter 6.

A review of the solubility of respiratory gases and the laws of diffusion whereby gases move from higher to lower concentrations would be helpful before undertaking Activity 3. The Learning Experiences involving enzymes in respiration show the complexity of living organisms and the fact that enzymes are essential for every biological activity.

After reviewing the concept of diffusion across concentration gradients, the activities on excretion and the artificial kidney machine would follow naturally. In discussing Reproduction Page 20 on the dialysis machine, be sure to point out the need for a variety of monitoring devices. This will remind students again of the many variables such as pressure, temperature, and pH that must be maintained at a specific level to ensure a proper functioning of the body. Included in the Content Overview is an excerpt from *When Your Kidneys Fail,* published by the National Kidney Foundation. It is a fine example of the total integration of the various systems of the human body.

During the unit on respiration, you may want to refer to the activities in Chapter 2 on salt-excreting organs in aquatic animals. Content Overview material on the transport of respiratory pigments in the blood may be used in activities on respiration, as well as those on the transport system.

Although the unit on the endocrine system is brief, it is very important and relevant to teenagers, who are undergoing drastic changes in their hormonal balance. A discussion of the relationship between the endocrine system and mental attitudes such as stress, depression, and sexual arousal may prove helpful in increasing their self-awareness and security.

PERFORMANCE OBJECTIVES

As a result of the Learning Experiences in this chapter, students should be able to:

1. Describe and compare the respiratory systems of aquatic and terrestrial animals.

2. Discuss the solubility of respiratory gases in water, and state the advantages and problems of air breathers compared to aquatic animals.

3. Define *metabolism, transport, respiration, excretion, respiratory pigments,* and *regulation.*

4. Identify at least four structures associated with the respiratory, excretory, and transport systems.

5. Trace a drop of blood from one part of the human body to another, following the paths of circulation.

6. Describe how the kidneys function and how the dialysis machine operates and compare them.

7. Compare the various organ systems of humans to another animal, such as the frog.

8. Name and give the function of five hormones in the endocrine system.

CONTENT OVERVIEW

Respiration

The release of energy from nutrients is accomplished by most organisms through cellular respiration: the oxidation of fuel molecules from food by molecular oxygen. The first step in this process is to obtain the needed oxygen from the surrounding environment of the organism. The two types of environments from which organisms may obtain oxygen are air and water.

The most obvious difference between the two is that air contains far more oxygen—at least twenty times more—than does water. About 21 percent of atmospheric air is oxygen, while the amount of oxygen dissolved in water depends on the concentration of oxygen in the air and on the water temperature. Water at 5° C that is fully saturated with air contains about 9 ml of oxygen per liter. Air, in contrast, contains about 210 ml per liter. The solubility of oxygen decreases as the temperature rises. This low concentration of dissolved oxygen is the greatest respiratory problem facing aquatic animals. Also, the diffusion of oxygen is much slower in water, and water is much denser and more viscous than air. Therefore, successful aquatic animals must have evolved very efficient ways of removing oxygen from water. Most advanced fishes have highly efficient gills and pumping mechanisms, yet even they may spend as much as 20 percent of their energy extracting oxygen from water. In contrast, mammals use only 1 or 2 percent of their energy to obtain oxygen during rest periods.

In general, animals have evolved one of two types of adaptations for obtaining oxygen: either evaginations of body surfaces, such as gills, which are best for aquatic respiration, or invaginations, such as lungs, which are most suitable for air breathing.

Excretion

The kidney is an organ that not only removes metabolic wastes but also performs highly important homeostatic functions that maintain optimal chemical composition of body fluids. The basic process that occurs in the nephrons of the kidney can be seen more clearly by studying an artificial kidney or dialysis machine.

In the artificial kidney, or dialyzer, blood flows through the blood compartment, which is surrounded by a semipermeable membrane. Outside the semipermeable membrane is the dialysate compartment, which holds the clear dialyzing solution that allows diffusion, the removal of waste products, and chemical balance to take place. All substances (including wastes) in the blood, except protein molecules and blood cells, can diffuse back and forth across the semipermeable membrane. The protein molecules and blood cells are too large to pass through the membrane. The electrolyte level of the plasma is controlled by keeping the dialyzing solution electrolytes at the same concentration found in normal plasma. (These electrolytes are ions of dissolved salts, such as ions of potassium, sodium, calcium, and chlorides.) Any excess plasma electrolytes move down the concentration gradient and into the dialyzing solution. If the plasma electrolyte level is normal, it is in equilibrium with the dialyzing solution, and the blood does not lose electrolytes. Since the dialyzing solution contains no wastes, substances such as urea move down the concentration gradient into the dialysate. Thus, wastes are removed, and normal electrolyte balance is maintained. By raising the pressure of the blood or lowering the dialysate pressure so that the blood is at a higher pressure than the dialyzing solution, fluids such as excess water are forced out of the blood through the membrane. This is called *ultrafiltration* and is another aspect of the dialysis process. Nutrients such as glucose or acetate may be added to the dialysate, in the first case to supplement nutrition and in the second to help maintain a proper pH balance in the blood. Thus the kidney machine accomplishes the principal function of the kidney.

Because the human body is such an integrated entity, if even one organ, such as the kidney, cannot function properly, the body can be affected in numerous, seemingly unrelated ways. The following excerpt from *When Your Kidneys Fail,* published by the National Kidney Foundation of Southern California, warns those with kidney disease about the possibility of bone damage:

> Bone disease is a medical problem that can affect all people with kidney failure to a certain degree. Calcium is a mineral needed by the body to form bone tissue, but which cannot be used unless Vitamin D is present. Because of a decrease in the amount of Vitamin D during kidney failure, calcium is not normally absorbed from food or from calcium pills. Because of this, the calcium level in your blood may drop. When phosphorus accumulates in the blood, a decrease in the level of blood calcium may occur. When the calcium decreases in the blood, a reaction in the body is triggered resulting in the release of calcium from the bones. This reaction is caused partially by the parathyroid glands, which are the tiny glands located in the neck. When the blood calcium level drops, these glands may release a hormone known as the parathyroid hormone which causes the calcium to be released from the bones. The calcium from the bones then goes into the bloodstream to increase the blood calcium level to normal. The released calcium from the bones may cause them to weaken and may result in bone pain and broken bones. To keep the calcium and phosphorus levels normal, your physician may prescribe calcium supplements and antacid therapy or phosphate binders. If your calcium level remains low, your physician may prescribe a special calcium preparation called Vitamin D or calcitriol.

Transport System and Respiratory Pigments

The discussion here is limited to two functions of the blood and the chemical composites that have evolved in order to carry out these functions. The first function is the transport of respiratory gases. In some invertebrates, oxygen and carbon dioxide are merely dissolved in body fluids. However, the solubility of oxygen is very low, and only animals with a low metabolic rate could survive with such a low oxygen concentration in their circulatory fluid. In almost all advanced invertebrates and all vertebrates, nearly all of the oxygen and a significant amount of the carbon dioxide is transported within special colored proteins called *respiratory pigments,* the most common of which is hemoglobin. Hemoglobin has a great affinity for oxygen; the amount of oxygen that attaches itself to the heme group depends on the oxygen partial pressure in the fluid surrounding the blood corpuscles. If there is a great amount of oxygen in the surrounding fluid, a large amount of oxygen binds with the hemoglobin; if a low concentration is present in the surrounding fluid, oxygen is released from the heme group. This is an important characteristic since it allows more oxygen to be released in the areas of low concentration where it is needed. About 25 percent of the carbon dioxide is carried out of the body by the hemoglobin in a similar manner. One possible problem in our technical society is that hemoglobin has a two hundred times greater affinity for carbon monoxide than for oxygen, and therefore carbon monoxide is highly toxic to animals with hemoglobin. Some other respiratory pigments are hemocyanin, chlorocruorin, hemerythrin, and myoglobin.

Although most of the oxygen entering the blood of higher organisms is transported through these pigments, only a small amount (25 percent) of carbon dioxide leaves the body in this manner. Most of it, about 67 percent, is converted in the red blood cells into bicarbonate and hydrogen ions. The hydrogen ions are buffered by several systems, the most important of which is hemoglobin.

There are many such mechanisms involved in maintaining a stable chemical composition in the blood and in supplying cells with needed materials and removing wastes. All of these body systems are coordinated by the interaction between the nervous and endocrine systems. Reproduction Page 24 has several schematic feedback diagrams for your use in discussing endocrine functions.

LEARNING EXPERIENCES

Respiration—Aerobic Metabolism

1. You might introduce the topic of respiration by asking students what it means. Since most answers probably will deal with external respiration, ask why the oxygen is needed, where it goes, and why we die if we do not get enough. In discussing cellular respiration, mention the term *metabolism*—the process of energy exchange—and that some organisms such as certain bacteria and yeast can carry on metabolism without using oxygen. This is called *anaerobic metabolism* or *fermentation*. Explain that during heavy exercise, cellular respiration in humans will also undergo an anaerobic phase, called *glycolysis*, which produces lactic acid, causing fatigue; under normal conditions, cellular respiration, which requires oxygen, produces carbon dioxide and water.

   Ask your students what happens to carbon dioxide levels in the blood during moderate exercise. Where does the carbon dioxide go? After students comprehend the relationship between cellular respiration and the production of carbon dioxide, inform your students that they can use an indirect method of demonstrating that the energy used in exercise comes from this process within the cells.

   First, divide the class into groups. Have each group prepare two beakers, A and B, each containing 25 ml of water and 4 drops of phenolphthalein solution. To Beaker A, add about 10 drops of dilute acid; to Beaker B, add an equal amount of dilute base. Tell students to record any color changes that occur. What does the color change denote? After stating that carbon dioxide forms carbonic acid when added to water, instruct the students to blow through a straw into the beaker containing the base for about 1 minute. They sould note a color change. Ask them to explain what has happened.

   Now have each group place 100 ml of water in a 250 ml flask and add 5 drops of phenolphthalein. One student should use a clean straw to blow into the solution for 1 minute. Ask if the solution at this point is acidic or alkaline. Have students slowly add dilute sodium hydroxide using a medicine dropper and count the number of drops needed to produce a faint color change. Be sure they shake the contents of the flask after adding each drop. Tell them to record the number of drops needed to cause a color change that remains after shaking the flask. Repeat the activity and obtain an average of the number of drops used.

   Instruct students to set up the experiment again, placing water and phenolphthalein in a new beaker. This time tell them to run in place as an exercise for 2 minutes before blowing into the solution for 1 minute. Again, have them count the number of drops of dilute sodium hydroxide required to cause a faint color change. Which test required more sodium hydroxide?

Therefore, when did the student produce more carbon dioxide? Explain that the cellular respiration required for energy production is the internal aspect of respiration, the way an organism obtains oxygen from its environment and eliminates carbon dioxide is termed *external respiration.*

2. Before going on to activities involving external respiration, you may want your students to see a demonstration of anaerobic metabolism where the energy produced is indicated by a rise in temperature and carbon dioxide is again a by-product. This demonstration involves fermentation by yeast cells. Using five Styrofoam cups and a flask, have your students construct the following three setups. Pour 70 ml of water into Cup 1, add half a package of dry yeast, and stir. Cut off the top half of a second cup and make a small hole in the center of the bottom. Invert this half over the mixture in Cup 1, and push a thermometer through the hole until the bulb is below the surface of the yeast solution. Gently turn the top cup until it fits snugly. Seal the opening around the thermometer with clay and label the cup "1."

   Mix 70 ml solution of 50% molasses with one-half package of dry yeast and shake it well. Pour this into another cup, marked "2", and proceed with the top as in Cup 1.

   Into a third cup pour another mixture of 70 ml of 50% molasses and yeast. This time through the hole in the top, place a glass bend large enough to extend into an adjacent flask containing phenol red solution. The glass tubing should be positioned at least 1 in. above the molasses-yeast solution. The flask and Cup 3 covering could be aluminum foil. (See Fig. 5.1.)

   Allow the 3 cups to remain undisturbed for 2 days. Check the temperature in Cups 1 and 2 during this period. After 2 days, have your students look at the contents of the 3 cups and flask and record any changes in color, odor, volume, or other property. If there was a change in temperature or color, elicit from your class the possible reasons for the changes. If your students have not used phenol red previously, have some mix it with a small amount of carbonated soda and others blow into it through a straw. They will note the same color change as occurred during the experiment. Since your students are aware from Activity 1 that they exhale carbon dioxide and since most teenagers know that carbon dioxide produces the bubbles in soda, they can conclude that carbon dioxide is given off during fermentation.

3. In order to give students a comprehensive understanding of the process of external respiration, begin by discussing the composition of air and the solubility of the various gases in water. This would explain how the oxygen and carbon dioxide are diffused through moist membranes entering or leaving the body while the nitrogen is not and why higher animals have evolved respiratory pigments in order to increase the carrying capacity (volumes) of oxygen and carbon dioxide carried by the blood. The table on variations in respired air, Reproduction Page 19, and material on the transport of gases in the Content Overview should prove useful during this discussion. It would be beneficial and interesting to follow the discussion with this experiment, which demonstrates the different amounts of carbon dioxide in inspired and expired air.

   Set up two flasks as illustrated on Reproduction Page 19. Pour enough limewater to cover about 1 in. of the bottoms of the long glass tubes. (Be sure

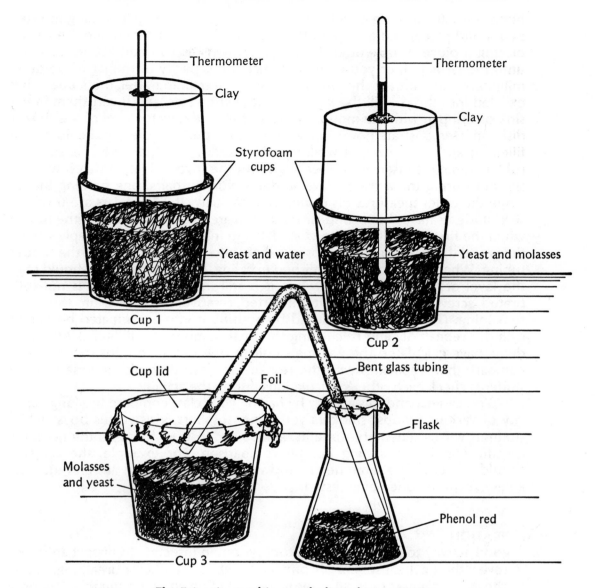

Fig. 5.1. Anaerobic metabolism demonstration.

the limewater is freshly prepared.) Invite a student to hold his or her nose and then inhale and exhale through the mouthpiece for about 2 minutes. Caution the student not to allow the liquid in the expiration flask to rise into the rubber tubing while inhaling. Have the students compare the milkiness or cloudiness of the limewater in the two flasks. Which had more carbon dioxide bubbled through it? Was this from the inhaled or exhaled air? Instead of limewater, you could substitute any of the following indicators: bromthymol blue, phenol red, or phenolphthalein.

4. Students are usually very interested in measuring their lung capacity. To do this you will need 2 1-gal. clear jars or bottles (1 2-gallon jar would be even

better), a 100 cm piece of rubber tubing with a piece of glass tubing inserted as a mouthpiece, and a large dishpan or a sink. You can calibrate the jars by placing a piece of tape at each new water level as you add 200 ml of water until the jar is full, or you could measure the capacity of the jar or bottle in milliliters and subtract the amount of water remaining after the student has exhaled into the jar. Fill the jars or bottles with water, and invert them in the sink or dishpan with the mouth of the jar below the water level of the sink or dishpan. Demonstrate how to invert the jar properly by placing the lid on the filled jar and unscrewing it while it is inverted under the water. Be sure the rubber tubing is inserted well enough into the inverted jar so that it will not slip out during the activity. Have students work in pairs, one holding the jar while the other measures his or her lung capacity. If 2 1-gal. jars are used, be sure students have the second jar ready and are prepared to switch the tubing when the first jar is filled. Instruct students to inhale and exhale deeply several times and then, holding their noses, exhale into the mouthpiece of the rubber tubing. When the student has finished exhaling, his or her partner should read the level of the calibrated jar while it is still inverted; if the jar is not calibrated, screw the lid on while it is inverted, remove it, and measure the water remaining. (The water is measured by pouring it into a graduated beaker or cylinder repeatedly and calculating the total number of milliliters.) After students have calculated the volume of air in one exhalation, instruct them to compare their capacities with the rest of the class. It would be wise to have students check each other's calculations during the activity.

You can expand this activity by having your class compare the lung capacity of various groups: smokers versus nonsmokers, girls versus boys, active students versus sedentary students, and so on. Instruct them on the need for specific controls in setting up the comparison. For example, the subjects should be about the same height and weight and similar in all relevant variables except the one being tested.

INSECT RESPIRATION

5. A good activity to show the respiratory system in insects is to dissect an insect to reveal the tracheal system of connecting tubes needed for breathing. These tracheae are connected to an external opening known as the *spiracle.* Students can readily identify these vital organs. Use a large insect, such as a grasshopper or a beetle.

6. Another activity showing how the respiratory system in insects operates is to secure several types of insects, such as a grasshopper, a common beetle, a cockroach, and a house fly, and place each separately into a special "gas chamber." This gas chamber can be easily constructed by using a bell jar with a tightly fitted cover and a one-hole spiget. Attach to the spiget a tube in which you generate various gases at different times. For example, place pure nitrogen gas in the chamber with a grasshopper. (*Note:* You do not need to have the air completely removed from the chamber. There should be a higher concentration of the gas you are testing.) Observe what happens. Another time, generate hydrogen. Be sure, as a control, to have another gas chamber

set up with a mixture of air, containing oxygen, as if it was a natural surrounding. Students should readily see how the spiracle operates and how important oxygen is to the survival of these insects.

7. Obtain a water scorpion (*hemiptera*), a mosquito larva, and a damselfly naiad from the field or through a biological supply house that supplies live materials. Have students observe the respiratory adaptations of these insects by observing them under a low-power binocular microscope or by using a hand lens. Each will show its specialization for obtaining oxygen through air tubes or tracheal gills. A discussion of these adaptations can follow.

ENZYMES IN RESPIRATION

8. This might be the time to introduce students to the action of enzymes in oxidation reactions during cellular respiration. For this purpose, you can explore the action of the enzyme catalase in decomposing poisonous hydrogen peroxide, which builds up in tissues. The advantage of using this investigation is that it is simple and the materials are readily available. Begin the lesson by pouring about 10 ml of fresh hydrogen peroxide (3%) into a large test tube and adding some dry yeast from a package. The tremendous reaction should elicit students' interest and questions. Ask what the presence of bubbles indicates. Give students the formula for hydrogen peroxide (H_2O_2) and ask which gas is probably being liberated and what product is left in the test tube. How can their theories be verified? If the peroxide was merely broken down to oxygen and water, what part did the yeast play in the reaction? Introduce your class to the enzyme catalase present in plant and animal tissue and discuss its function. Then guide your students in devising a setup for collecting and measuring the gas liberated, and use the following activity in the next session.

9. Students, working in groups, may use different living tissues containing catalase, such as minced raw potatoes, raw ground meat, yeast cells, fresh blood from a frog, or ground leaves from bean seedlings about 3 weeks old.

   Each setup requires one large test tube and one very small one. The small test tube should be filled about one-third full of fresh hydrogen peroxide (3% solution) and placed in the larger tube containing one of the catalase sources. Collect the gas produced by displacement of water. Using rubber tubing and a glass bend in a one-hole stopper, connect the large test tube to an inverted graduated cylinder in a beaker of water, as shown in Fig. 5.2.

   Each group can test two or three different tissues, or each group can test one type of tissue and work out a series of control tests on that sample. For example, they may boil the tissue before adding the peroxide, or they may test the effect of temperature variations on the activity of the catalase by adding a small amount of distilled water to the tissue and keeping the large test tube in a water bath at different temperatures. After tilting the large test tube, point out the production of bubbles, which indicates tremendous activity of the catalase, and have students measure the volume of gas caught in the graduated cylinder. You may wish to have them test the gas with a glowing splint to identify the gas being generated.

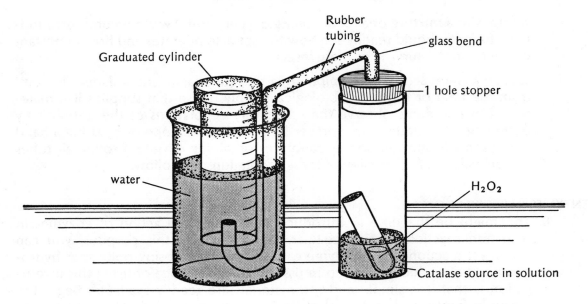

Fig. 5.2. Enzymes in respiration.

10. Using the setup from Activity 9, have students determine the effect of pH on catalase activity. Grind bean leaves from ten seedlings about 3 weeks old and add this to 40 ml of distilled water. Place this mixture in the large test tube and again pour fresh hydrogen peroxide in the small tube until it is one-third full. At the start of the timed interval (5 minutes), tip the tube, mixing the peroxide and enzyme solution. Begin with a trial run using an enzyme-buffer solution at 7.2 pH, and let the reaction continue for about 5 minutes. Vary the pH of the enzyme-buffer solution by adding weak acids or bases and carry on other runs using pH buffers at 3.6, 4.4, 5.2, 6.0, and so on.

    Students can determine the optimum pH concentration for catalase by noting which buffer solution produced the greatest amount of oxygen in the 5-minute period.

11. In the same way, you can demonstrate the inhibiting effect of strong metallic salts on the action of enzymes by adding a small amount of a metallic salt such as mercuric chloride to the enzyme solution at an optimum pH concentration.

    Such an experiment could be used to introduce a discussion on the effects of different substances on the body's absorption of important nutrients—for example, insulin aiding the absorption of sugar, milk inhibiting the absorption of tetracycline, caffeine inhibiting the absorption of vitamin C. Have students research the possible effects of alcohol or other substances on the absorption of food. You might mention here that although most substances are absorbed into the bloodstream from the small intestines, a few substances, such as some water and salt, certain drugs, and alcohol, can be absorbed through the wall of the stomach, therefore requiring much less time to reach the bloodstream.

12. A novel way of investigating the effects of varying enzyme, pH, and water concentrations and the presence of heavy metals or drugs on enzyme activity

is through the study of bioluminescent reactions. Start by explaining to students that the mechanism of bioluminescence occurs when luciferin, a heat-stable substrate, is oxidized in the presence of oxygen, water, and the heat-sensitive enzyme luciferase. Have students place a bit of powdered marine crustacean, cypridina (which contains both luciferin and luciferase), in the palm of their hands and add a few drops of water. A brilliant blue light results. Be sure the room has been darkened before beginning the demonstration. You may obtain small quantities of pulverized Japanese marine crustaceans from biological supply houses.

Then, using 20 ml of distilled water in each beaker, begin changing variables. You might start by adding a small amount of the powder to one beaker of distilled water and twice as much in a second beaker of water. Compare the maximum intensity of luminescence in each. Try stirring one solution to add more oxygen. Does this affect the brightness? Mix the same amount of powder in solutions of varying pH concentrations; compare again. Try adding heavy metals or various drugs to the distilled water, and see if any of these affect the intensity of the reaction. The effects of these variables should follow the usual patterns characteristic of enzymatic reactions: a certain pH concentration is optimum, heavy metals inhibit the reaction, and so forth.

Excretion

13. Discuss the role of the kidney with your class and compare the structure and function of the kidney with that of an artificial kidney called a dialysis machine. A diagram of the kidney can be found in any biology text. Reproduction Page 20 has an illustration of a closed-system dialysis machine, which offers life support to thousands of people. A more detailed explanation of dialysis and the function of the kidney can be found in the Content Overview. Discuss the need for the various monitors used in regulating conditions during dialysis and what would happen if these conditions were not controlled.

14. You may want your students to write to the National Kidney Foundation Inc. in your area for more information about kidney disease and treatment. Kidney transplants and new treatments will be discussed in Chapter 10.

15. Have students construct a simple kidney machine using two clear plastic cups separated by a piece of dialyzing membrane. Fill the first cup to the top with a prepared dialyzing solution containing known concentrations of salt and acid. Cut a hole in the bottom of the second cup, invert it, and place it over the first cup separated by the dialyzing membrane. Place a strip of tape around the cups where they are joined. Now pour a different solution through the hole in the second cup. Perhaps this solution contains twice as much salt as the first (or none) and is alkaline. You may want to use a copper salt in one so you can see the diffusion. Seal the opening at the top. Test the solutions the next day for pH concentrations. Have your students design a dialysate that will remove salt from the second solution or neutralize an acidic one.

16. Read the excerpt from *When Your Kidneys Fail* in the Content Overview and elicit from your students some of the many problems that may be caused by kidney disease.

17. A dissection of a calf's kidney, which exposes the tubules and network of blood vessels, can prove interesting. This activity can then be compared to the "kidney" systems of insects and earthworms.

18. If you wish to demonstrate the action of the enzyme urease to the class, you can do so quite simply. This enzyme converts urea found in urine into carbon dioxide and ammonia. You can dissolve urea (available from a biological supply house) in water and divide the solution into two beakers. To each beaker add phenolphthalein until the solution turns a milky white color. By adding a few crystals of the enzyme urease (available from a biological supply house) to one beaker, you can observe the solution changing from milky white to a red color in the presence of ammonia. This solution may be compared to that in the second beaker. Once you have demonstrated the action of this enzyme, you might try it on a sample of urine. See Activities 21 and 22.

19. By using a model of the urinary system, students can trace a drop of urine from the place it enters the system from the blood to the place it is excreted from the body. This serves as a good review of the system.

20. A good film that reviews the uses of the kidney, lungs, and skin as organs of excretion is *The Human Body: Excretory System* (Coronet Films).

21. In order to test urine for the presence of glucose, ask students to bring a sample of urine to the class (similar to the sample they would bring to a doctor's office). It is best to keep the samples anonymous. Place 5 ml of Benedict's solution in a test tube and add *exactly 8 drops* of urine to the tube. (You may wish to have a tube for each student.) Boil for 2 to 3 minutes and allow to cool. A precipitate will form when there is about 3% glucose present in the sample. You can also use commercially available strips of paper or tablets to check for sugar in the urine. These strips or tablets may be secured at any pharmaceutical house.

22. To test for albumin in the urine, pour 5 ml of concentrated nitric acid into a test tube. Tilt the tube and slowly add, drop by drop, a sample of urine to the test tube. Observe any stratification of liquids with a white precipitated protein area at the point of contact where the urine and acid meet. This indicates the presence of albumin in the urine.

23. An activity using a common wood tick can demonstrate the attractiveness the animal has for butyric acid, which is found in a warm-blooded animal's sweat. Secure some butyric acid from a chemical supply house. Place 3 drops on a small piece of cotton gauze. Place 3 drops of water on another guaze pad, and on a third pad, place 3 drops of household vinegar. Place all inoculated pads in an aquarium containing 6 ticks, which were gathered in a forest or purchased from a supply house. Cover the aquarium and observe. Students can record the data. A discussion of how adaptive this organism is to securing a blood meal can be elaborated on. To kill the ticks once the activity has been completed, place the ticks carefully into 70% methyl alcohol. Be careful not to have the tick attach to you or the students.

Transport

PLANTS

24. To show movement of water in a plant, you can use an impatiens plant, which has a clear stem so the fibrovascular bundles can be seen when the plant is held up to the light. To demonstrate water movement, remove an impatiens plant from a flowerpot, wash off the roots, and immerse the roots in a colored solution of phenol red or red ink. The colored solution can be traced along the bundles in the stem. You can also use a stalk of celery to show how transport up a stem takes place.

25. Root hairs in plants play an important role in providing water to the rest of the plant for use in the photosynthetic process. To show root hairs, soak radish seeds in a covered petri dish for several days. Using a hand lens, students should be able to see the root and its hairs growing. This can lead to a discussion of the importance of root hairs in the absorption of water, helping to save large areas of land from erosion.

26. You can pin a bean seed to a cork and place it in a vial of water in which the seed is kept moist. In this way, the root will develop, and its hairs can be readily viewed in the vial. (Be sure to keep the vial upright so the root grows into the water.)

27. To show that plants take up water and transport it throughout its structures, you can use a radioautograph, which will show the accumulation of uranium nitrate in the leaf. First prepare a 10% solution of uranium nitrate (which can be purchased from a biological supply house). Stand a plant stem in the solution. A geranium plant may be used. As the stem absorbs the solution, you can place the leaves on unexposed photographic film. The leaves are held on the film with a block of wood for about 10 days in the dark. Then develop the film and see the results. A good control for this experiment would be to use a leaf from a similar plant that has been standing in water. Compare both films. See the dramatic results.

28. To understand transpiration in plants, students should be aware of stomates found on leaves of plants. To demonstrate these important structures, spread a thin film of collodion over the upper and lower surface of a leaf of a healthy plant, such as a geranium. Do not remove the leaf from the plant; it should remain intact on the plant. After a few hours, students will observe that collodion remained transparent over the region of leaves that remained dry and unaffected by transpiration, whereas the moist parts of the leaf turned a whitish color.

29. Use Reproduction Page 21 to develop an activity in which students count the number of stomates per square millimeter of leaf on various plants. By having the students use the low power of a compound microscope, they can, with patience, count the stomates and draw conclusions in terms of the type of environment various plants live in, even if they have never seen the plants before. The first page of Reproduction Page 21 should be distributed the first day, and the second page, the following day to compare findings.

30. Transpiration may be demonstrated on a plant by using cobalt chloride paper (blue), which is placed on the upper and lower surfaces of a leaf of a healthy growing plant. The paper will turn pink when it is moist. Place a piece of plastic over the paper to avoid the addition of moisture from the air. Clip it and observe the degree of color change of the paper. You can make your own indicator paper by soaking strips of filter paper in a 3% cobalt chloride solution. When saturated, the solution and paper will be red in color; on drying, it will turn blue.

31. A simple demonstration to show loss of water from twigs of trees uses two freshly cut woody twigs. From one of them, remove the leaves; the other should keep its leaves. Prepare a ring stand with two flasks inverted, each having a one-hole rubber stopper. Place one twig through each of the one-hole rubber stoppers, positioning the leaf part of the twig inside the flasks. Use wax to seal off the rubber stopper. Place the freshly cut part of each twig in a beaker of water and observe. A comparison may be made of the amount of condensation within each flask. Ask the class to determine the control. This demonstration is a good introduction to the concept of transpiration in plants.

32. A more sophisticated demonstration of transpiration is to measure the water loss using a potometer. To make a potometer, connect the bottom ends of two burettes with a short rubber tube. Fill the apparatus with water, and plug one burette with a one-hole stopper through which a woody stem has been inserted. Seal the stem at the stopper connection with wax. Plug the other burette with a no-hole stopper. The water level in the burette should be marked at the start so that as the transpiration continues, the amount of water absorbed may be measured by the change in the water level. See Fig. 5.3.

33. To show the lifting power of leaves in a plant, fit a leafy stem into a one-hole rubber stopper, airtight. Add some water to a U tube apparatus in which the

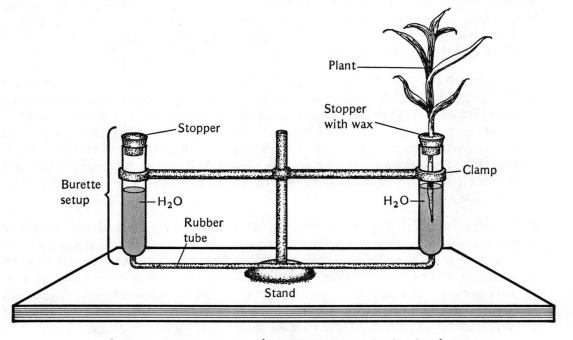

Fig. 5.3. A potometer to demonstrate transpiration in plants.

plant will be placed. To the other arm of the U tube, add a small amount of mercury so that an equal level in both arms of the U tube is maintained. In about 1 hour, students will be able to see the mercury level displaced in the direction of the tube containing the water.

ANIMALS

34. A good heart demonstration is to dissect a freshly killed frog and remove the entire heart with the pericardial sac. Place the heart in a petri dish and add Ringer's solution. Note the rate of heartbeat. To make Ringer's solution, dissolve 0.14 g of KCl, 6.50 g of NaCl, 0.12 g of $CaCl_2$, and 0.20 g of $NaHCO_3$ in 1 l of distilled water.

35. You can observe heartbeats in a clam by cracking one shell of the clam and cutting the anterior and posterior adductor muscles with a sharp knife. Remove the mantle and observe the heartbeat. Use Ringer's solution to speed up the rate.

36. You may wish to have your students see circulation in the capillaries of an organism. By wrapping the body of a goldfish in wet absorbent cotton so that only the tail is exposed, you can illustrate such circulation. Place the fish, wrapped in cotton, in a petri dish with a small amount of water. Cover the tail with a glass slide in the dish. Examine under low and high power of the microscope.

37. A good film to show the class about blood and circulation is *Hemo, the Magnificent,* distributed free of charge by Bell Telephone Co.

38. A good exercise is to trace a drop of blood from one place in the body to another place. In order to perform this exercise, students need to understand the pathway of circulation and the role of the heart. Using Reproduction Page 22, have students place arrows in the direction of the blood flow, and then ask each to trace a drop of blood using the problems listed below the schematic.

39. Using the notes in the Content Overview, discuss the function of respiratory pigments in the blood and mention specific examples. You may wish to tie this in with a lab on testing the blood for hemoglobin levels. For this, you will need a Tallquist Scale pad and color chart. Discuss various types of anemia and how they may be related to diet.

40. Since blood pressure is one of the basic physiological indicators of a person's health and can be used to test the effect of various substances or activities on the body, it would be beneficial for students to learn the technique of measuring blood pressure. Try to obtain several sphygmomanometers and stethoscopes from various sources: the school nurse, public health clinics, physicians, students with relatives in the medical profession. Have students read Reproducton Page 23. Then you demonstrate the technique on one student. Caution students that the cuff may not be left inflated for more than 30 seconds. Have some students take the blood pressure of others while you circulate among the groups. After students have mastered the technique, invite them to measure the effect of exercise on blood pressure. Instruct them to measure the subject's normal blood pressure; then, immediately after the subject has completed 2 minutes of exercise (running in place or jumping rope, for example),

take the measurement again. Tell your students to repeat the measurement every 2 minutes until the blood pressure has returned to normal, and record the data. In a similar manner, they can measure the effect of deep relaxation (use a prepared exercise on relaxing), of various types of music, of different substances such as caffeine, and, if possible, also measure the effect of smoking on the blood pressure of an adult smoker who works in the school.

Although the last example may require special permission, it has proved to be a very effective demonstration of the negative effect of smoking on the body. The systolic pressure often rises at least ten points right after smoking. A relaxing exercise is also very effective in lowering blood pressure. Such exercises can be used to stimulate discussions on the effect of drugs and stress, biofeedback techniques, and physiological illnesses.

Endocrine Activities

41. This is a simple investigation to study the effect of a plant hormone (such as auxin or gibberellin) on a plant's growth. First, obtain two potted bean seedlings, and have your students make a rough sketch of each. Label one A and one B. Obtain auxin or gibberellin from a supply house and mix thoroughly with 0.1 of beta-indoleacetic and 1 ml of 70% ethyl alcohol and add this to 50 g of hydrous lanolin. With a toothpick, apply the lanolin-hormone mixture to one side of the stem of Plant A. Apply plain lanolin to the same location on Plant B. Instruct students to observe the plants for 1 week and record their observations in their notebooks. During a discusson on the effect of the hormone, ask students why one plant was treated with plain lanolin.

42. The following exercise demonstrates how hormones affect the regulation of the transport system in animals. This activity uses the neurohormone acetylcholine. Explain to your class that although such chemicals as acetylcholine are not produced by endocrine glands, they act very much like hormones. They are, in fact, secreted by axons when impulses pass over neurons; thus the term *neurohormone*.* During this activity, students, in pairs, will investigate the effects of adrenalin and acetylcholine on the heart rate of daphnia. Instruct students to place a drop of daphnia culture on a slide and locate the daphnia's heart under low power. Then, while one student keeps time for 1 minute, the other counts the number of heartbeats. Marking a slash on scrap paper every fifth beat may help them to keep an accurate count. The procedure should be repeated three times and an average calculated. Now a drop of acetylcholine is added to the slide. Students again record the heartbeat several times and calculate an average. Students can remove most of the acetylcholine by blotting the liquid on the slide, adding a few drops of water, and repeating this procedure a few times. After about 5 minutes, they should again find the average heartbeat.

Now have your students determine the effect of adrenalin on the daphnia's heart rate by repeating the experiment using a drop of adrenalin.

---

*A more recent term is neurotransmitter.

Discuss the different reactions with your class, correlating the effect of the two chemicals on the daphnia with their effect on the human body. Ask which of the two chemicals might influence their heartbeat when they are frightened or angry. From there, you might go into a discussion about the effect of hormones on the muscles of the arms, neck, stomach, and intestines. Would this explain the common relationship between stress and neckaches or backaches or the phenomenon of a nervous stomach? Even such disorders as dental problems may be stress related. You can use a current magazine article on the effect of stress on health and longevity. You may follow this activity with one showing the effect of relaxation on heartbeat and blood pressure (activity 40).

43. A good way to give students an appreciation of the sensitivity of the endocrine system and an awareness of the integration between their emotional and physical nature is by listing common physical responses people have to different emotions and stimuli. For example, embarrassment may cause a blush, sadness may cause tears, and fright may cause tension. Point out the split-second speed of the response and the usual lack of control in reacting in each case. Mention common responses to physical stimuli as well: mouth watering (salivating) when smelling food, sexual arousal on seeing an attractive date, and so on. Use a list of common hormones of the endocrine system found in college biology texts to determine which hormone(s) would be responsible for the reaction in each case.

44. In order to study the influence of the hormone thyroxin in this investigation, you will need about 9 to 15 tadpoles, pond water, and a small sample of thyroxin. Set up and label three shallow containers: one with 250 ml pond water, the second with 250 ml pond water and a drop of thyroxin solution, and the third with 250 ml pond water and 3 drops of thyroxin solution. (Thyroxin tablets can be obtained from a biological supply house. Prepare solution by placing one tablet in 5 ml of distilled water.) If the results are not obvious, increase the concentrations of thyroxin solution. Place 3 to 5 tadpoles in each container. Have students observe the appearance and behavior of the tadpoles the first day, recording the approximate size of each and their overall behavior. Repeat this procedure daily over a period of about 6 weeks. Feed the tadpoles a small amount of hard-boiled egg yolk every other day. Change the water once a week, maintaining the same level of thyroxin in each container. Ask students if the thyroxin affected the tadpoles and, if so, which container showed the greatest change.

Discuss the influence of the pituitary gland on the thyroid and on other organs. At this time, you may want to talk about the physical changes teenagers undergo during puberty through the influence of the endocrine system and the resulting emotional volatility that usually accompanies this period.

45. Use Reproduction Page 24 for examples of feedback illustrations in the endocrine system. Have students give examples of the various stimuli, senses, and organs involved in the first two illustrations. Then have students fill in examples C and D on their own. Encourage them to construct a similar chart using an original example from their own experience.

ASSESSING ACHIEVEMENT OF OBJECTIVES

For an evaluation of students' ability to recognize the importance of respiration and excretion, assign an in-class essay developed from Reproduction Pages 19 and 20.

Several of the activities in this chapter can be used for evaluating students' achievements. Among the Reproduction Pages that can be used for evaluation purposes are 21, 22, and 24.

To determine students' ability to master the skill of taking blood pressure, use Reproduction Page 23. By observing the amount of time it takes the student to accomplish the task, you can readily assess his or her ability.

To assess the students' ability to understand the functions of the endocrine glands, review the hormones involved in one system, such as the female reproductive cycle of the mammal, and ask the students to write a descriptive essay on how the endocrine system functions.

RESOURCES FOR TEACHING

Following is a selected list of materials and resources for teaching about metabolism and physiology. These materials—and those in other chapters—are meant to update and supplement the extensive bibliographies that exist in most teachers' guides. We have listed materials and resources that meet our criteria of being especially useful to teachers.

Books, Pamphlets, and Articles

Anthony, Catherine P., and Norma J. Kolthoff, *Textbook of Anatomy and Physiology*, C. V. Mosby Co. A beginners' text with wonderful illustrations and explanations of the human systems.

BSCS, Human Sciences Program, *Feeling Fit* (teachers' edition), National Science Products. An excellent curriculum study using hands-on experiences in the health sciences.

Jacob, Stanley W., Clarice A. Francone, and Walter J. Lossow, *Structure and Function in Man*, W. B. Saunders Co. A classic approach to studying the human structure and function.

National Kidney Foundation of Southern California, *When Your Kidneys Fail*. An introduction to the physiology of the kidneys and dialysis.

Schottelius, Byron A., and Dorothy D. Schottelius, *Textbook of Physiology*, C. V. Mosby Co. A technical treatment of the facts on anatomy and physiology.

Turner, C. D., *General Endocrinology*, W. B. Saunders Co. One of the best textbooks in the field of endocrinology. Detailed and concise information on research in this field.

Other Resources

Excretion (29 min.), McGraw-Hill. Film explaining the basic functions of this system.

Excretory Systems in Animals (16 min.), Indiana University. Film explaining the various adaptive excretory systems in vertebrates.

Endocrine Glands (16 min.), Encyclopedia Britannica. A classic approach to the six most common glands. A good introduction.

Circulation and the Human Body (10 min.), Churchill Films. A film exploring the essentials of blood transport throughout the body.

Respiration in Man (26 min.), Encyclopedia Britannica. Shows how one breathes and the respiratory functions of the human body. Film developed by the National Safety Council.

The Open Alveolus (20 min.), Contact Corp. Film includes fine shots of lungs and capillary action during oxygen exchange in the blood.

The Human Body: Excretory System (16 min.), Coronet Films. A good introduction to the human excretory system in both anatomy and physiology.

Hemo, the Magnificent (36 min.), Bell Telephone Co. An excellent animated film on blood and circulation in humans.

6

Responses

INTRODUCTION

Think how many times your students have observed animals and plants in their natural environments and wondered about such phenomena as how animals know when it is mating time, whether the brain controls the way in which animals perceive their environment, and whether their cat or dog sees the world as they do. These questions as well as many others are raised and discussed in this chapter.

The topic of sensory perception and responses of organisms covers some of the most interesting aspects of biology, such as the evolutionary adaptations of sense organs in different species and how each structure is remarkably suited to fulfill a specific function.

In the previous chapter, we discussed the structure and function of the systems that process materials from the external environment. In this chapter, we offer concepts and activities to demonstrate how the senses of an organism enable it to obtain those materials necessary for survival. For example, a carnivore, in order to maintain an internal environment, requires flesh, hence its eyes are well adapted for chasing and catching prey. The regulatory system discussed previously was viewed in terms of the internal functioning of the organism. Here we see its influence in controlling external behaviors of the organism necessary for its survival. An understanding of the functions of the senses and the nervous system discussed in this chapter will provide the necessary background to grasp better some of the concepts pertaining to reproduction in the next chapter.

The most astonishing aspect of studying the senses is how the brain is able to decipher the myriad impulses and translate them into varying impressions. It may even take distorted stimuli and adjust its interpretation to give a correct impression. An interesting way to present this concept to students is to discuss the work of G. M. Stratton contained in Activity 35.

We advise using Activity 49 on pheromones; besides being fascinating, it provides background information for use in later units on regulatory systems and behaviors in animal societies.

It usually takes too much time to do behavioral experiments with higher animals, but through readings and audiovisual production, concepts of biological clocks, migration, imprinting, and communication can be readily illustrated. Several films and readings are mentioned in the activities on coordination of animal responses.

PERFORMANCE OBJECTIVES

As a result of the learning experiences in this chapter, students should be able to:

1. Distinguish between tropisms and taxes and give examples of the various types.

2. Identify main structural parts and functions of three sense organs (eye, ear, and skin).

3. Compare the adaptive aspects of the structure of sense organs to the needs of organisms.

4. Distinguish in higher animals the differences between involuntary and voluntary responses.

5. Distinguish between the structure and functions of the brain and spinal cord as they pertain to sensory perception and motor responses.

6. Explain how structure and function of the nervous system regulates behavioral responses in animal societies.

CONTENT OVERVIEW

Sight: Monocular versus Binocular

The eyes of animals are well adapted to their specific needs and environments. The amazing variety and effectiveness of these adaptations can be seen if we look at various animals as they are categorized in the prey-predator relationship. Animals that are classified as prey are dependent on a wide, panoramic view in order to survive. They must be able to spot a predator approaching from any direction and well enough in advance to make their escape. To accomplish this, the eyes of most prey have evolved a lateral position—one on each side of the head. Since the angles of vision of each eye are separate, each encompasses a different field of vision. If the eyes are positioned at a strategic location on each side, the field of vision of an animal—such as the jerboa—may encompass a full 360° field or periscopic vision. A horse's vision is almost periscopic, encompassing everything but the area directly behind it. However, since each eye has a separate field of vision with very little overlap, such animals have monocular or two-dimensional vision. They have very little depth perception.

The eyes of predatory animals such as tigers, wolves, and eagles are usually positioned in the front of the head, with the angles of vision overlapping to a great extent. This gives the animal stereoscopic or binocular vision. Hence, they have a much better depth perception. Since predators must be able to estimate distances accurately and rely on their ability to judge form and depth when chasing their prey, binocular vision is a great advantage.

The shape of the pupil can also serve to extend the field of vision. Horizontal slits extend vision laterally; vertical slits extend the vision below and above the animal.

Interpretation of Stimuli by the Brain

Although scientists are aware of the way in which stimuli affect sense receptors and how impulses are transmitted through nerve cells to the brain, they are far less cognizant of how the brain is able to decipher these signals. The problem becomes much more complicated when we look at the work of scientists, such as G. M. Stratton, who test the brain's ability to interpret distorted images. Stratton wore inverting lenses for days on end, making him the first person to have retinal images not upside down. Initially the brain inverted the image, giving him an upside-down view; it eventually adjusted to the distorted stimuli, giving Stratton normal vision.

Some investigators expanded the experimentation to include animals, fitting them with goggles of various kinds. In general, the displaced images immobilized the animals; their brains did not appear to have the capacity to readjust the distorted stimuli. Detailed accounts of these experiments can be found in *Eye and Brain: The Psychology of Seeing* by R. L. Gregory.

LEARNING EXPERIENCES

Phototropisms

1. Review with the students the term *tropism* as a growth response of plants. Mention that in a phototropism, the stimulus is light, and the response is the growth of a plant toward or away from the light. Have students observe plants in an open field. Note the plants and their leaf position in the field; compare those growing in the shade of a tree with those leaves growing on a vine. For example, you will notice grape leaves climbing up a tree to reach the sunlight for their growth, showing a positive phototropism. Another example would be the growth of more leaves on a tree on the side facing the sun.

2. You can demonstrate phototropism by using either a coleus or a geranium plant placed on a window sill. Rotate the plant every 2 weeks. Students can observe the movement of the leaves.

3. Soak seeds of a radish, bean, and grass overnight and plant them just under the surface of moist, clean sand in a paper cup. Place the cup under a shoe box to exclude light. You can also arrange another box with a similar set of cups and seeds, but this time place the cups under a shoe box that has a small slit on the side. Set both boxes in the light. After a few days the effects the light will play on the positive movement of the seedling stems toward the light will become obvious.

4. Since roots of plants show negative phototropism and a positive geotropism (toward gravity), you can illustrate both these simple tropisms very easily. Soak radish seeds overnight. Spread a piece of cloth across the top of several jars and secure with rubber bands. Sprinkle the soaked seeds on the surface. Enclose some of the jars in a dark box; place some jars in a box with a slit. Discuss with your class why the roots in the first box grew directly down, while those in the second box are also growing away from the light. Another way to construct a darkened area for phototropism is to place aluminum foil around and over the plant material. You can cut a small slit into the foil and get the same results as using the boxes.

Geotropisms

5. Review with the students the term *geotropism*, in which the earth's gravity is the stimulus, and the plant's response is growth toward or away from gravity. To demonstrate negative geotropism, lay a flowerpot with a coleus on its side in a dark closet. The plant will straighten itself in a few days. To demonstrate positive geotropism, soak corn seeds and encase them in a petri dish stuffed with wet cotton. As the roots germinate, stand the dish on its edge and rotate the dish 90° every 3 or 4 days. Observe the changing position of the roots. Have students discuss the reasons for this movement.

6. Place bean seeds soaked overnight on a moist blotter. Attach each seed to the blotter with a fine wire. Place the blotter in a petri dish, cover, and place the dish on its side. The next day, you will notice the roots developing. You may rotate the dish 90° each day, observing the following day that the roots still grow down. See Fig. 6.1.

7. Place cuttings of a plant, such as Swedish ivy, in soil in three test tubes. By attaching the test tubes to a clamp or ring stand, you can give each plant varying orientations: one on the side, one stem facing down, and one in a normal position facing up. After a few hours, note the growth of the stem away from gravity. This is a very dramatic demonstration. (Remember to seal the opening of the test tubes with wax or the water will run out.)

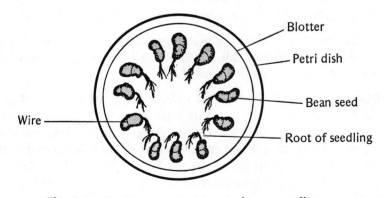

Fig. 6.1.   Positive geotropism in bean seedlings.

8. In discussing tropisms, have the students develop a special project, called the pocket garden. See Reproduction Page 25.

9. At this point, you may wish to describe to the class the classical experiments of Boysen-Jensen on the production of auxin, the growth hormone, which can be found in his book, *Growth Hormones in Plants* (McGraw-Hill). His work can be studied through some simple experiments in which you use oat seedlings. Have students soak oat seeds overnight and place the soaked seeds in boxes containing moist sphagnum moss. Keep the boxes in the dark for a few days until the seedlings appear. When the seedlings are about 1.5 cm in length, cut the tip with a sharp razor blade. Mention to the students that they are cutting the tip of the coleoptile of the oat seedlings, which is the cylindrical sheath that enclosed the first leaves of the seedling. Now you are ready to have the students place a thin layer of gelatin on the cut end of the stump and then place the tip back on the gelatin. See Fig. 6.2. The tip has been separated from the rest of the coleoptile by the thin layer of gelatin. Students should notice that the coleoptiles will resume growing even when separated. You may now place the experimental seedlings near a light source. Students should notice that the tip has sent a chemical message across the thin gelatin layer to the stump, causing the stump to bend toward the light. See Fig. 6.3.

Note: For control purposes, you may wish to have a plant in which the tip is removed totally and the thin gelatin layer is present. This can show that the hormone is not present in the stump.

Students might ask how you know a chemical is produced by the coleoptile. You can prove that auxins (the chemical) are produced by removing the tips from coleoptiles of oat seedlngs and placing the tips base down on sterile agar in a petri dish for about 1 hour. Remove the tips from the agar and discard. Now cut small blocks of agar out, and place these blocks back on the stumps of the cut seedlings. The students will notice that the stumps behave as though their tips had been replaced. The students should be able to conclude that a chemical must have diffused from the tip onto the sterile agar. For more specific information on these and similar experiments, you may refer to *A Sourcebook for the Biological Sciences* by E. Morholt et al. (Harcourt Brace Jovanovich).

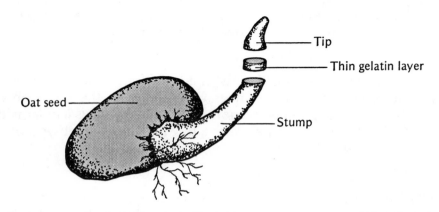

Fig. 6.2. Auxin production in seedlings: Separation of tip from oat seed.

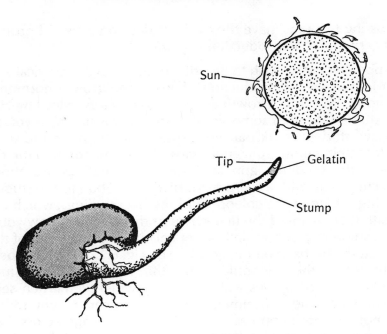

Fig. 6.3. Experimental seedling with tip reattached.

Hydrotropisms

10. Review with the students the term *hydrotropism,* mentioning the fact that water is the stimulus to which the plants respond. To show hydrotropism, place soaked radish seeds on a dry piece of blotter that is adjacent to a wet blotter. Once germination takes place, you can readily see the roots move toward the moist blotter.

Taxes

11. Direct observation is probably the best way of introducing students to the concept of taxes. As students observe the simple responses in lower animals that are outlined in Activities 12 through 15, you can use Reproduction Page 26 to record data and compare taxes with tropisms.

GEOTAXIS

12. Observe paramecia in a small jar with a hand lens. They will swim up to the top of the container away from gravity. Substitute the common land snail (helix), which shows a similar response. Place a few snails in a jar with a cover and note that they immediately move upward in the jar. If you place the jar on its side, you will also note their negative geotaxis.

CHEMOTAXIS

13. A behavioral response to chemicals can be readily demonstrated by adding a lettuce leaf with vinegar to the jar containing the snails. Earthworms may be

substituted. Notice how the snails move away from the acid. Set up a control for comparison by using a piece of lettuce without vinegar in another jar.

THIGMOTAXIS

14. Demonstrate this taxis using a common cockroach, noting the animal moving along walls and corners, preferring contact with a solid surface rather than open spaces. You can demonstrate negative phototaxis using the same roach, and observing its response while shining a light on it.

THERMOTAXIS

15. A fascinating example of a simple animal's response to temperature is the common tick. Note that ticks determine whether a warm-blooded animal is passing by the change in its surrounding temperature. Once the temperature of its surroundings changes by a degree or so, the tick will drop on to this animal for a blood dinner. Demonstrate this by presenting to a tick a piece of meat warmer than its surroundings. It will move toward its prey. Ticks can be secured in wooded areas or purchased from a biological supply house.

Responses in Higher Animals

16. A good way of introducing the topic of reflex action in higher animals is to have students break up into groups of two or three and test their own reflexes. It is important to demonstrate that the student actually reacts before perceiving the stimulus since reaction movement is initiated by the spinal cord before the impulse reaches the brain. Students can perform the following activities:

    a. Blinking reflex: Have one student simulate a punch toward another student. Direct the student receiving the fake punch not to blink. Note results. For another blinking reflex, have one student hold a blank overhead transparency sheet against his or her nose, thereby also covering the eyes. Allow a second student to toss a paper ball at his or her eyes. Note the blinking reflex. Ask students to explain the reasons for this response.

    b. Iris contraction: Have one student shine a penlight beam in his or her partner's eye. Note the contraction of the pupil. You might want students to note that one iris can contract or dilate independently of the other.

    c. Knee jerk: Have one student lightly tap the other student's kneecap or patella with the side of his or her hand. Note the reaction. The knee jerk is especially effective if the subject is reading aloud, clearly demonstrating the lack of brain activity in the knee jerk.

17. If time permits, have students discuss their reaction to light after leaving a dark movie theater or dark tunnel. Elicit from them the relationship between this phenomenon and the activity on iris contraction they just performed. (*Warning:* In giving directions, instruct your students to be very careful and business-like during these activities. Use your discretion as to which reflex activities would be best for your class.)

18. In discussing responses of higher animals with your class, you might find various films and readings on instinctive behavior and conditioning to be of assistance. Begin with a film showing instinctive behavior, such as *Dance of the Bees,* a description of von Frisch's work or other films on behavior from the AIBS series, currently available from McGraw-Hill Company. Have students define and discuss instincts and compare this behavior to reflexes. There are also good readings in reports from *Scientific American* on various instinctive behaviors, such as "How an Instinct Is Learned" by Jack P. Hailman and "The Homing Salmon" by Arthur D. Hasler. These, as well as others, can be secured from W. H. Freeman & Co.

19. An excellent way to demonstrate conditioning behavior to a class is to instruct the class to draw a continuous line on a piece of paper every time you say the word *draw.* The class should stop after 2 seconds and wait for the signal "draw" again. Do this about every 2 or 3 seconds about 20 times. Be sure that every time you state the word *draw,* you tap your desk with a ruler. After about 20 times of repeating these signals (tap of ruler plus word *draw*), continue to tap the ruler but stop using the word *draw.* Note that many students will continue to draw the line at the sound of the tapping. They are temporarily conditioned.

20. Have students explain the factors needed for conditioning. How could this type of conditioned behavior become unconditioned? You can discuss the historic experiment of Ivan Pavlov and his dogs. Some accounts can be found in the book, *Ivan Pavlov,* by Jeffrey A. Gray.

21. As a good follow-up lesson, ask your class to explain in writing how they would teach a pigeon to play Ping-Pong or a dog to fetch a softball. You will be surprised at the discussion generated.

22. Introduce to the class a habit. To illustrate the habit formation idea, discuss common habits with the class and compare these to conditioned behavior in young children or animals. You can discuss with the class how children are often encouraged to form a habit through conditioning with an artificial reward, such as a gift for studying. Then when the artificial reward is absent, there is no motivation to continue the habit. You may wish to ask a student to describe how he or she ties a shoelace. Note the difficulty in undertaking a description.

23. Have students write as quickly as possible a dictated paragraph or poem. Read the material at a fair pace and record the time it takes for the students to copy the material dictated. Now read the paragraph again, this time instructing the students *not* to dot any i's or cross any t's in the words they copy. Have the students score the number of dotted i's and crossed t's they actually wrote.

24. Finally, briefly discuss learning as a special human response. You can compare learning under differing conditions and by trial and error. For example, place on the chalkboard a list of words, and direct the students to memorize the list in vertical order. Cover the words after 15 seconds, record the learning time, and ask the class to write the words. Uncover the list for another 15 seconds

and see how many more students can duplicate the list. Be sure the list contains words that make no sense. Such a list might be:

These
I
Whose
Know
Are
Woods
I
Think

Do the same exercise, but this time place a list of words that makes sense when read vertically, such as:

Whose
Woods
These
Are
I
Think
I
Know

After noting the results, it should be obvious to students that there is a need to understand main ideas so that reading and writing in school fits into a meaningful category rather than nonsense. You can elicit from the class the idea of distraction while learning and demonstrate it by playing distracting noise while they attempt to memorize the words. This short exercise can illustrate the importance of studying properly and utilizing study time profitably.

The Nervous System: Brain and the Spinal Cord

25. Diagrams of the brain indicating the activities controlled by various sections appear on Reproduction Page 27. Using these diagrams, discuss some of the results of experimentation carried out by neurosurgeons. For example, during brain surgery, doctors have stimulated various sections of the brain using electric impulses. When the portion of the temporal lobe controlling the memory for music was stimulated, a patient "heard" melodies listened to previously. When the area containing the memory for sights was stimulated, the person "saw" a scene from the past. Discuss the parts of the brain and the types of activities controlled by each. Be sure to mention that the brain is divided into two hemispheres, right and left, and that, in general, the left side of the brain controls the right side of the body and the right side of the brain controls the left side of the body. The area controlling speech is on the left side of the brain.

26. One way of demonstrating the function of the spinal cord in reflex actions is by performing reflex tests on a spinal frog. (A spinal frog is a living frog in

which the brain is destroyed but the spinal cord is left intact.) Directions for preparing a spinal frog may be found in many biology texts or manuals. One such manual is Morholt's *A Sourcebook for the Biological Sciences*. When the toes of a spinal frog are pinched, the legs jerk up close to its body. Another reflex to demonstrate is the scratch reflex. When the back of the frog is rubbed with dilute acetic or nitric acid, it will try to brush off the irritant with its hind leg. Since some students may be sensitive to the use of a live frog during these tests, it is advisable to discuss the use of laboratory animals for experiments prior to the testing.

27. Another way of approaching the topic is by referring to the expression "running around like a chicken without its head." Discuss why a chicken can still move about for hours after its brain has been severed from the rest of its body. Mention that vital organs in people, such as the kidneys and heart, may still function for days after the brain has been severed provided the person is hospitalized and on life-supporting machines. You may want to initiate a discussion on the topic of what determines the moment of death. When the heart stops? When the brain is not functioning?

28. Begin a lesson on the autonomic nervous system with an activity demonstrating its effect. Have students take their pulse (instruct them to place their right hands so that their palms are facing upward and to place the three middle fingers of their left hand in the depression of their wrists directly behind the thumb). Then have them place one foot on a chair and jump up and down ten times. Immediately take their pulse rate again; wait a minute and again take the pulse rate. See how many minutes it takes for the pulse rate to return to normal.

The Senses

SIGHT

29. Introduce the unit on vision by asking how many students have gone walking in a campsite or rural area at night. Have them describe what "pitch black" means to them. After determining the necessity of light for vision, use a diagram of the human eye to discuss the parts and functions. (A diagram of the eye may be found on Reproduction Page 28.) You may want to show the parts of the eye by dissecting a sheep's eye obtained from a local butcher or biological supply house.

30. An excellent way to demonstrate the principles involved in the functioning of the eye is by having the class construct a model of the human eye. The *World Book Encyclopedia* contains a lesson on building a model eye using two magnifying glasses, a rubber ball, frosted acetate, and two mailing tubes. the project is part of a discussion under the subject heading "Eye."

31. The following is a simple but effective lesson demonstrating how the pupil of the eye adjusts to receive the proper amount of light. Have students bring in a pocket mirror. Tell them to cover one eye for a minute, then remove the hand and immediately look in the mirror. They will note that the pupil of the

eye that was covered is larger or dilated, but it immediately begins contracting as it adjusts to the light. Students may need to try this several times to observe the effect. Another way of obtaining the effect is to darken the room for a minute and have students observe their eyes in a mirror when the light is turned on suddenly. You might point out in the first method that the pupils can contract or dilate independently of each other. Also have students work in pairs, noting the size of their partner's pupils as the partner focuses first on a nearby object and then on a distant object.

32. Numerous activities can show different aspects of visual perception. One possibility is testing for binocular, or two-eyed, vision. There are important advantages to performing the test for two-eyed vision besides the fact that it is extremely simple. The first is that although students are tested for distant vision, people can have 20/20 vision in both eyes and still not have developed the proper visual coordination necessary for binocular vision. Students who have difficulty obtaining the proper results in this experiment may have this sort of vision problem (sometimes a person favors the use of one eye more than the other, for example). The second advantage is that it may lead to a better understanding of the differences between monocular (one-dimensional) and binocular (two-dimensional) vision, which will be discussed later in the activities on animal vision.

    To test for two-eyed vision, have students set up an open text about 16 inches in front of them. Encourage them to form the habit of tilting the book at an angle convenient for reading. Then instruct them to hold a pencil midway between their eyes and the book. They should have no difficulty reading the page without moving either their head or the pencil. The pencil becomes transparent since they can see the letters behind it. They will begin to see two pencils in their view. Mention that this is a normal effect of two-eyed vision when focusing on a point more distant than the pencil. Stress that depth (seeing around objects) is created when the angles of vision of both eyes overlap.

33. Another aspect of visual perception is the blind spot in our field of vision. Before demonstrating the blind spot, explain that it is the point at which the optic nerve leaves the retina; hence there are no visual receptors (rods or cones) in this area. Have students work in pairs. Instruct them to draw a small cross on a large sheet of white paper, placing the cross a bit left of the center. Direct one student to close the left eye and stare at the cross with the right eye while holding the paper 12 inches from the eye. Have the subject's partner bring a pencil point into the subject's field of vision, starting 2 to 4 inches to the right of the cross on the paper. Note at what point the pencil point disappears. Mark the point on the paper and repeat the activity, this time bringing the pencil from another angle. By bringing the pencil from different directions toward the cross, students can plot the boundary of the blind spot.

34. If you would like to teach the uses of concave and convex lenses in overcoming eye defects, set up a demonstration using both types of lenses, a projection screen, and a candle. Hold the convex lens in a straight line between the candle and the screen. Have a student light the candle and turn out the lights and show how the inverted image is projected on the screen.

After inconspicuously substituting a concave lens for the convex one, ask the student using the substituted lens to project the image once again onto the screen. Ask the students why the demonstration cannot be repeated. Eventually someone will realize the lens is different. Explain the differences between a concave and convex lens. Then, using Reproduction Page 29, discuss some common defects of the eye—nearsightedness, farsightedness, and astigmatism—and show how glasses containing different lenses can solve the problem.

35. Many students have heard that the eye inverts images so that the scene viewed is actually projected upside down on the retina but the brain interprets the scene right side up. Review this concept. Then ask students what they think would happen if a person received images right side up on the retina. Would the brain then interpret the images upside down or right side up? Discuss or read some accounts of the experiments of G. M. Stratton. A brief summary of these experiments is given in the Content Overview; more detailed recordings of the experiments can be found in R. L. Gregory's *Eye and Brain*. Mention that the results of the experiments demonstrated that animals show far less adaptation to shift or reversal of images than do human observers.

    This difference between the perception of the human brain and that of animals should be emphasized here and in the later activities on animal vision Stress that although scientists know how our brain would view the world through the compound eyes of insects, we do not know how the insect's brain interprets the optical stimuli it receives.

36. The brain can present a distorted view of a scene for various reasons. Elicit from students occasions when the brain may give a distorted view of reality (hallucinations from drug-induced states, mental disease, solitary confinement, and dreams, for example). Then discuss how in normal states our eyes—or rather our brain—can be deceived by optical illusions. A series of optical illusions can be found on Reproduction Page 30. Allow students no more than 5 to 10 minutes to answer the questions on this page. Then go over the answers and ask students what difficulties they experienced in choosing the correct answers.

37. The sense organs of animals differ according to the needs and environments of each species. An interesting and unusual lesson is to study the different adaptations found in animal sense receptors, such as the eye. Reproduction Page 31, showing pupil shapes, is available for use in conjunction with this lesson.

    The top diagrams of pupil shapes list several animals that demonstrate each type. Have students discuss the advantages of each shape, noting, for example, that vertical slits expand vision in lower and higher directions while horizontal pupils widen the field of vision beyond that obtainable by round and vertical pupils. Then elicit from students why specific pupil shapes are suitable for the animals that possess them. This might best be done by dividing the class into small groups and having them list the animals mentioned on the Reproduction Page. Instruct them to write which animal behavior they think would warrant the advantages discussed previously. For example:

Animal	Pupil Shape	Behavior
Cat	Vertical slit	Jumps up and down
Horse	Horizontal slit	Must be aware of approaching predators

After 10 to 15 minutes, each group should share their results with the class. You may wish to discuss the reason for the pupils of nocturnal animals dilating from slits to circular shapes in dim light. This will be a good summary and reminder of the lesson on pupil dilation.

38. Activity 37 can lead to a discussion on eye position. Some sketches and information on eye position can be found on Reproduction Page 32. Again encourage students, in small groups or alone, to discuss why each type of vision is suited to the animal that possesses it. For example, predatory animals need to judge depth and distance while hunting. Prey, on the other hand, must be able to view approaching predators without making the slightest movement that would give away their position.

    You might wish to include lens shape in this lesson since the round lenses of seals, fish, and small rodents also enable them to see objects throughout a wide periphery without moving their heads.

39. Have students research the special visual adaptations found in the following animals: chamelion, eel, anablep, bolas spider, jerboa, turtle, fiddler crab, owl, and crayfish. They can investigate such topics as eyeshine, color vision, and aquatic vision. Encourage students to share the results of their research with the class, either by short oral presentations or group discussions. They may wish to write reports on their findings for extra credit. Allow students to choose whichever form of presentation they feel most relaxed with so that investigatory experiences will prove enjoyable.

40. Another fascinating adaptation of animal vision that stimulates interest is the compound eye of invertebrate animals. Introduce the lesson by asking how many students have tried to swat a fly or a mosquito with their hands. How is it that an insect always seems to know when we are approaching? One possible explanation is the theory of scientists that insects see a mosaic pattern of images instead of a single uninterrupted picture. That means that since a fly has approximately 4,000 facets or lenses, it will see your hand move in 4,000 different images, thereby giving it 4,000 simultaneous warnings. Use Reproduction Page 33, which contains diagrams of the compound eye, to make an overhead transparency and student copies. During an explanation of the diagrams, mention that scientists are not sure how the invertebrate brain interprets the visual stimuli. Insects may not "see" the mosaic picture we imagine but merely receive a sufficient change in light patterns to initiate movement. On the other hand, it seems that some insects can distinguish colors not visible to the human eye. (Bees see ultraviolet.) Have students discuss the advantages of seeing many images of the same scene rather than one.

41. You might want to show to the class an excellent film, *Eyes: Their Structures and Care* (Coronet).

HEARING

42. One very important concept to present in introducing the unit on hearing is that sound waves require a medium through which to travel, as well as a receptor capable of receiving the waves. Begin by asking students why astronauts must use radio communication when talking to each other on the surface of the moon. Another common query is, "If a tree falls in a forest and there is no animal or person there to hear it, is there a noise?" I like to ask students, "Who can hear the music in this room?" (assuming no audible music is playing). Then I show by turning on a radio that there is plenty of music carried on the radio waves into the room, but that these waves must be changed into sound waves to be heard. This leads to a discussion on how our ears pick up sound waves that travel through the atmosphere. The diagram of the human ear on Reproduction Page 28 can be used to discuss the parts and workings of the ear.

    Mention that sound waves also travel through solids. Discuss the use of a walkie-talkie made with two paper cups and string.

    You might include in this lesson the role of the semicircular canals of the inner ear in maintaining balance. Draw the diagram shown in Fig. 6.4 on the blackboard. Explain how, as we move, the fluid in the semicircular canals also moves to maintain its level (just as the water in Fig. 6.4 is touching different parts of the glass as the glass is tilted). This motion of the fluid causes changes in the pressure in different parts of the canal and nerves alert the brain to these changes. The brain then sends messages to the muscles, which act to maintain balance.

43. Another way of presenting the concepts involved in the structure and function of the ear is by having the class build an artificial ear. *World Book Encyclopedia* contains a project on building an artificial ear using a paper cup and plate, nails and thumb tack, a mailing tube, a button, string, and two small pieces of lumber.

44. An interesting way of reinforcing an understanding of the scientific principles involved in hearing is by studying the sense of hearing in various animals. Mention that the hearing organs of different animals may be able to vibrate at lower or higher speeds than ours and therefore pick up sounds at lower

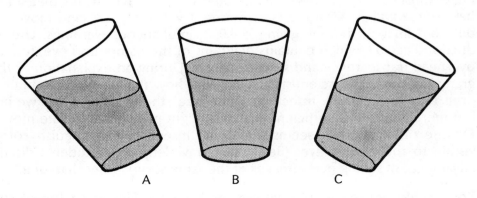

A   B   C

Fig. 6.4. Motion of fluids.

or higher frequencies than the human ear can hear. Explain or have students research the principle of a dog whistle, how a bat navigates, and the ability of some moths to detect the bats' ultrasonic cries and respond accordingly ("Moths and Ultrasound," by Kenneth D. Roeder, *Scientific American*, April 1965).

45. To demonstrate sound location, have students close their eyes. Move quietly to some point in the room and click a ballpoint pen. Have the students, with their eyes closed, point to the spot where the sound originated.

    Why is this ability to locate the origin of a sound lost when a scuba diver is submerged?

SMELL

46. Have students work in pairs to show the strength and specificity of the sense of smell. Instruct students on the day prior to the activity to bring in substances suitable for the lesson (leather, oranges, coffee, lemons, apples, garlic, cinnamon, Ivory soap, and so on). Tell them to be sure to wrap each item separately so the odors are not intermingled. The day of the lesson, the students take turns blindfolding one another and presenting the substances they brought in for their partners to identify. Where possible students could go outdoors and try to identify various shrubbery, such as evergreen needles, sassafras leaves, and so forth.

47. While students are writing notes on their activities, inconspicuously open a plastic bag of freshly chopped onions in the back of the room. Ask students to raise their hands as they notice a special odor in the room. Discuss how the odor diffuses through the atmosphere in the room. In discussing how odors travel, ask why a predatory animal is more likely to spot prey if the predator is in a downwind location relative to the prey. You might refer to movies that show fugitives escaping hound dogs by submerging in water.

48. Demonstrate the influence of smell on the sense of taste by means of the following experiment. Blindfold several students, and have them hold their noses or use nose plugs. Offer the students cubes of raw potato, apple, and onion. Have them chew and identify the materials. Repeat the experiment with different students, this time offering coffee and grated chocolate. Have students try to identify other foods without using the senses of vision or smell.

49. You might begin a lesson on pheromones by asking students, "Where is the nose of an insect?" and "Does an insect smell?" Inquire why a person can be walking past a swarm of bees unnoticed when suddenly the whole swarm attacks (alarm pheromone). Introduce students to the invisible signal system of pheromones prevalent in nature.

    First, distinguish between pheromones and hormones. Then, using the information given on Reproduction Page 34, discuss the difference between primer and releaser pheromones and the various types of pheromones categorized according to their functions.

    After discussing the types, functions, and examples of pheromones, encourage students to relate this information to their own knowledge of insect activities. For example, ask how many have seen lines of ants following each other along the same trail. Be sure to stress the idea that insects do not function solely on one type of sensory apparatus. Explain also that the chemical system of pheromones is not an isolated entity but operates within a certain environmental and multiple-sensory context. For example, the primer queen substance of bees is not merely "smelled" by the antennae of the insect but also licked from the queen. The effects are more intense when supplemented by the visual and tactile stimuli that result from contact with the queen. In the same way, the effect of odor trails is supplemented by the visual stimulation produced by the "dance" of the honey bees.

50. Where possible, try an experimental lesson on pheromones by setting up an odor trail using a strong perfume. An outdoor setting would be ideal, but you might be able to use halls and lavatories or empty laboratory rooms as convenient settings. Before class, dab traces of a strong perfume at equal intervals along a given route, increasing the dosage as you approach the desired object (a candy bar, a poster, or some other object). Depending on the size of the class, you may set up several trails, dividing the class into smaller colonies and assigning each group to a different trail. After the "foraging" is completed, allow students time to discuss their experience, and encourage them to figure out ways in which the same chemical can be used for different signals (differences in concentration, location, accompanying visual or tactile stimuli, etc.).

51. Pheromones are used in conjunction with pest control in order to eliminate insect pests without causing undue harm to the environment. You can demonstrate the procedure to your classes by this activity, which should be performed in late spring. Purchase the female sex attractant pheromone of the japanese beetle from any garden supply shop. Place some in a beetle trap jar, and set it up in a location where the beetles are present. Since the sex attractant will attract only the male beetles, you might want to add a substance with a sweet flowerly scent to attract female beetles. Even after the potency of the purchased pheromone has faded, the beetles will still be attracted by the pheromones present in the dead beetles in the jar. A beetle trap jar may be purchased in any garden supply store or constructed by attaching a narrow-tipped metal funnel upright in the mouth of a jar.

TOUCH

52. In introducing the separate aspects of the sense of touch (touch, pressure, pain, heat, and cold), have students perform the following activities working in pairs. Arrange to have the following materials on hand: glass rods, beakers of ice water and hot water, and markers of washable red ink and washable blue ink. One student will be the investigator and the other the subject in each pair. Have the investigator chill a glass rod and apply it to the skin on the back of the subject's hand and also to the forearm. The subject must keep his or her eyes closed during the testing. Ask the subject to tell when he or she is aware of the temperature of the rod (cold). Locate the receptors for cold and mark them with the blue marker. Students then repeat the experiment using a glass rod warmed in the hot water. Caution them to be sure the rod is not too hot. Locate the receptors that sense the stimulus of heat (mark them in red). Areas that indicate touch but not hot or cold should be marked with a pencil.

Refer to the diagram of the skin on Reproduction Page 28. Have students compare the relative number of receptors for hot or cold with the number of receptors for touch, in both the diagram and their actual experience.

53. You might wish students to locate receptors for touch through one of the following activities with students working in pairs. Have the investigator touch the hand of the blindfolded subject with the pointed end of a soft pencil, leaving a mark. Then, using a blunt probe, the subject locates the place on the skin where he or she received the stimulus. Have the investigator measure the distance between the two points—the probe and the pencil mark—in millimeters. Repeat this several times on the fingers, hands, and forearms.

Another method for localizing the receptors for touch is by using a cork with two pins inserted closely together. Have the investigators gently touch the subject's hand, forearm, and fingertips with the pinpoints. Repeat the experiment several times, increasing the distance between the pins in the cork before each trial. When the pins are closely spaced, the sensation is that of one pinpoint; as the distance between the pins increases, the subject feels two separate stimuli. Note at what distance the subject is aware of the two separate points first on the fingertips, then on the hands, and last on the forearms. Where are the receptors grouped most closely?

54. Another way of demonstrating the keen sensitivity of the fingertips to touch is by having students develop their own system of braille. Using beaded pins on cardboard sheets or Styrofoam lunch trays, make an alphabet of ten letters. Each letter is represented by a given number of pin heads in a certain position (such as A-∴, E-⋮). After agreeing on the representation for each letter, have students send messages consisting of a word or a simple sentence to a classmate nearby. The receiver must "read" the message using his or her fingertips. The alphabet could be expanded to include more letters. Have students try to read the message using the palm of their hands. Note the differences in sensitivity.

55. Have students attempt to identify objects using the sense of touch. Besides presenting them with objects of different textures (such as glass, wool, fur, metal, sandpaper, cactus plant, leaf), encourage them to estimate size and shape, as in a doorknob or a table. Note the different aspects of the tactile sense used to identify objects: sensing coldness in metal, warmth and texture in fur, pain from a cactus plant, pressure in the heaviness of an object.

TASTE

56. Open discussion on the sense of taste by asking students the different types of substances they can taste in foods. After eliciting the four types of substances—bitter, salty, sour, and sweet—ask students if they have ever tried a new food or drink that at first tasted good but then had a bitter after-taste. Why does this occur? Are we more sensitive to one type of substance than another? Are taste buds specialized on different parts of the tongue? Ask students to answer the questions by mapping out the area of the tongue sensitive to sweet, salty, sour, and bitter substances. Set up the following solutions:

A. Salty: 10% NaCl solution.

B. Sour: 2 parts H₂O to 1 part acetic acid (vinegar or the juice of a half a lemon in a half a cup of water).

C. Bitter: A weak solution of aspirin in water.

D. Sweet: 5% sugar solution.

Mark the bottles of solution A, B, C, D so that their contents are not known. Have students use a glass rod to apply the solution during the test or apply small squares soaked in each solution to different areas of the tongue using a forceps. Instruct students to wash out their mouths and the glass rods between tastings. Direct students to draw four diagrams of the tongue in their notebooks, using one for each substance tested. Again working in pairs, tell students to start with solution A (the salt solution) and apply it to the tip, sides, center, and back of the tongue of their partner. After locating the area of the tongue sensitive to salt, they can mark it on their diagram. Instruct them to repeat the test using solutions B, C, and D, applying each of the solutions to the same regions of the tongue as before. After each test, students mark their findings on the proper diagram. (It might be wise to test students with tap water, Solution E as a control test to eliminate the factor of suggestion.) Have them compare their findings with the areas shaded in Fig. 6.5.

57. Discuss inherited taste sensitivity. Start by naming several foods (be sure to include liver) and asking who likes each food. Bring out the fact that people may not have the same sensitivity to different substances. This can be demonstrated by having students taste PTC (phenylthiocarbamide) paper. About 70 percent of all people can taste PTC; the rest find it tasteless. Whether we can taste this chemical is determined by genes.

58. Another factor in tasting substances is the effect that some foods have on taste buds. One such food is the artichoke. Contrary to common opinion, artichokes do not make good appetizers since they block out all sensations of taste except sweet. Currently they are being tested for use with diabetics to bring out the sweet taste in unsweetened foods in order to make them more appetizing. It might be interesting to have your students test this theory as a home assignment (artichokes are rather expensive for class consumption). Instruct the class to eat a piece of artichoke (perhaps the heart), wait a few

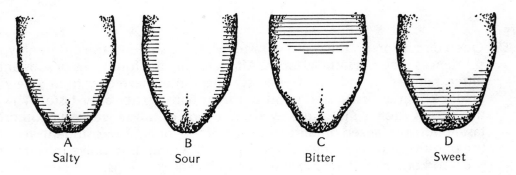

A   B   C   D
Salty   Sour   Bitter   Sweet

Fig. 6.5. Tongue diagrams illustrating the sense of taste.

minutes, and taste another substance. Vary the substances after each piece of artichoke to include bitter, salty, sour, and sweet. Discuss the results in class.

59. Point out to students that the taste organs of animals are not always in their mouths. Some fish have taste receptors all over the outside of their bodies, and insects can have taste organs on their antennae, feet, or ovipositor, as well as on their mouthparts. Students can research the location of taste organs on common insects.

60. A good way of summarizing the unit on the senses is to show the film *Gateways to the Mind* (Bell Telephone System).

Coordination of Animal Responses

61. Some of the best readings on animal behavior are found in reprints of *Scientific American*. These are compiled in a paperback book, *Reading from Scientific American—Animal Behavior*, selected by Thomas Eisner and Edward O. Wilson (W. H. Freeman & Co.). An excellent laboratory and field book in behavior is Allen W. Stokes' *Animal Behavior in Laboratory and Field* (W. H. Freeman & Co.).

62. Some good films to introduce students to the topic are *Animal Communities*, Animal World Series Filmstrip (McGraw-Hill); *Imprinting* (Appleton-Century-Croft); and *A Time of Migration* (Potomac Film Prod.).

63. Briefly discuss social behavior in animals. Include discussions on aggression, dominance, and sexual behavior. Some good basic books for interested students are K. Z. Lorenz's *King Solomon's Ring* (Thomas Y. Crowell Co.) and N. Tinbergen's *Curious Naturalist* (Doubleday). These two books are highly motivating so students may wish more detailed readings on specific animals.

64. Finally, you might wish to use Reproduction Page 28, which reviews through diagrams the senses of smell and taste. These diagrams can be used to generate discussion on these important but often neglected senses.

ASSESSING ACHIEVEMENT OF OBJECTIVES

Ongoing Evaluation: The extent to which students have learned about animal and plant behavior can be measured by having them submit for evaluation the final products of activities in this chapter.

Final Evaluation: For an overall evaluation of students' ability to recognize the brain and sense organs, assign an in-class essay developed from Reproduction Pages 27, 28, 29, 32, 33, and 34.

Several activities in this chapter can be used for evaluating students' achievements. Among the Reproduction Pages that can be used for evaluation purposes are 25, 26, and 31.

RESOURCES FOR TEACHING

Following is a selected list of materials and resources for teaching about behavior, the senses, and the nervous system. These materials—and those in other chapters—are meant to update and supplement the extensive bibliographies that exist in most teachers' guides. We have listed materials and resources that meet our criteria of being especially useful to teachers.

Books, Pamphlets, and Articles

Allington, Richard, *Touching*, Raintree. A beginning book on the sense of touching and the physiology of the skin.

Boysen-Jensen, P., *Growth Hormones in Plants*, McGraw-Hill. A classic study of the famous plant hormone, auxin.

Eisner, T., and E. O. Wilson, *Readings from Scientific American: Animal Behavior*, W. H. Freeman & Co. A collection of reprinted articles on the subject.

Freese, Arthur, *The Miracle of Vision*, Harper & Row. A good book explaining how we see and eye functioning.

Freese, Arthur, *You and Your Hearing*, Scribner. An informative guide to the ear and hearing.

Gray, Jeffrey A., *Ivan Pavlov*, Macmillan. A biographical study of the man and his work.

Gregory, R. L., *Eye and Brain*, McGraw-Hill. An excellent book on the sense of sight and its relationship to the human brain.

Hailman, Jack P., "How an Instinct Is Learned" *Animal Behavior: Readings from Scientific American*, W. H. Freeman. An excellent article on instincts in animals.

Hasler, Arthur D., "The Homing Salmon," *Animal Behavior: Readings from Scientific American*, W. H. Freeman. A classic study of the behavior of migrating salmon.

Hornaday, William, *The Minds and Manners of Wild Animals*, Arden Library. A unique treatment of how and why animals behave the way they do.

Lorenz, K., *King Solomon's Ring*, Thomas Y. Crowell. A wonderful and easily read account of how animals behave. A must for all interested students.

Morholt, E., et al., *A Sourcebook for the Biological Sciences*, Harcourt Brace. The definitive source book on demonstrations and experiments in the field of biology.

Roeder, K. D., "Moths and Ultrasound," *Scientific American* (April 1965). An article illustrating the responses of moths to hearing and behavior.

Schubert, E. D. *Hearing: Its Function and Dysfunction*, Springer-Verlag. A technical treatment of how we hear and the various diseases associated with hearing and hearing loss.

Stokes, Allen W., *Animal Behavior in Laboratory and Field*, W. H. Freeman. An excellent collection of laboratory exercises on behavior in animals.

Tinbergen, N., *The Curious Naturalist*, Doubleday. A great introduction to studying nature. A must for young people.

Wilson, Edward D., *Animal Behavior: Readings from Scientific American*, W. H. Freeman. A collection of articles from *Scientific American* on behavior and the nervous system.

Other Resources

Dance of the Bees (15 min.), AIBS Series, McGraw-Hill. A wonderful visual account of Von Frisch's study of bee dances.

Eyes: Their Structure and Care (12 min.), Coronet Films. A brief review of the anatomy of the eye and proper care.

Gateways to the Mind (30 min.), Bell Telephone System. Explores the brain and nervous system. Excellent film.

Imprinting (35 min.), Appleton-Century-Croft. Explains the psychological phenomenon of imprinting, with emphasis on chickens.

A Time of Migration (30 min.), Potomac Films. Investigates the behavior of migratory patterns.

Animal Communities, Animal World Series, McGraw-Hill. Filmstrip that describes how animal populations can survive together. A good introduction to behavior.

7

Continuance

INTRODUCTION

Once students have grasped an understanding of the importance of processing, they are ready to understand the importance of species continuation or reproduction.

In approaching the topic of reproduction, students usually think only of sexual reproduction. It is important to clarify at the start that reproduction can be nonsexual, such as fission and budding, as well as sexual, involving the fertilization of gametes. Mention that *sexual reproduction* is a term that includes courtship and mating behavior in animals but that biologists make a clear distinction between this behavior and reproduction. Sexual reproduction can occur without this behavior (as in plants) and mating can occur without reproducing offspring (as in humans).

This chapter contains many activities devoted to various aspects of species continuation. Included are activities involving skills of observation, in both the field and laboratory; data gathering; and chart and graph interpretation as well as comparative studies of both plants and animals.

The theme of the book is developed in this chapter by showing how the external environment plays an important role in setting the clues for organisms to "know" when to reproduce. Much research has been done on biological clocks, courtship, and mating behavior because it is vital to the survival and variation of species on the earth.

Another important theme that has been stressed in this guide is that biology should be conceptual, and students, therefore, must be shown relationships among structure, function, and environment, as well as evolutionary trends. With this in mind, the Content Overview contains a summary of the evolutionary development of reproductive adaptations in vertebrates. It also includes an account of the courtship and mating behavior of pigeons.

Little emphasis has been placed on cellular reproduction, flowering plant reproduction, and forms of internal and external fertilization in animals, since information on these topics can be found in basic biology texts. There are, however, several good activities for these areas.

A good teaching strategy to follow as you explore this chapter is to begin by discussing human reproduction. Students are usually highly motivated by this topic, and by first discussing the human aspects of anatomy and physiology, you can initiate a discussion on reproduction, moving from known animals to less familiar species. It has been found that if you start with animals, you can proceed to flowering plants with ease since the students have a firm foundation and means for comparing the animals with the plants. Cellular reproduction (mitosis and meiosis) is best approached in genetics and is left for development after a sound foundation of reproduction in organisms has been acquired.

We advise approaching the sensitive topic of menstruation delicately. Although it is best presented in a mixed group of boys and girls, girls are often embarrassed by the topic. We advise setting the atmosphere by first discussing physical changes (secondary sex characteristics) that occur in boys as well as girls during puberty. Mention the various hormones that influence the development of both male and female gametes and discuss where the gametes are stored and how they leave the body. The discussion then naturally leads to the menstrual cycle.

In order to help your students develop an integrated self-image, mention that both male and female sex hormones in different proportions are present in each of us and that these hormones greatly affect our emotions as well as our physical development. This is especially true during adolescence.

PERFORMANCE OBJECTIVES

As a result of the Learning Experiences in this chapter, students should be able to:

1. Compare courtship, mating, and reproduction, giving examples of each.

2. Describe the reproductive cycles of flowering plants, frogs, and mammals.

3. Identify the sex parts of flowering plants and describe how each structure functions.

4. Identify the reproductive structures found in mammals and frogs and describe their functioning as it pertains to species continuation.

5. Observe several flowering plants in both the field and laboratory, and identify the methods employed to continue their species.

6. Observe several vertebrate animals in both the field and lab, and identify the methods of courtship and structures involved in mating behavior.

7. Describe the development of embryos from fertilization to birth, in flowering plants, frogs, and mammals.

8. Describe the evolutionary development of reproduction in vertebrates relating the adaptations found in fish, amphibians, reptiles, birds, and mammals to the number of eggs produced.

CONTENT OVERVIEW

Asexual versus Sexual Reproduction

Just as animals have different ways of processing materials from their external environments, so there are different styles of reproductive behavior. The term *reproduction* means nothing more than "producing again." There is no requirement that the production of new individuals should involve the interchange of genetic material between organisms that defines sexual behavior. It is consistent with one of the themes of this guidebook to ask what evolutionary advantages are to be gained from the often elaborate adaptations involved in sexual reproduction. The principal advantage stems from the increase in genetic variability and the rapid dispersion of resulting genetic innovations throughout the population. Such increases in variability improve the capacity of the species to respond to environmental variety and change. However, asexual reproduction has its advantages—simple organisms can reproduce quickly, without having to find a mate—and at times is employed by rather highly developed animals when favorable conditions exist in the external environment. Such is the case when daphnia reproduce by parthenogenesis.

During parthenogenesis, new offspring develop from the ova of the female without fertilization by the male. Daphnia are able to reproduce without mating as long as the environment is favorable. Then they produce as many offspring as they can, as fast as they can, to make use of the good nutritional possibilities, as well as desirable temperature and rainfall. Reproduction becomes sexual when living conditions become poor—for instance, when the available space is exhausted.

Therefore, although reproduction in general serves the continuation and extension of the species, the particular type of reproduction employed fulfills the specific needs of a certain species, at times changing to suit specific conditions. Alternation of generation in plants, budding in plants and lower animals such as the hydra, conjugation in paramecia, and parthenogenesis in some insects exemplify the use of alternate forms of reproduction used by a species to ensure survival.

Evolutionary Development of Reproductive Systems

Variations in reproductive methods and structures are both a result of and a cause of evolutionary development. In general, asexual reproduction is the principal means of continuation in lower forms of life, and sexual reproduction is the chief means in higher organisms. Varying degrees of sophistication are found in the reproductive structures and techniques of organisms using sexual reproduction. The succession of evolutionary development of reproductive systems, techniques, and behavior in vertebrates is evident when related to the degree of success in the survival of offspring from egg to fully formed young. For example, lower vertebrates such as the fish usually produce by means of external fertilization and oviparity, with little or no care of their young. Therefore they must produce enormous numbers of eggs to ensure the survival of relatively few; for example, the female codfish usually lays about 1 million eggs in one season.

While most amphibians such as the frog and toad do not have internal fertilization, the fertilization of most of the eggs is ensured by a process known as *amplexus*. During amplexus, the male mounts the female and discharges his seminal fluid containing the sperm over the eggs of the female as she is laying them. Since the process of fertilizing the eggs is more efficient in amphibians than in fish having external fertilization, fewer eggs are produced by amphibians. (The female leopard frog lays from 500 to 5,000 eggs during amplexus.)

Fertilization is internal in reptiles, achieved through copulatory organs, which may be single, as in crocodiles and turtles, or paired (hemipenes), as in lizards and snakes. Also, embryonic membranes—such as amnion, yolk sac, allantois, and chorion, which are used for nourishment, protection, and respiration of the embryo, first appear in the reptile. Since the reptile employs internal fertilization and embryonic membranes and often provides a degree of protection for the eggs, there is another drastic reduction in the number of eggs needed to ensure survival. A female snapping turtle may lay twenty to thirty eggs.

Although a few birds, such as geese and ducks, have well-developed copulatory organs, internal fertilization in birds is usually achieved by bringing the cloacal surfaces of the male and female into contact. Besides employing internal fertilization and embryonic membranes, birds show very advanced courtship, nest building, and epimeletic behavior. Hence, few eggs are needed for continuance of the species. The number of eggs in a clutch ranges from one or two in some hawks and pigeons to eighteen or twenty in a quail.

Since mammals also exhibit these evolutionary adaptations and possess structures for the internal development and nourishment of the egg (*viviparity*), they also require only a small number of eggs to ensure survival. The number ranges from one to about twenty. Usually the larger the animal, the smaller the number in a litter.

Courtship and Mating Behavior

The distinction between courtship and mating behavior can be explained by illustrating both in a specific animal such as the pigeon. One can note courtship behavior in pigeons by observing the male, which struts around the female with his puffed-out chest and irridescent neck. In his strut, he bows down and then stands up tall again. The female makes a cooing sound while the male struts. If the male is successful in his first attempt (and many times he is not), the female will respond by rubbing her bill to his. Shortly, the female will insert her bill into the male's, and the courtship continues in this fashion. The male is feeding the female as part of his courtship. Once the pair has accepted one another through this initial courtship behavior, the next phase of mating behavior may take place.

During mating, the female shows her readiness to mate by crouching down in front of the male. The male then climbs onto the female's back and balances himself by flapping his wings. Copulation occurs when the male stimulates the female's cloaca, enabling a coordination of these structures to meet (*cloacal kiss*) so the male can transfer his sperm into the female for union with her eggs. This is the essence of sexual reproductive behavior.

During such behavior, some organisms are monogamous—after courtship and mating, the pairs remain with each other for life—such as the pigeons. Some species of animals are polygamous—a male may mate with more than one female, and a female may mate with more than one male, such as the elephant seal.

Too often we may confuse students by mentioning the idea of parental behavior. In the true sense, this is misleading. There are animals who are raised in communal societies (termites and bees) in which care and protection is given to the young but not by the parents. Such care-giving behavior is termed *epimeletic behavior*. Some offspring may need a great deal of care (*altricial*) on being hatched or born compared to those who can fend for themselves as soon as they enter the world (*precocial*).

LEARNING EXPERIENCES

For convenience, this section has been divided into three parts: plant reproduction, animal reproduction, and human.

Plant Reproduction

1. One of the best ways to involve students with plant reproduction is take a field trip around the school yard or local community and examine parts of flowers found on trees and shrubs. Have students identify parts of flowers, such as petals, pistils, and stamens. Ask students to state the purpose of each of the parts. Have students keep a log in order to see if there is a pattern of similarity among groups of plants based on their flowers (three petals, five petals, three stamens, etc.) and if there are dominant flowers found within the community. If there are such flowers, ask reasons why they survive and any adaptations they may have for your local area. See Reproduction Page 35 for a sample data log, which may be duplicated.

2. Have students prepare a plant reproduction collage or bulletin board. Students can cut out pictures from magazines or take photographs to show various asexual methods of reproduction. This is a good way for students to begin seeing the diversification found within plants, as well as setting the stage for lessons on sexual reproduction.

3. Prepare a solution by placing a package of dry yeast in 250 ml of warm distilled water. Keep in a warm place overnight. The next day, prepare a wet mount and examine the solution for yeast cells budding.

4. Have students grow bread mold (Rhizopus) in a dish and observe parts under the microscope. See if students can identify the methods by which mold grows.

5. Students can graph the rate of growth each day for the bread mold being grown in class. Through such an exercise, students can readily see the rapid growth rates and learn something about exponential growth.

6. In season, crush stigmas of flowers on a glass slide and observe under the microscope any growth of pollen tubes. Have students describe how a sperm nucleus in the pollen grain reaches the nucleus of an egg cell in the ovule so that the egg cell is fertilized.

7. An innovative activity for students to undertake is finding out which concentration of sugar solution can serve as an artificial medium for the germination of pollen grains of various flowers. Since different species require different concentrations of a carbohydrate to germinate, students can experiment and determine the concentrations needed for different species.

8. A good exercise to develop as a month-long project is to determine the germination time of seeds for different species of plants. Secure packets of six different flowers or vegetables, and set up an experimental design in which you develop a "germination chamber," consisting mainly of a clear plastic shoe box containing Jiffy Mix or sphagnum moss that has been well moistened. Place seeds—one seed group into one container—and observe their germination by removing some of the seeds in the soil mixture daily and recording the amount of time (usually in days) it takes for the seeds to germinate. This activity can be developed further by observing how long it takes the seedling to push through the soil and develop its first set of leaves. You can begin to develop a set of standards for different plants. These data can then be graphed to show time span for species, being sure all other variables—moisture, temperature, and so on—have been controlled. A quicker method for seed germination might be to use a wet blotter in a covered clear container in which seeds are placed. You can observe the time it takes for them to germinate.

9. There are twelve excellent films from the AIBS series "Reproduction, Growth, and Development." Select some of these films to use as review, motivation, or summaries.

10. An interesting activity for students is to observe the two generations of ferns in their life cycle. From underneath an adult fern frond (adult sporophyte generation), remove some spores (brown dust) and place in moistened sterilized sphagnum moss in a sterilized container with a lid. It will take about six weeks for fern gametophytes to grow in the moss. You can identify this generation by its heart-shaped "leaf." Once these are observed, remove half the number of plants to provide adequate space. In the remaining plants, you will eventually have sperm and eggs produced, forming a young sporophyte plant on the old gametophyte generation. This exercise will help students to understand the concept of alternation of generations.

11. Using Reproduction Page 36, have students identify the parts of a typical flower, especially the reproductive parts. After completing the diagram on Reproduction Page 36, have students dissect a flower, such as a gladiolus or lily, and see if they can identify the various sexual parts and compare them to their diagrams.

12. Using a lily flower, ask students to identify the sexual organs, especially the ovary. Let students view microscopic slides showing the cross-section of the ovary of the lily. Bring in pea pods from a vegetable store, and let the students dissect the pod to identify the ovary, ovules, and placenta. See Reproduction Page 37.

13. Use Reproduction Page 38 to illustrate the reproductive cycle of flowering plants. Discuss with the class each step shown on the diagram.

14. Bring in bean seeds, such as kidney beans, which have been soaked overnight, about ten for each student in your class. Ask each student to cut open one bean carefully and identify the parts. Plant the remaining seeds in a container. See Reproduction Page 39 for illustration.

15. Students can observe pollen grains under the microscope. Students can discover the different shapes and patterns of each grain for different plant species. Mount in water or xylol. Students may also determine pollen in the air by placing slides, coated with Vaseline on one side, out of doors. After a few hours, students can bring in the slides and observe the quantity, as well as identify which pollen belongs to which plant. You may wish to stain the pollen grains for easier identification. Add a small amount of crystal violet to a small amount of aniline oil, so a light purple color tint is produced. Mount the grains in a few drops of this tinted solution on one part of a slide. Hold the slide carefully over a small flame until the grains stain a deep color. Be careful not to let the slide get too hot. Observe under the microscope.

16. Another good activity is to have students examine fruits and seeds from various plants. Bring to class some exotic fruits, such as a coconut, an avocado, and a banana, and ask the class to show you the ripened ovary (fruit) and the ripened ovule (seeds). The banana has degenerate seeds, which are not functional, but this plant is propagated vegetatively. (This is a good point to develop a lesson on vegetative propagation.) Have students discuss seed adaptations to dispersal within their environments. A scrapbook or collage could be made illustrating wind dispersal, water dispersal, and other means of dispersal.

Animal Reproduction

17. In addition to viewing budding in yeast cells, you can show this process in hydra. Prepare a microscopic slide of a hydra culture and observe over a few days this budding process. An innovative experiment students can perform is to starve, overfeed, or overcrowd hydra populations to see the effects on the budding process. Encourage students to experiment, and discuss methods of experimentation, observation, and recording of data.

18. An excellent microscope activity is to view the development of embryos in horseshoe crab eggs. Eggs may be obtained in the spring by digging up egg cases along the beach where horseshoe crabs have been sighted. By placing them under a dissection scope (40x power), you can see clearly the different stages of development of the horseshoe crab. Students (and teachers) are usually fascinated by the activity.

19. Insects provide a good source for studying sexual reproduction. In the early spring, students can collect egg masses of the tent caterpillar or of the praying mantis. Place the egg masses in a terrarium, where the eggs will hatch in a few days or weeks. Have students study the nymph stage of the mantis, which is incomplete metamorphosis. You may compare this with complete metamorphosis of the tent caterpillar. Have students examine the pupae stages by

cutting open the cocoons of moths or butterflies found in the field. The entire reproductive cycle of insects can be discussed.

20. In order for students to view gametes (sperm and egg), use a freshly killed frog. Remove the testis and place in a dish containing 10 ml of Ringer's solution. Tease the organ apart with clean forceps. Mount a drop of the suspension onto a clean slide and cover with a clean cover slip. Have students examine the slide under the microscope. They may have to wait a few minutes for movement. To see the flagella of the sperm, add a drop of methylene blue to the slide (the dye will, however, kill the sperm cells). Egg cells are easier to observe since you simply remove them as large black and cream colored masses from a freshly killed female frog. Examine with a hand lens or under the microscope. If the eggs are fertilized, you may be able to view stages of cleavage.

21. Have students dissect a frog to uncover the reproductive organs. Use Reproduction Page 40 as a guide. If possible, secure frogs from a source that will provide half males and half females. In this way, you can give half the class one sex and the other half the remaining sex. Members of the class can then compare their dissected frogs.

22. If frog eggs are available, you may wish to fertilize them artificially. This exercise can be valuable since students see how the process is accomplished and also the various embryological steps. If the eggs are not available, visit a local fish hatchery where students can view the fertilization process.

23. Have students examine prepared slides on the various stages of frog development, from fertilized egg to tadpole. Use Reproduction Page 41 to illustrate what they view. These stages can be used as comparison to mammals later on.

24. Use Reproduction Page 42 to discuss the critical stages in frog reproduction. Compare these stages with that of the flowering plants.

25. The study of live chick embryos is a fairly simple undertaking. Secure a few dozen fertilized eggs from a supply house or local farm, incubate, and let develop for about 3 weeks. An incubator may be made by obtaining two cardboard cartons, one smaller than the other but of similar proportions. Place the smaller box inside the larger. Fill the space between them with an insulating material such as Styrofoam or crushed newspaper, and seal the mouth of the space with duct tape. Cover with a plate of hard plastic or glass. You can use a light bulb to heat this home-made incubator. To start, you need to have your incubator at 37° C, with a thermometer inserted at the tray level where the eggs will be placed. Include a pan of water in the incubator to keep a uniform humidity. Place the fertilized eggs on a tray or rack in the incubator carefully, being sure not to wash off the protective film on their surfaces. Turn the eggs daily to prevent adhesion of membranes. Have students mark the eggs with a pencil so they know which surface to turn. After the eggs have been incubated for about 36 hours, they are ready for examination. (Be aware that about 10 percent of the eggs might not be fertile and that many will be lost during the first 36 hours.) Remove an egg from the incubator, being sure to hold it in the same position it was in when you removed it. Crack the egg

carefully on the edge of a bowl containing a saline solution, such as Locke's solution, which was in the incubator overnight to ensure proper temperature of the solution. Let the egg contents flow into the warmed solution so that the embryo is submerged in the solution. Using a hand lens or binocular microscope, examine the early embryo.

Each day remove another egg and observe the various embryonic stages of development. Students can draw diagrams of each stage. You may also purchase from a biological supply house prepared slides showing the various stages of chick development. By referring to these slides and photographs in a basic embryology textbook, students should be able to see and identify the stages of development.

26. An interesting activity for students to observe, in which they collect and analyze data and then make graphs to represent the results, is the mating behavior of the fruit fly, drosophila. This exercise is a good introduction to this animal, which will be used in the next chapter on heredity. To begin, keep several species of drosophila (purchased from a supply house or secured from a university that keeps stocks of the fly), with sexes and age groups separate. The male is recognizable by its smaller size, black-tipped abdomen, and the sex comb on the front pair of legs (the comb looks like a black spot halfway down the leg). Sexing can be easily accomplished by anesthetizing flies and separating males from females. Be sure to record the species and sex. Detailed instructions on identifying and separating the male and female drosophila and breeding them can be found on Reproduction Page 50. Techniques and answers for the activity are discussed in Learning Activity 12 in Chapter 8. You are now ready to begin your study of mating behavior.

Transfer male flies to containers with females, as follows:

a. Male type A matched with female type A.

b. Male type B matched with female type A.

c. Male type C matched with female type A.

d. Male type B matched with female type B.

(Type refers to wingless, white eyed, etc.) First observe with the naked eye. Watch for initial responses on their encounter. Next, bring containers under a low-powered binocular microscope and identify behavioral actions, as described in Allen W. Stokes, *Animal Behavior in Laboratory and Field*. Make a data sheet listing type, behavior, time, and sex involved. Record all observations and draw conclusions.

27. Another activity is to observe the sexual behavior of field crickets (acheta), which may be secured locally in the field or purchased through a supply house. They are easily kept in the laboratory in a terrarium with oatmeal, pieces of apple or pear, and a watering bottle. It is easy to recognize the sexes since the females have a distinctive ovipositor, which the male lacks. Place a male and a female in an observational container and note the initial responses. Ask students to answer the following questions:

a. How does the male know that she is a female and not a rival male?

b. What happens to his song?

c. Does the female sing?

The class should be able to view the female mounting the male from behind and the male attaching a spermatophore to her genitalia. Students can observe the length of time and any postcopulatory activities.

For comparison, you may wish to have students carry out the above activity using two males or two females.

28. In studying mammals, it is best to use models and charts to describe the male and female reproductive organs. There are many good models and charts commercially available. If possible, have students make large charts of both systems on a plain white window shade. Using Reproduction Page 43, students may copy a large version of the reproductive systems illustrated. Be sure to point out that the urinary system is separate from the reproductive system in females. In the diagram, the bladder is in front of the vagina.

29. If available through a butcher or meat processing plant, secure the uterus of a pig. You will receive a bifurcated uterus with several fetuses. Carefully cut through the uterine wall to reveal the chorion and amnion. Also cut through the amnion to reveal the amniotic fluid. Students will easily identify the placenta and umbilical cord as you lift out the fetus. Remove the fetuses and preserve in alcohol for future study.

30. If time allows, dissect fetal pigs, both males and females, revealing the reproductive system. This system can be compared to the human system.

31. Now that students have studied the reproductive systems of a variety of animals, this is a good point at which to introduce a conceptual model of the evolutionary development of reproductive systems in vertebrates. Start by reviewing the purpose of reproduction.

If a species is to continue, the female must produce enough eggs so that a sufficient number will develop and survive the hazards of climatic changes, predatory enemies, and food limitations until they themselves can reproduce. Ask students how many eggs are produced by various vertebrates. Have them research the topic in biology texts, the encyclopedia, and library books. List the results, and group the animals that show similar numbers.

Then elicit from students the types of fertilization and embryonic development found in each species. Using the information on reproductive systems found in the Content Overview, show how reproductive adaptations that evolved in the higher vertebrates eliminated the need for enormous numbers of eggs. Point out that internal fertilization occurs mainly in terrestrial animals and is a logical evolvement since sperm requires fluid for mobility. Conclude by having students make a chart listing the reproductive adaptations and approximate number of eggs for each type of vertebrate: fish, amphibian, reptile, bird, and mammal. Be sure to point out various species that do not conform to the general pattern; examples are hammerhead sharks and various tropical fish (guppy) that show viviparity.

Human Reproduction

32. If the social and intellectual atmosphere in the community is permissive, you may wish to study the psychosocial sexual patterns in human beings. This type of discussion usually stimulates interest and intellectual curiosity, which can be used to undertake a detailed discussion of human sexuality and reproduction.

33. Use Reproduction Pages 44 and 45 to identify and describe the human reproductive system. Both male and female systems are illustrated. From such illustrations, discuss the process of coition and the special adaptive features of the organ system. If you use a model or chart, you may wish to white out the labels in the diagrams of the Reproduction Page and have the students name the parts.

34. Using Reproduction Page 46, summarize the critical stages of the human reproductive cycle.

35. The female menstrual cycle is a series of very interesting changes of which all adolescents should be aware. Use Reproduction Page 47 to illustrate and discuss this cycle. Have the students answer the questions at the bottom of the sheet. Be sure to mention that the onset and length of the cycle may vary in different individuals and the length may even vary from month to month in the same individual. Such factors as seasonal temperatures, stress, and physical condition may affect the cycle. Adolescents are often concerned that their body may not be developing "normally," and such information is reassuring.

    If your school district permits lessons on birth control, you can explain how oral contraceptives affect the cycle in order to inhibit ovulation. Mention, however, that the pill was actually designed to regulate the cycle in some women so that they might become pregnant.

36. You are now ready to discuss with the class how and where the embryo develops. Use models and charts to assist you in this discussion. Reproduction Page 48 can be used to illustrate some of the important structures involved in embryo development. Compare the human system with the flower and frog.

37. It is important for students to realize how the embryo grows. Some excellent film loops that are commercially available illustrate this point in a matter of minutes. This can then be followed up by using Reproduction Page 48 with a discussion of the various stages of development.

Courtship and Mating Behavior

38. You could use information on the pigeon given in the Content Overview to introduce courtship and mating behavior. After discussing sexual behavior in the pigeon, ask students to research and compare the rituals, physical changes, and epimeletic behavior found in a variety of animals.

39. Have some students research the relationship between environmental changes and biological clocks in various animals.

40. A relevant activity would be to research how biologists are investigating the biological clocks of salmon in order to use this information in the process of aquaculture. By finding out the exact age at which to release the young salmon into streams near hatcheries, they can ensure the return of these salmon to the same stream for spawning purposes.

41. In certain environments, students can readily observe courtship and mating behavior in organisms, such as farm animals, aquarium fish, and frogs. Ask students to keep a log of signals the animal exhibits during each phase of sexual reproduction.

42. There are many good journal articles on courtship. W. H. Freeman and Company has reprints available from *Scientific American,* which may prove helpful. Check with their updated indexes.

ASSESSING ACHIEVEMENT OF OBJECTIVES

Ongoing evaluation: The extent to which students have learned about the structure and function of reproduction in plants and animals can be measured by having them submit for evaluation the final products of the various activities in this chapter.

Final evaluation: For an overall evaluation of students' ability to compare courtship, mating, and reproduction—including the reproductive cycles in flowering plants, frogs, and humans—assign an in-class essay developed from the facts found in the various activities of this chapter.

Have students write an essay describing the evolutionary development of reproduction in vertebrates.

Several of the activities in this chapter, such as questions and identification of structures found on Reproduction Pages 35 through 48, can be used for evaluation purposes.

RESOURCES FOR TEACHING

Following is a selected list of materials and resources for teaching about reproduction and the continuance of species. These materials—and those in other chapters—are meant to update and supplement the extensive bibliographies that exist in most teachers' guides. We have listed materials and resources that meet our criteria of being especially useful to the teacher.

Books, Pamphlets, and Articles

Barnett, S. A., *The Human Species,* Harper and Row. An excellent paperback indicating how humans develop from egg to adulthood.

Bermant, G., *Biological Bases of Sexual Behavior,* Harper and Row. A fine book discussing sexual behavior from a neuroendocrine approach.

BSCS, Lab Block on *Animal Growth and Development,* D. C. Heath. A description of projects that students can undertake and the various laboratory techniques required.

Daly, M., and Margo Wilson, *Sex, Evolution and Behavior,* Duxbury Press. A discussion of sex strategies employed by animals.

Halliday, Tim, *Sexual Strategy,* University of Chicago Press. A clearly defined book in which biological principles of sexual behavior are discussed, with many examples.

Montagna, W., and W. A. Sadler, eds. *Reproductive Behavior,* Plenum. A comprehensive text on reproduction.

Readings from Scientific American: Reproduction and Development, W. H. Freeman. A compilaton of all past articles in the area of embryology and reproduction.

Rugh, R. *Experimental Embryology: Techniques and Procedures,* Burgess. A classic in the field of development in which the various techniques are described for studying embryos.

Tortora, G., *Plant Form and Function,* Macmillan. A clearly written text illustrating many plant life cycles.

Wilson, Carl, Walter E. Loomis, and Taylor A. Steeves, *Botany,* Holt, Rinehart and Winston. One of the best basic botany texts, with an exceptionally good section on plant reproduction.

Others Resources

Growth of Seeds (14 min.), Encyclopedia Britannica (EB). A simple film showing the actual growth process by speeding up the photographic process.

Reproduction, Growth and Development (set of 12 films, 28 min. each), developed by AIBS Film Series in Modern Biology, McGraw-Hill. A definitive set of films covering all aspects of continuance and development.

A Tree Is Born (29 min.), Syracuse University, College of Forestry. A fine film showing the developmental stage of arboreal growth through the years of its development to adult.

Amphibian Embryo (16 min.), EB. A short silent film showing the stages of frog development, from fertilization to adulthood.

Chicks, set of 12 transparencies, Carolina Biological Supply Co. A fine set of overhead projection sheets on chick embryology.

The Fish Embryo (12 min.), EB. A short silent film showing the developmental stages of the fish.

Flowers: Structure and Function (11 min.), Coronet Films. A short film illustrating the various structures of the reproductive system of flowering plants.

Handling Drosophila (4 min.), Ealing. A fine loop giving students a clear illustration of

working with the fruit fly. Adapted from the BSCS Techniques.

Human Reproduction (21 min.), McGraw-Hill. A fine introductory film on the human sex role. Sensitively done.

The Thread of Life (50 min.), Bell Telephone Co. A good summary of reproduction and an introduction to genetics. Free of charge.

Understanding Puberty, 4 filmstrips, 4 cassettes, Teaching Aids. A four-part series discussing male and female physical changes and addressing the emotional and social aspects of puberty.

The Reproductive System and Sexual Response of the Male, Teaching Aids. Filmstrip discussing the male reproductive system, the phases of male sexual response, sperm production, and the endocrine gland system.

The Reproductive System and Sexual Response of the Female, Teaching Aids. The functions of the female reproductive system are discussed, as well as the phases of female sexual response.

Human Reproduction: What You Should Know, 4 filmstrips, Guidance Association. An award-winning, contemporary, four-part filmstrip that uses scanning electron microscope images and stunning in utero photography in a straightforward presentation of the male and female reproductive systems and the entire process of fetal development and birth.

REPRODUCTION

Have a Healthy Baby: Pregnancy (22 min.), Churchill Films. Through animation, details the growth of the human embryo from conception through pregnancy, emphasizing organ development in the first three months. Avoidance of drugs and good nutrition are stressed.

Have a Healthy Baby: Labor and Delivery (29 min.), Churchill Films. Depicts the experience and feelings of two couples through the stages of labor and prepared delivery and uses animation to explain the physiology of birth.

Boy to Man (15 min.) and *Girl to Woman* (17 min.), Churchill Films. Updated revisions of the earlier, award-winning versions, which use animation and conceptual framework to construct a fresh look at physiological changes during puberty. Both films, good for junior high level, are classics.

8

Heredity

INTRODUCTION

The concept of genetic inheritance is a natural sequence to the chapter on continuance. Why offspring of one species look like their parents and not like other species and what is the physical basis for the inheritance of characteristic traits within species and families are questions that have puzzled scientists for centuries. The first few Learning Experiences present this enigma in various ways and prepare students for the findings of biologists from Mendel to the present.

The activities are, in general, sequential, beginning with the basic laws of Mendel and continuing through the chromosome theory to DNA coding. For the most part, each basic concept of genetics, such as segregation, sex linkage, and multiple alleles, is presented in at least two or three activities. The activities have been varied to include laboratory experimentation, genetic problems, group activities, class lectures, and individual research. If time and facilities permit, it would be ideal to use some of each type.

During the labs using drosophila, it is important to caution your students about the dangers of using ether. Be sure your classroom is well ventilated. Since your students may have worked only with preserved animals previously, you might relate the humane method of killing the drosophila to present controversies over the treatment of animals during experimentation.

During activities on genetic problems, it would be helpful to have your students bring in calculators in order to speed up data analysis.

Since the study of evolution is a course in itself, it has only been touched on in the activities on mutations. Space has also prohibited an expanded discussion on inherited diseases (though several are listed in the Content Overview). However, such connections as the concentration of genes for certain diseases in a given population and the concept of natural selection should be made where possible. (For example, people with sickle-cell anemia survived in areas where malaria was epidemic because the first disease acts as a natural immunity to the second.) A lesson on mutations would also lead naturally to a discussion on the dangers of insecticides, drugs, and various synthetic food products.

While we have not included an activity on genetic counseling, a discussion on the topic would be relevant and a good preparation for activities on genetic engineering found in Chapter 10.

PERFORMANCE OBJECTIVES

As a result of the Learning Experiences in this chapter, students should be able to:

1. Discuss Mendel's laws of dominance, segregation, and independent assortment, giving examples and phenotype ratios for each.

2. Define genetic terms such as *dominant, recessive, homozygous, heterozygous, genotype, phenotype, hybrid, homologous chromosomes, testcross,* and *haploid and diploid conditions.*

3. Successfully identify, breed, and analyze genetic characteristics in offspring of drosophila.

4. Analyze counts of contrasting genetic traits in organisms such as corn and garden pea plants to determine the genotypes of parent organisms.

5. Use Punnett squares to predict numbers of offspring exhibiting dominant and recessive traits in monohybrid and dihybrid crosses.

6. Discuss and give examples of such concepts as autosomal and sex linkage, incomplete dominance, multiple alleles, mutations, and chromosomal aberrations.

7. Relate the process of meiosis to oogenesis and spermatogenesis.

8. Discuss the biological basis (chromosome theory and nucleic acids) for genetic inheritance.

CONTENT OVERVIEW

Mendel: Father of Genetics

Gregor Mendel was the first person to understand the quantitative principles of heredity. Between 1856 and 1864, he conducted breeding experiments on thousands of garden pea plants, carefully examining the progeny of calculated crosses and formulating his principles from an analysis of the results. Mendel studied seven basic traits (fourteen characteristics) in the first (F_1) and second (F_2) generation offspring resulting from crosses of pure strains (one dominant, one recessive) of the garden pea plants. Table 8.l lists the results of his classic experimentation.

From these results, Mendel postulated his principles of heredity: first, the law of dominance; second, the law of segregation; and third, the law of independent assortment. While Mendel did obtain some results that conflicted with these principles, he ignored traits that offered confusing data and concentrated on those that verified his theories. Thus, he was able to formulate a basic foundation for the study of genetics.

Table 8.1. Seven Contrasting Traits.

	Seeds		Flowers		Flowers		Plants	
	Round	Wrinkled	Colored	White	Axial	Terminal	Tall	Dwarf
F$_1$	all		all		all		all	
F$_2$	5474	1850	705	224	651	207	787	277
Ratio	2.96	1	3.15	1	3.14	1	2.84	1

	Cotyledons		Pods		Pods	
	Yellow	Green	Green	Yellow	Inflated	Constricted
F$_1$	all		all		all	
F$_2$	6022	2001	428	152	882	299
Ratio	3.01	1	2.82	1	2.95	1

Table 8.2 lists the results of ten of Mendel's F$_1$ hybrid plants. As these data show, an individual cross often does not achieve the predicted ratio for a dominant trait. The total phenotypes, however, result in a ratio that is close to 3 : 1.

Mendel's Laws and the Chromosome Theory

Mendel's findings went unrecognized until the turn of the century when scientists, in particular, Theodor Boveri and W. S. Sutton, saw the relationship between concepts of cell organization and Mendel's principles of inheritance. During the later nineteenth century, scientists had discovered chromosomes, their longitudinal separation into daughter chromosomes in mitosis, the constancy of chromosome numbers in a species, and the significance of meiosis. Now Boveri and Sutton realized the parallel behavior between these chromosomes and Mendel's genetic "factors" (later called *genes*). Mendel had said these factors (genes) occur in pairs, one from each parent. Chromosomes also exist in pairs, one from each parent. Mendel postulated that when reproductive cells are produced, the paired factors separate and are distributed as units to each gamete (segregation). In meiosis, homologous chromosomes separate and are

Table 8.2. Seed Production in F$_1$ Plants

Plant	Round	Wrinkled
1	45	12
2	27	8
3	24	7
4	19	16
5	32	11
6	26	6
7	88	24
8	22	10
9	28	6
10	25	7
Total	336	107

distributed one to each sex cell. According to Mendel's law of independent assortment, in a dihybrid cross, the distribution of one pair of factors is independent of the distribution of the other. During meiosis, maternal and paternal chromosomes are distributed randomly. If genes for two traits are located on different chromosomes, the law of independent assortment holds true during meiosis. Of course, scientists realized that organisms possessed many more traits than chromosomes and so concluded that many genes must be located on one chromosome. This would also explain some of the conflicting results Mendel obtained during his experiments. Thus concepts such as autosomal and sex linkage were later formulated.

Inherited Human Disorders

There are many recessively inherited disorders among humans. Some common examples are cystic fibrosis, galactosemia, phenylketonuria, thalassemia (blood disorder), and Tay-Sachs disease. Diseases such as hemophilia and color blindness are recessive, but, because they are sex linked, only one recessive gene is needed to produce the trait in males.

Although most genes for diseases are recessive, some are dominant. A few such disorders are achondroplasia (dwarfism), chronic simple glaucoma (some forms), Huntington's chorea, hypercholesterolemia, and polydactyly (extra fingers or toes).

Diseases such as sickle-cell anemia, in which the hybrid genotype is said to have the trait, show incomplete dominance. Genes for sickle-cell anemia and Tay-Sachs disease are found mainly in certain gene pools, the former among African Blacks and the latter in East European Jewish populations.

Some disorders, such as Down's syndrome, are due to chromosomal aberrations where there is an extra or a missing chromosome. Other disorders of this type are Turner and Klinefelter syndromes and females with an extra X chromosome (XXX). Often individuals with an extra X chromosome are mentally retarded.

LEARNING EXPERIENCES

Inherited Traits

1. Show pictures of various adult animals; then show separate pictures of young animals of the same species as the adults. Do the same with plants. Ask students to indicate which young organisms are the offspring of which parents. What causes offspring to look like their parents? Elicit the idea that information that determines structure and appearance of a species must be passed in some form from generation to generation.

   Ask students how they think this information is passed on. Allow students to mention such words as *genes* and *chromosomes,* but remind them that when people first questioned this phenomenon, the microscope was not invented. The existence of cells and microorganisms, let alone chromosomes and genes, was unknown. Discuss early theories of heredity: preformation versus epigenesis.

2. You could use several introductory lessons on heredity. One that arouses a great deal of interest and involvement is to have students bring in pictures of their parents and see if students can identify which parents belong to which child. Caution those who know the parents of friends not to give away the answer.

   Ask students if they were told they look like an aunt or uncle or grandparents. Do brothers or sisters show a family resemblance?

3. Another good way of introducing the topic of heredity is to sit a boy and girl with obvious contrasting traits in front of the class. Ask students to observe their traits and describe the contrasting characteristics. Have them construct a chart:

   Trait: *Contrasting Characteristics*

   1.

   2.

   Elicit from students where these traits come from and what we call the transfer of traits from parent to offspring (heredity). Ask what branch of biology studies how heredity occurs (genetics).

Mendel's Laws and Punnett Squares

4. Read or have students read an account of Gregor Mendel's first experiments on heredity in a biology text or a book on genetics. You can use some of the information given in the Content Overview. Discuss why the garden pea was an excellent choice for experimentation. Elicit the facts that gardeners had developed pure strains, which were much simpler to study, and that the garden pea is self-pollinating and can be cross-pollinated.

   At this point you may want to introduce and define such words as *pure, hybrid, cross-pollination, generation, dominance,* and *recessive.* Stress the fact that Mendel could not use the terms *chromosome* and *gene* and referred to heredity determinants as "factors."

   Ask students to describe the plants that resulted when Mendel cross-pollinated a short and a tall plant. How did he explain these results? Since these new offspring, although tall, obtained two different factors for the trait of size (tall "T" and short "t"), ask what term Mendel called them. What term did he use for the parents? What happened when he crossed the hybrid plants? Use letters to represent contrasting traits in the cross: *Tt* x *Tt* can give *TT, Tt,* or *tt* offspring. Ask which of these offspring would be tall.

   In discussing the seven traits of garden peas that Mendel studied, elicit from students which were dominant and which recessive. Relate dominance to eye color in humans. Ask how a man with brown eyes and a woman with blue eyes could have nine children all with brown eyes. Be sure to mention that, unlike garden pea plants, tallness is not dominant in humans.

5. Using the information in the Content Overview, make a chart on the chalkboard showing Mendel's F_2 offspring from F_1 hybrids. For example:

	Smooth		Wrinkled
F_1:	all		0
F_2:	5474		1850
Ratio	2.96	:	1

Note that the recessive trait (wrinkled seed), which was not exhibited in the F_1 generation, reappears in the F_2 generation in approximately a 1:3 ratio. Ask students how this occurred. Encourage them to employ capital and lower-case letters representing traits when demonstrating their theories.

Explain how each parent of the F_1 generation can produce two types of gametes and that either type from one parent can fertilize either type from the other parent.

Demonstrate this on the chalkboard.

F_1: Ss × Ss   (S = smooth   s = wrinkled)

F_2: SS,Ss, sS, ss

Since "S" (smooth) is dominant, which combinations would have smooth seeds? Note the 1:3 ratio of the recessive trait evidenced in Mendel's results. Ask, "What did Mendel call this principle?" (segregation).

6. This would be a good point at which to introduce the Punnett square and terms such as *genotype, phenotype, heterozygous,* and *homozygous.* Reproduction Page 49 explains the Punnett square, incorporating the example presented in Activity 5, and presents ratios using the above terminology. Have the Reproduction Page read aloud, and stop after each section to be sure students understand the instructions and analysis. Ask them to predict the offspring in the concluding problem by means of a Punnett square.

7. The principle of segregation can be demonstrated concretely using seeds of hybrid corn or hybrid sorghum, which possess a recessive gene for albinism. When numerous seeds are planted, the recessive trait of albinism will show up in the seedlings in approximately a 1:3 ratio; therefore about one-fourth of the seedlings will be white (or lack color).

8. Have students practice making predictions of traits in offspring by using the Punnett square method. Give them various problems, including some that ask for the genotype of the parents. The following problems are good examples since they involve only one trait in each.

   a. Both the husband and wife in a family are hybrids for freckles. If freckles are dominant, what are the chances that their children will have freckles?

   b. Both you and your brother or sister have blue eyes, yet your parents have brown eyes. What are the genotypes of your mother and father?

c. In one family, all the children have dimples. The father has dimples; the mother does not. If dimples are dominant over no dimples, what is the probable genotype of all members of the family?

Since problem c is most difficult, you may want to assist students by eliciting the mother's genotype and showing where it would be placed in the square. Stress that ratios for traits in actual families do not necessarily follow predictions based on Mendel's laws.

9. In order to aid students in figuring out the answers to such problems, you may construct a Punnett's square out of plywood or on a felt board. Hooks may be placed in the plywood in such a manner that the genotype of parents is shown as diploid, the gametes as haploid, and the offspring within the squares as diploid. Fig. 8.1 illustrates the setup.

   Ask students to make cardboard models of plants or animals showing parents with a contrasting or similar trait (such as a black and white rat or two black rats) and hook the models on the board. Be sure to have students mark the genotype on each. Gametes might be represented by circles with appropriate letters and offspring as small black or white rats, again with genotypes visible.

   The same setup may be used on a felt board. Students become much more involved in making the models and working on a chart visible to the entire class.

10. You can involve your students in several lengthy experiments demonstrating dominant and recessive ratios.

    One is to germinate seeds from a cross between pure tall and dwarf peas and at the same time plant seeds that were produced in a cross between two hybrid tall pea plants. Seeds may be purchased from most biological supply houses. Have students germinate the seeds in paper cups containing moist sand. By comparing the second set of seedlings with the first, students will see the resulting ratio of three tall to one short plant. A variation on this experiment would be to use pea plants hybrid for a smooth-wrinkled trait.

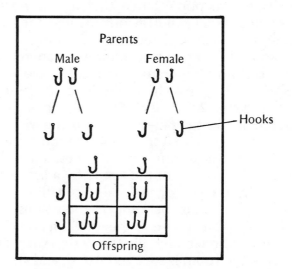

Fig. 8.1. Punnett square of plywood.

Sorghum is another plant that can be used for this activity. When grown in sufficient sunlight, red-stemmed sorghum is dominant over green-stemmed. You can purchase seeds produced by inbred hybrid plants from a supply house. Seeds germinate in about 5 days; the color differences are most obvious after 7 to 10 days.

Remember that the larger the number of seeds used, the closer the results will demonstrate the expected ratios.

You might have the entire class work on one plant at a time or half experiment with one type of plant while the rest of the class works on a different type.

11. If time, space, a lack of green thumbs, or other conditions limit your ability to carry out long-term experiments, ears of corn may be a marvelous—and practical—answer to your problem. Ears of corn purchased from supply houses offer excellent opportunities for counting segregating traits, and the resulting numbers are usually close to theoretical Mendelian ratios. Two common traits are color (purple aleurone dominant over yellow aleurone) and endosperm (starchy dominant over waxy). Have students count and record the number of kernels showing each trait. Progeny of a hybrid cross will give a 3:1 ratio for each trait; a cross between a hybrid and a recessive parent will give a 1:1 ratio. (Mention that the latter is a back cross used to determine the genotype of a plant showing the dominant trait.)

12. For a more adventurous class—and if you are an adventurous teacher—experiment with the classic *Drosophila melanogaster* to demonstrate the laws of dominance and segregation. If you do this activity, we encourage you to have your students first complete the lab exercise on Reproduction Page 50 to familiarize themselves with the fruit fly and to learn the techniques necessary to breed them.

Prior to the experiment, have students read over the entire lab and discuss the life cycle of the fruit fly, as well as the techniques to be used. Mention that a new female does not mate for approximately 12 hours after emerging from the pupa. Stress that it is important to use a virgin since females retain sperm from previous matings for a considerable time. For this reason, they are usually isolated as soon as they emerge.

The life cycle from egg to adult may range from 10 to 15 or more days, depending on the temperature. It is advisable to keep the temperature at about 25° C (77° F), which results in a 10 day-cycle. Lower temperatures prolong the cycle; 20° C (68° F) results in a life cycle of about 15 days. Remember that the temperature inside the vial is slightly higher than the room temperature due to fermentation of the medium.

Mention that in transferring the flies, students may tap the vial on the table or hold the bottom of the bottle by a light source in order to keep the flies toward the bottom of the vial. (Fruit flies show a positive phototaxis.) Stress that the vials must be kept on their sides until the flies awaken since unconscious flies will adhere to the medium and drown. Students will know if they have over-etherized the flies since the wings of a dead fly stand out at an angle. Be sure the room is well ventilated, and stress the importance of safety when using ether.

Discuss the findings and conclusions your students obtained, and have them present their ideas for demonstrating Mendel's principle of dominance.

13. The next activity, breeding two strains of fruit flies to demonstrate Mendel's principles of dominance and segregation, takes from 3 to 4 weeks. All of the techniques introduced in Activity 12 are used during the labs, and the Punnett square is used in analyzing the results. Reproduction Page 51 describes five labs, performed over a 21 to 24 day time period, giving step-by-step procedures needed to carry out a valid study. Relevant questions and charts are included to record and clarify the resulting data.

   Have students read the Reproduction Pages prior to the first lab. Review the techniques learned previously, and have your students focus on the purpose of the study.

   Pure cultures of drosophila possessing vestigial wings and pure cultures with normal wings should be obtained from a supply house just prior to the study. The "morgue" mentioned in the second lab may be constructed by placing some mineral oil in a bottle and sealing it with a rubber stopper.

   It is advisable to discuss with your students why it is necessary to kill the fruit flies during the experiment.

   After completion of the study, have students write their results on a chart on the chalkboard and calculate the class ratios. You may want to spend several periods analyzing and discussing the results of the study and the difficulties encountered.

14. In order to reinforce the skills learned in the previous activities, you can have students conduct a backcross (a hybrid of the F_1 generation crossed with a vestigial-winged virgin). Remind students that this is a test cross used to determine the genotype of an organism exhibiting a dominant trait.

15. As students will find in experiments involving segregation, the ratios actually obtained do not always conform to those predicted. Sometimes, especially with a small sample, they are extremely different. On the chalkboard, show the data Mendel obtained from ten of his F_1 hybrid plants used to study smooth versus wrinkled seeds. (Data may be found in the Content Overview.) Point out that while the total numbers were close to a 3:1 ratio, offspring from some individual plants were very far from it; 19 smooth to 16 wrinkled were the offspring of one F_1 plant.

   The activity on Reproduction Page 52 is excellent for demonstrating the role chance plays in genetic ratios. Tell students to bring in a set of dice for the activity, or two coins may be used (TT–TH–HH). Relate their findings to Mendel's predicted ratios and those obtained in their past experiments. Note that the greater the samples, the closer the results are to the expected ratios.

16. You can use the following example in order to relate the role of probability in genetics to zygote formation in fertilization. Two mice, hybrid for black coloring, are mated (Bb × Bb). Fig. 8.2 represents the cross.

   After placing the chart on the board, ask students the following questions:

   a. If four zygotes are produced, how many of the 200 million sperm joined with egg nucleii?

   b. How do we know which sperm will join?

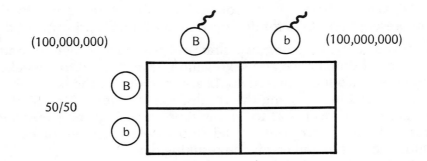

Fig. 8.2. Cross of black hybrid mice.

Stress that with such a small number of offspring, the ratios may be very distorted.

17. To introduce Mendel's law of independent assortment, pose a hypothetical question such as, "How smart are tall people?" or ask students, "If you inherit your father's eye color, must you also inherit his sex?" Students can readily see that such traits are inherited independently.

    Read an account describing Mendel's investigation of combined inheritance of two pairs of traits in peas; for example, he studied numerous crosses between pea plants showing differing traits for height and color of cotyledons. Show how crosses between pure dominant and pure recessive strains resulted in dominant phenotypes, while crosses between the F$_1$ hybrids resulted in four different phenotypes in the ratio of 9:3:3:1. Place the Punnett square shown in Fig. 8.3 on the chalkboard, using T = tall, t = recessive gene for dwarf, Y = yellow, and y = recessive gene for green. Demonstrate that the 9:3:3:1 ratio is a combination of 3:1 × 3:1.

    Have your students use a Punnett square to show possible offspring for two different traits—for example, normal versus vestigial wings and red versus white eyes in drosophila. Mention that Mendel did find exceptions to the principle, but he ignored them. Today we know that the genes for some traits are linked together and therefore do not follow the expected ratios of independent assortment.

18. You can use ears of corn obtained from a supply house to show simply, but concretely, the resulting phenotype of a dihybrid cross. Kernels may be purple (dominant) or yellow and starchy (dominant) or waxy. Have students make a chart for the four phenotypes: purple/starchy, purple/waxy, yellow/starchy, and yellow/waxy. After counting and recording each phenotype, they can work out the resulting ratios.

19. Ask students to solve the following problems using Punnett squares:

    a. What is the genotype of the children in a family where the father is homozygous dominant for freckles and homozygous recessive for attached earlobes, while the mother is homozygous recessive for no freckles and homozygous dominant for unattached earlobes?

	TY	Ty	tY	ty
TY	tall TTYY yellow	tall TTYy yellow	tall TtYY yellow	tall TtYy yellow
Ty	tall TTYy yellow	tall TTyy green	tall TtYy yellow	tall Ttyy green
tY	tall TtYY yellow	tall TtYy yellow	short ttYY yellow	short ttYy yellow
ty	tall TtYy yellow	tall Ttyy green	short ttYy yellow	short ttyy green

Possible gametes = TY, Ty, tY, ty

Fig. 8.3. Crossing hybrids (Tt Yy × Tt Yy)

b. If the offspring for this cross marries someone of the same genotype for these traits, what are the chances that this couple will have a child who has no freckles and has attached earlobes?

Incomplete Dominance

20. Discuss the existence of red, pink, and white four o'clock flowers. Explain that the pink flowers result from a cross between the red (RR) and white (rr) and so are hybrids (Rr). In this type of blended inheritance, the expected ratios are different. Have your class use a Punnet square to predict the offspring from a cross between two pink flowers (Rr × Rr).

    Explain that the resulting ratio 1:2:1 indicates the presence of blending. When presenting multiple alleles in later activities, you can show that blending can be distinguished from multiple alleles by this ratio. You might show charts of Andalusian fowl or other organisms that exhibit incomplete dominance.

21. Another way of studying incomplete dominance is to have your students research the hair texture in their families. Explain that there are basically three types—curly, wavy, and straight—and that one is the phenotype for the hybrid. Tell them to record this trait for their brothers and sisters, as well as their parents, and try to figure out which characteristic is a blending. Have them compare their results with other students in groups of four or five. After the investigation is finished, show them how a cross between two parents with wavy hair can result in offspring showing the three different phenotypes: curly, wavy, and straight. Remind them, however, that chance can distort the expected results.

Biology of the Cell and Genetics

22. Before introducing other factors involved in the transfer of genetic traits, such as multiple alleles and sex linkage, it is wise to present the biological basis for

the laws of heredity. Once students understand that genes are located on chromosomes and relate genetics to the process of meiosis, the concept of sexual fertilization and the laws of genetics become logical and obvious. If genes are inherited half from the male and half from the female parent, then gametes must possess a haploid condition, and homologous chromosomes in the zygote would be a natural progression. While meiosis explains segregation and the law of independent assortment, it also gives the biological basis for linked genes, crossovers, and so forth.

You can give a brief account of the historical work of such scientists as Theodor Boveri and W. S. Sutton, who, realizing the parallel behavior of genes and chromosomes, presented the chromosome theory as a working model for the transfer of inherited traits. Information on their study may be found in the Content Overview.

Then review both mitosis and meiosis, showing how the former results in a diploid condition, while the latter results in a haploid one. Show how fertilization again produces a diploid cell containing a full set of chromosomes for a particular species. Students can research the number of chromosomes normal for different species.

23. A concrete way of reinforcing this concept is by using a string of pop beads to show the linear arrangement of genes in a definite sequence. Ask what structure is represented by this model, and why, if it were in a cell, it would be only half a dictionary of information. Present a second string and elicit the meaning of homologous chromosomes. After discussing where each member of the pair originated, again review meiosis and fertilization.

24. Reproduction Page 53 unifies these concepts concretely, incorporating the processes of spermatogenesis and oogenesis with the law of segregation. Have students read and discuss the diagrams and directions on the page and list the phenotypes and genotypes of the resulting zygotes. This activity has proved to be excellent for clarifying and strengthening a comprehensive concept of the chromosome theory and provides a means of evaluating students' understanding of the previous lessons.

Beyond Mendel

LINKAGE AND CROSSING OVER

25. After establishing the fact that genes are located on chromosomes, it is easy to introduce the concept of linkage. Mention that when Mendel worked out the ratios he presented in his law on independent assortment, there were many traits of peas that did not result in the predicted ratios. To simplify his study, he ignored these exceptions and worked with traits that confirmed his theories.

Present the work of Thomas Hunt Morgan on drosophila or Harriet Creighton and Barbara McClintock's study of linkage in corn. Ask how long-winged drosophila usually have gray bodies, while short-winged drosophila usually have black coloring. Describe similar phenomena of linkage found in corn (colored kernels and waxy endosperm versus colorless kernels and starchy endosperm). Use strings of pop beads—four representing those from the male and four those from the female—to show how certain traits are grouped or linked together when they are passed on to offspring. You should use different colored beads to represent genes for different traits.

Mention that after exhaustive studies, geneticists have established that the number of linkage groups in an organism is equal to the number of homologous pairs of chromosomes in that organism. Make a chart of several organisms studied, similar to the following:

Organism	Number of Linkage Groups	Number of Homologous Chromosomes
Drosophila	4	4
Corn	10	10
Neurospora	7	7
Tomato	12	12

Have students research the numbers of chromosomes found in different organisms.

26. Show students a Punnett square representing a dihybrid cross with linked genes such as drosophila with long-winged gray bodies and short-winged black bodies (Fig. 8.4). Analyze each square and ask students which of Mendel's three principles seems to be contradicted by linkage. Have students make Punnett squares of other linked traits.

27. Review the work of T. H. Morgan and mention that in the above cross, he discovered a few flies with long-winged black bodies and short-winged gray bodies. Present the idea of crossing over. Pop beads are again an excellent way to show the concept. Have students read about the evidence of Creighton and McClintock, which confirmed the theory of crossing over.

28. If a lesson on sex chromosomes has not been presented, introduce your students to the existence of the X and Y chromosomes and their relation to sex determination before proceeding to the next activities. Show pictures of homologous chromosomes in different organisms such as drosophila, and point out that the sex chromosomes in the male are the only pair that do not match.

Be sure to mention that in some animals, such as birds, the XY chromosome constitution is found in females and XX in the males. You might also mention that in cases where XY constitutes a male, the genes for maleness are not always found on the Y chromosome. Such is the case in many insects such as the fruit fly where genes for male traits such as the penis, copulatory bristles, and abdomenal pigmentation are probably carried on the autosomes. Scientists think that it takes two X chromosomes in such insects to mask the effect of male determinants on autosomes and produce a female. Mention,

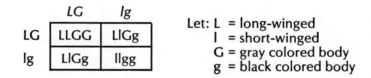

	LG	lg
LG	LLGG	LlGg
lg	LlGg	llgg

Let: L = long-winged
    l = short-winged
    G = gray colored body
    g = black colored body

Figure 8.4. Punnett square for drosophila.

however, that in human beings, genes for maleness are found on the Y chromosome.

Ask your students which parent, the man or the woman, has the gene that decides the sex of their children.

29. To introduce traits that are sex linked, return to the work of T. H. Morgan and discuss his study of the white-eyed drosophila. If you have performed the previous labs on drosophila, you may want to duplicate Morgan's experiment. First review the procedures on Reproduction Page 50 for recognizing and separating the males and females. Be sure to obtain your pure red-eyed and white-eyed specimen just prior to the lab date. Have your students read Reproduction Page 54 and review the back cross as a test of genotype. Have students perform the experiment and compare their results with those of Morgan.

30. A simpler activity to show sex-linked inheritance would be to study the pedigree chart of Queen Victoria found on Reproduction Page 55. Ask students if they notice anything unusual about the inheritance of hemophilia. Elicit which pair of the 23 chromosomes found in humans probably carries the genes for normal versus hemophilia and which chromosome, X or Y, carries the gene for hemophilia. Inevitably some students answer the Y chromosome. If so, mention that Victoria carried the recessive gene.

Draw three chromosomes and indicate that the shorter Y chromosome lacks information. (See Fig. 8.5.)

Have students describe the following:

(1) $X^{-N} X^{-N}$

(2) $X^{-N} X^{-h}$

(3) $X^{-h} X^{-h}$

(4) $X^{-N} Y$

(5) $X^{-h} Y$

Stress that the $X^{-h}Y$ individual has only one recessive gene yet shows the recessive trait. You might mention that there is a blood test to diagnose a carrier ($X^{-N}X^{-h}$). Discuss other diseases that are sex linked.

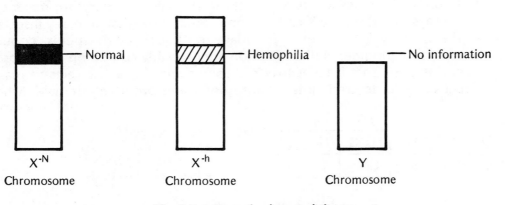

Fig. 8.5. Gene for hemophilia.

MULTIPLE ALLELES

31. An interesting way of introducing your class to the concept of multiple alleles is to present them with the following situations involving paternity suits:

    a. A woman with type O blood claims Mr. X (type O blood) is the father of a child with type A blood.

    b. A hospital is being sued by the parents of a newborn. The mother has type A blood, and the father is type B. Since the child has type O blood, the couple claims that the hospital gave them the wrong child.

    Using a chart or the chalkboard, show students the possible genotypes for all blood types. Then refer back to the motivational problems and see if they can solve them. Ask you students what the total number of alleles is with respect to blood type. How does this compare with other traits? Discuss other examples of multiple alleles, such as coat color in rabbits where there are four alleles in a dominance series: normal, chinchilla, himalayan, and albino. Mention that multiple alleles arise through mutations at the gene locus.

32. In order to distinguish between multiple alleles at one gene locus and multiple gene inheritance involving several sets of alleles, have students act as different alleles in the following manner. First, show multiple alleles. For this, use two rows to represent homologous chromosomes. Have six students represent the alleles for blood type, each holding a card with one letter on it: two with A, two with B, and two with O. Since only one chair in each row represents the locus for that gene, only two students will be positioned at the loci at any given time. Show all the various possible combinations and ask students what the resulting phenotypes will be (AA, AO, BB, BO, AB, OO).

    Then go on to show how multiple genes involve more than two loci. The degree of pigmentation in crosses between the black and white human races illustrates this type of inheritance. Although scientists believe many genes are involved in skin pigmentation, tell your students that you will assume only two independently assorting genes are involved in order to simplify the explanation. Now set up four rows to represent two pairs of homologous chromosomes, with one chair in each row representing the gene loci for skin pigmentation. Be sure to place the loci in corresponding positions for homologous chromosomes. With two possible alleles for each locus, show all of the possible combinations: (AABB), (AaBB), (aaBB), (AABb), (AaBb), (AAbb), (Aabb), (aabb). Explain how cumulative genes in such crosses have a quantitative expression, with each dominant allele contributing one unit of pigment. Ask your students to describe the resulting phenotypes.

DNA AND MUTATIONS

33. Before performing the following activities, introduce or review with your class the two types of nucleic acid and the function of each. Since students are often skeptical about how scientists can arrive at theories without actually seeing molecules interact, tell them that you will describe two of the most famous experiments that led biochemists to the belief that the gene is composed of DNA. Use Reproduction Page 56 to present the work of Avery, MacLeod, and McCarty. Read the page with your class, stopping at each question to elicit answers.

34. Reproduction Page 57 illustrates the second classic experiment proving that DNA carries the genetic coding. Before reading about the experiment, review the function of ribosomes in the cell, and discuss the ability of bacteriophages to destroy bacteria by taking control of bacteria ribosomes. Use Reproduction Page 57 to show how the virus attacks the bacteria. Spend some time on the question of setting up an experiment to determine which part of the bacteriophage, the protein or the DNA, directs the production of more viruses. Since students may have difficulty understanding how radioisotopes are used as indicators, you may want to simplify the account of the experiment in the following manner.

   Ask, "If Drs. Chase and Hershey could have stained the protein blue and the DNA red, how would this have indicated which part of the bacteriophage entered the bacterial cell?" (Red DNA would have shown up in the bacterial cell.) Tell them that instead of stains, the scientists used radioisotopes of sulfur and phosphorus. Explain that since the protein shell contains sulfur and the DNA contains phosphorus, whichever radioisotope is found in the content of the bacterial cell indicates the part of the virus carrying the genes.

35. Introduce your avid readers to the charming and interesting autobiographical account of James Watson's work, *The Double Helix*. Have these students present their reactions to the book to the class.

36. After students have a basic understanding of how genes are coded on a DNA molecule, you can introduce the idea of genetic mutation by telling them that the coding can be changed by various chemicals, such as colchicine and DDT, or by radiations, such as X-rays, ultraviolet, and cosmic rays, or even by high temperatures. An interesting way of illustrating mutations in species is by studying the adaptability of various insects, such as the cockroach to insecticides. Discuss why farmers and exterminators must change pesticides frequently if the pesticides are to be effective. Relate this to the fact that pesticides are one of our greatest environmental problems.

   At this time, you may want to digress to show how mutations relate to Darwin's theory of evolution.

   Be sure to distinguish between genetic mutations and chromosomal aberrations, which cause such disorders as Down's syndrome.

37. Have students research various phenomena such as human babies born with a tail or albino offspring from a line of normal-colored kangaroos. Some students may want to investigate the relationship between mutations and cancer. Stress that if the mutation is to be passed on to the next generation, it must occur in a sex cell.

Environment and Heredity

38. Students should be made aware of the tremendous influence of environment on hereditary traits. A simple illustration such as growing some potato seedlings in poor soil or in unfavorable conditions with little water or sunlight, while others grow in favorable conditions, would make the concept obvious. Discuss how skin and hair color are affected by sunlight and how children

brought up on proper diets and healthy living conditions are generally taller than their parents who were not. (You might discuss the low ceilings and doorways of average houses that were built 100 to 200 years ago.) Have students research studies of identical twins who were raised in different environments.

An impressive and extremely unsettling activity is to study the effects of poor living conditions, especially diet, on the health and mental ability of infants. Accounts of the effects of food programs such as one illustrated on the television documentary, "The Unfinished Child" (a Lirol Production), are both uplifting and tragic. The documentary showed how pregnant women in poverty areas were given food supplies to maintain a well-balanced diet during their pregnancy, and extra food was given to the newborn infant until he or she was one year old. The results were astounding. Children born to the same parents prior to the food program were unhealthy, mentally slow or retarded, and in some cases even deformed. Those receiving proper nourishment during gestation and infancy were normal, intelligent, good-looking children. The only difference was diet. How tragic for those who did not receive the proper nourishment! (Studies such as these not only develop social awareness as well as cognitive understanding in your students but also foster attitudes that will ensure proper health habits in raising their own children.)

General Activities

39. "Characteristic Traits in My Family" is an activity that will not only evaluate your students' understanding of several genetic principles but is guaranteed to captivate the interest of every pupil. The activity can be found on Reproduction Page 58. Assign the table entitled "Your Genotype" for homework the first night. Be sure to supply your class with enough phenylthiocarbamide (PTC) paper or phenylthiourea for each family member to taste.

    The next day, assign a "mate" for each student and have the two students work together in filling out the table entitled "Your Future Children." "Mates" can be chosen by randomly picking names from two boxes—one box containing boys' names, one containing girls'. If there are more of one sex than the other, you may have to have several groups of three where one student "shares" their genes with two students of the opposite sex. (You can always group this activity with controversial issues!)

    After explaining how to construct the pedigree chart, have students complete the activity for homework and discuss their results in class the following day.

40. Reproduction Page 59 discusses how modern genetic principles are applied in breeding plants and animals. By using such principles as hybridization, vegetative propagation, and induced mutations, among others, breeders are able to increase the quantity and quality of food sources and have also produced some organisms that are immune to common diseases. Read the page with your students, and have them solve the problem at the bottom. They may feel more secure and accomplish more by working in small groups rather than individually. Assign several other similar problems.

ASSESSING ACHIEVEMENT OF OBJECTIVES:

Ongoing evaluation: Students' understanding of genetic concepts and their ability to analyze results from experiments on heredity can be measured by having them submit for evaluation the final products of the various activities in this chapter.

Final evaluation: Have students construct Punnett squares for crosses involving homologous and hybrid parents for one and two independently assorted traits and for dihybrid crosses involving linked traits. Students should write out an analysis of the phenotypes for each square.

Have students write an essay showing how the behavior of chromosomes explains the various genetic principles such as segregation, independent assortment, sex linkage, and multiple alleles. Activities found on Reproduction Pages 51, 54, 56, 58, and 59 can be used for evaluation purposes.

Have students construct a pedigree chart of their family for various traits such as eye color, hair texture, and blood type.

RESOURCES FOR TEACHING

Books

Asimov, Isaac, *The Genetic Code,* Mentor. An account of the discovery and significance of DNA.

Asimov, Isaac, *The Wellsprings of Life,* Mentor. Discusses the chemistry of the cell and its relation to evolution, heredity, and development.

Berry, R. J., *Genetics,* McKay. A teach-yourself series in which students progress in the learning of the principles of genetics.

Cooke, Robert, *Improving on Nature: The Brave New World of Genetic Engineering,* Time-Life. An excellent account of a changing technology and tampering with genes.

Davern, Cedric, *Genetics: Readings from Scientific American,* W. H. Freeman. A collection of great articles on all aspects of genetics—classic and modern.

Frankel, Edward, *DNA: The Ladder of Life,* McGraw-Hill. A fine treatment of DNA molecule and its research and relationship to heredity.

Hershowitz, Irwin, *Principles of Genetics,* Macmillan. A comprehensive textbook on the entire field of genetics. An excellent reference book.

Mendel, F., "Experiments in Plant Hybridization," *Classic Papers in Genetics,* ed. James A. Peters, Prentice-Hall. A clear presentation of Mendel's experiments and his interpretation of his results.

Nagle, James J., *Heredity and Human Affairs,* C. V. Mosby. A comprehensive text discussing reproduction, evolution, and genetics as they relate to humans.

Watson, James D., *The Double Helix,* Mentor. A delightful account of the work and the personalities that led to the discovery of DNA.

Films and Filmstrips

Genetics (set of 12 films, 28 min. each), McGraw-Hill. An excellent set of films on all aspects of heredity as developed by AIBS.

Genetics: Mendel's Laws (14 min.), Coronet. A fine short film depicting the three laws of Mendel. Good visualization.

Genetics, Techniques of Handling Drosophila (3 min.), Thorne. A must for all teachers, developed by BSCS. Excellent demonstration on drosophila study for genetics.

Handling Drosophila, (film loop) Ealing. An excellent loop illustrating techniques in using fruit flies in genetics.

9

THE LITTLE-KNOWN ENVIRONMENTS

INTRODUCTION

This chapter explores some of the little-known environments, and requires a special attitude and willingness to understand phenomena that are not clearly defined. In order to understand how life-forms function within the relatively known and familiar environment humans inhabit, it is interesting to take a journey into less-known environments, such as the oceans or outer space, to see how life would—or would not—function in these alien conditions. In these environments, organisms could encounter extremes in pressure, temperature, sunlight availability, and other conditions. By contemplating the effects of these alien conditions on humans and other life-forms, students will better understand the adaptations and biological principles by which living things survive and function in normal surroundings.

After examining life-forms in the depths, the activities move on to techniques used in coastal marine studies so that students might have first-hand experience of how information is gathered while they are discovering interesting life-forms close at hand. Just as we are interested in the exploration of space and the seas, we need to learn more about the world beneath the microscope. If we ask any person on the street what is the most dangerous "living organism" they know besides humans, what do you think they would answer? The answers probably would range from lion to whale, but very few, if any, would think of the virus. Yet it is an entity that has such destructive abilities that it could wipe out an entire race or generation in a matter of days. It is important to explore what we know of these creatures, as well as other disease organisms, and try to search out their place in the scheme of living things on the earth.

In the Content Overview, we discuss the new five kingdom system of classification, in which microbes are reclassified into another division; some of the basic structural components of microorganisms are discussed, as well as a new method of cultivating microorganisms through the use of membrane technology. A brief discussion of the possible effects of the marine environment and space travel on life-forms and the adaptations that some creatures have evolved will also be presented as background information.

The Learning Experiences section presents various exercises designed to help students better grasp microorganisms and disease. An excellent exercise with a step-by-step approach to cultivating bacteria is presented using a membrane filtration system. In addition, replications of student activities on disease are presented from the BSCS Human Sciences Program, *Feeling Fit*. In these activities, students can explore various diseases by becoming disease detectives.

As a means of learning more about the ocean environments, several activities involve setting up a marine aquarium and on-site field exploration. Through such projects, activities can be developed in which students observe, record data, and draw conclusions about the ocean environment. There are recommendations for articles in science journals on both the oceans and outer space to be used in classroom discussions. Such activities can play an important role in understanding these little-known environments.

PERFORMANCE OBJECTIVES

As a result of the Learning Experiences in this chapter, students should be able to:

1. Classify microorganisms and marine life according to the new five kingdom classification system.

2. Identify the various steps in culturing microorganisms, using a membrane filtration system.

3. Observe various microorganism types and identify the type as beneficial or harmful to humans.

4. Describe the abiotic and biotic components of the ocean environment and observe the various factors that keep things alive in a marine environment.

5. Discuss the physical and biological aspects of outer space and techniques physicists have devised to overcome some of the ill effects of space travel on human beings, based on the various readings from the scientific literature.

6. Describe some organisms found in the ocean depths and the adaptive mechanisms that enable them to survive in this environment.

CONTENT OVERVIEW

Membrane Filtration Technology

Occasionally a new technology emerges that presents a refreshingly simple and new approach to solving certain scientific problems. Membrane filtration is such a technology.

The precise separation made possible by membrane filters enables workers in science and industry to perform tasks that were once thought to be impossible or impractical. Precise separations with membrane filters also permit biology students to isolate more easily and positively microorganisms from air, water, soil, foods, and the human body.

The key to the technology lies in the unique way that a membrane filter screens out particles. Ordinary filter paper, which is essentially a nonuniform fibrous material, will trap particles throughout the entire depth of the material. Some particles, particularly individual bacterial cells, will find their way through the maze of fibrous material and emerge in the so-called filtered fluid. By contrast, a membrane filter, such as the Millipore filter, a thin plastic disc, works by screening out particles on its surface. It traps and holds all particles, including bacterial cells, in a single plane of focus, allowing high magnification and identification of the entrapped particles of microorganisms. With this unique membrane, students can analyze environmental conditions, such as air, water, and themselves.

The Millipore Corporation of Bedford, Massachusetts, publishes a manual describing this simple process. To summarize this filtration process briefly, you should use an *aseptic technique*, which means free from disease-causing microorganisms but is generally broadened to mean free from *any* microorganisms that are unwelcome at the particular place and time. Although the great majority of microorganisms are not pathogenic, a good microbiologist treats all cultures as if they were. To accomplish this, you must make sure that all equipment you are using is sterile and prevent the escape of microorganisms from the experiment. Techniques for equipment sterilization can be found in any handoook on culturing microorganisms. The equipment needed for virtually every membrane filtration investigation is a vacuum filter holder, a vacuum source, a pair of non-serrated forceps, and a membrane filter disc of the appropriate pore size and diameter. The most versatile type of filter holder for investigations is a Millipore Sterifil Filter Holder, a modified Buchner funnel made of autoclavable plastic (Lexan polycarbonate), which will withstand rugged use (or abuse) by students.

Five Kingdom Classification

In order to understand microbiology and other little-known environments, biologists are changing their views on the old two-kingdom classification system of taxonomy (plants and animals) to a more diverse system of five kingdoms. Within this system, eighty-nine phyla are distributed among five kingdoms. The greatest division is not between plants and animals as one might expect but within the once-ignored microorganisms—the prokaryotic Monera and the eukaryotic Protista. The five kingdoms are represented as three great levels of life: the prokaryotes (bacteria of the Kingdom Monera), the eukaryotic microorganisms and their derivatives (Protista), and the eukaryotic larger forms (Plantae, Animalia, and Fungi). These last three familiar kingdoms represent the three great ecological strategies for larger organisms: plants (production), animals (consumption), and fungi (absorption).

Before undertaking any activities with your students on this new classification scheme, you should review the major differences between prokaryotes and eukaryotes.

Oceanography

Since the benthic zone of the ocean reaches a depth of over 6 miles in some areas, life-forms have to contend with extreme physical conditions such as tons of pressure per square inch, total darkness, temperatures as low as 2° C, and usually a scarcity of food sources. Benthic animals have adapted to these conditions by evolving various structures and behaviors usually uncommon in more familiar regions (for example, large, protruding eyes, bioluminescence, and tremendous internal pressures). These adaptations would be useless or even harmful in other environments.

Recently scientists have discovered a totally new type of ecological community living near rifts at the bottom of the ocean. This type of system is based on chemical synthesis rather than sunlight as an energy source. Two such sites are located along the Galapagos rift and the 21° north site. In these areas, seawater seeps deep into cracks and through porous rocks and percolates up saturated with minerals. As solutions of hydrogen sulfide, estimated to be about 350° C, rise to the ocean floor, bacteria metabolize the hydrogen sulfide and multiply, creating the primary food source for higher organisms.

One population found in this community are red-tipped worms, up to 12 feet tall, that have no eyes, mouth, gut, or anus. They have large amounts of hemoglobin and thousands of tiny tentacles arranged on lamellae, which absorb food and oxygen from the water.

There are golatheid and brachyuran crabs. Although they resemble cancer crabs of the shallows, the latter type are blind. These crabs had to be placed in pressure vessels set at 250 atmospheres in order to keep them alive for experimental studies.

Foot-long clams, which filter microorganisms and organic debris, have startlingly red meat containing hemoglobin with an unusually high affinity for oxygen. This is probably an adaptation to periods of low oxygen.

One of the prettiest organisms existing in these communities is a siphonophore scientists dubbed the "dandelion" because of its appearance. Consisting of a gasbag for buoyancy surrounded by hundreds of mesenteries, this relative of the Portuguese man-of-war is very fragile and falls apart as soon as it is brought to the much lower pressure at the ocean surface.

The concentration of suspended food available at the vents is estimated to be four times greater than in productive surface waters; however, scientists have postulated that these oases of the deep are short-lived phenomena.

Space Exploration

With all the dangers astronauts have faced while in the alien environment of the moon, probably the greatest problems to their health, and certainly the most uncomfortable, are during the space travel when they experience zero gravity. Physical changes in the body are quickly apparent even in the shortest space ventures. No longer drawn by gravity, blood and other body fluids redistribute themselves toward the head, and the semifluid intestines float upward. This fluid redistribution causes a nasal and sinus stuffiness much like a bad head cold and is probably a contributing factor to the space sickness termed space adaptation syndrome (SAS). Scientists think another cause of SAS, which induces nausea and vomiting, is the conflicting information that the brain receives from the eyes and inner-ear system during disorienting shifts in body positions.

Another effect of fluid redistribution is that the brain is fooled into eliminating too much water with the urine, eventually causing a 10 percent drop in blood plasma and a 15 percent reduction in red blood cells. Along with the water, calcium from bones was also passed in the urine at an alarming rate of 0.5 percent of total body calcium each month.

Besides the muscle atrophy that occurs in spite of exercise, the heart shrinks about 10 percent as it grows weaker. Doctors think this change occurs after only 48 hours in space, and it can take the heart almost a year after the space mission to return to normal. Ingenious space suits have been devised by the Soviets to overcome these problems: one that creates a vacuum around the legs, reversing the effects of weightlessness, and another, called the penguin suit, which pulls the body into a half-sitting position, forcing cosmonauts to use their muscles to avoid contracting into a fetal position. In spite of these remedies, reports from recent long-term Soviet space flights indicate problems still exist.

LEARNING EXPERIENCES

Classification Tree

1. To start, you might wish students to develop a classification tree in which the five new kingdoms are placed. Using Reproduction Page 60, have the class research which groups of organisms can be placed with which kingdoms on the tree. Students can be asked to give reasons why certain phyla are placed in one kingdom and not in another. You can test students' understanding of this new classification scheme by asking them to place the following groups of organisms into their respective kingdoms: nitrogen-fixing bacteria, yeast, bread mold, euglena, seaweeds, penicillium mold, paramecia, rotifers, insects, pine trees, and rosebushes. If possible, try to have students observe these organisms in order to make comparisons and see why they are classified as they are.

Membrane Filtration System

2. Secure a Millipore Filtration System or any other commercially available membrane filtration system from a biological supply house, and give students the following directions on how to use such a system:

   a. Unscrew the funnel portion of the Sterifil, and, using a smooth-tipped forceps, place a membrane filter in position.

   b. Replace the funnel.

   c. Attach a vacuum source, such as a hand vacuum assembly, purchased from a supply house.

   d. Add water or other liquid to be filtered to the Sterifil funnel.

   e. Apply vacuum and draw the liquid through the membrane.

   f. Release the vacuum, carefully remove the filter, holding it with smooth-tipped forceps, and proceed to analyze the filter in accordance with the objectives of the specific investigation.

These simple instructions usually accompany each filtration system you purchase. It is suggested that you use one system per two students. In this way, students can assist each other.

3. Now explore a few applications of this technology. First, students should gain some understanding of size when working with microorganisms. Use Reproduction Page 61, a diagram illustrating size scale. Have students answer the questions concerning microorganisms.

4. A good application of using membrane filtrations is to study life in a drop of pond water. Sometimes, however, the population density of the protozoans is quite low, leading students to get somewhat frustrated while trying to find even one organism. By applying the membrane filter technique, however, a sample of pond water can be concentrated by drawing a portion of it through the filter. Releasing the vacuum will stop the filtration. By this method, a volume of 100 ml pond water can be concentrated ten-fold, with a corresponding increase in the population density. A drop of this concentrated sample is now teeming with unicellular life and provides the students with some very exciting viewing.

5. The most important biological indicator of bacterial pollution in water is a common class of organisms known as coliform bacteria. This organism is easy to recognize and acts as a possible indicator for a source of disease-producing organisms. The attribute that makes coliform bacteria so easy to detect is their special ability to break down a complex sugar into a simple one, which will combine with a fuchsin stain to form an iridescent green coating over the coliform colony. These colorful "sheen" colonies are easy to distinguish from their less colorful counterparts. Since these bacteria are found in the intestines of warm-blooded animals, they usually indicate waste products in a water source, which may lead to pathogens present.

   The simplest and most widely used test for coliform bacteria consists of filtering a water sample through a sterile bacterial-retentive membrane filter. The microscopically small filter pores let the water through, leaving the organisms trapped on the filter surface. At this point, the microorganisms are invisible to the naked eye, but when the filter is placed on a paper pad soaked with nutrient Endo medium, the nutrients are absorbed through the filter pores to keep the microbes fed and multiplying. The nutrient Endo medium contains lactose plus basic fuchsin and can be purchased through a supply house. The selectivity of the test is achieved in the color reaction that takes place when coliform organisms break down lactose to form an acid aldehyde. The latter metabolic end product reacts with the basic fuchsin and gives the coliform colonies the characteristic green sheen.

Microorganisms in the Air

6. Use Reproduction Page 62 to detect and identify microorganisms found in the air outdoors and in the classroom.

Microorganisms and the Human

7. Once students have mastered the membrane filtration technique, they can undertake an exciting exercise on the bacteria found on the human body. Use Reproduction Page 63, a good summary of previous activities using this technology.

8. Using the mastery of the membrane technology, students can make a survey of local water sources. What evidence do they find of pollution? Compare water from the tap, swimming pools, beaches, rivers, ponds, and lakes. Which has the highest coliform count? Which has the least? Have students find out what the allowable coliform levels are in their state for drinking water.

9. Have students go to the library and research the work of Alexander Fleming. They can repeat his classical "zone of inhibition" experiment using membrane technology. It is fairly easy to secure penicillium mold from a rotting orange. It is blue-green in color. Let students devise an experiment based on their readings of Fleming's work.

10. You can demonstrate the antiseptic effect on the growth of bacteria. One effective method is to incubate six petri dishes containing harmless bacteria from previous activities using membrane filtration. Once the colonies are visible, set aside two as a control. To one add a filter paper disc that contains 2% tincture of iodine; to others, use other commonly known antiseptics. Incubate all petri dishes, including the control dishes, to see any further growth. You should be able to determine which chemicals were effective in 24 hours, 36 hours, and so on. Another variation of this activity is to place a drop of the antiseptic on the absorbent pad containing the food media. Be sure to have some controls. Incubate, and you can see which are effective in halting the growth of the bacteria.

Disease

11. An excellent activity to undertake with your class or have students undertake individually is "Be a Disease Detective," using Reproduction Page 64 as a guide.

12. An activity you may wish to do with your class is preparing a sirius stain, which can illustrate how disease can spread through a population from a single unnoticed source. To prepare the stain, which is undetected in normal light, add 0.5 g of sirius stain, a fluorescent salt, to 15 ml of glycerol. Stir until the stain is completely dissolved. The solution will be a bright yellow-orange color. Now you are ready to place the stain in various parts of the classroom before the students enter. Cover a commonly used area with a generous amount of the stain. Spread the oily substance around so that it is not in clumps and noticeable. You may place some on the pencil sharpener, a doorknob, and other surfaces. As students enter, they will touch various items, some containing the stain. You are now ready to check for the spread of the "contamination." To do this, have students line up and check their hands

under the ultraviolet lamp, which is set up in a dark corner of the classroom. Have students record on a sheet of paper the names of the contaminated people. Ask the class to figure out the location of the original source(s) of the contamination.

13. If possible, visit a university or hospital that has an electron microscope and request a special viewing of viruses under the scope. Students will be amazed as to what can be learned about these "living organisms." From their observation of the electron microscope, you may have your students go to the library and research information on how the electron microscope operates and information on the structure and function of viruses. Both the electron microscope and viruses are relevant topics in the study of disease.

14. The Shell Oil Company has a wonderful 35-minute color film, *Unseen Enemies*, that illustrates the sources of disease organisms and the diseases they cause.

15. Secure mosquito eggs or pupae from a nearby pond or supply house and hatch out to secure specimens of living mosquitos. Examine closely both male and female members of the species (after they have been anesthetized) under the microscope, and try to figure out how microorganisms can be transmitted to humans from these carriers.

16. Another fine activity is to review the various mouthparts of insects in order to understand how disease organisms might be transmitted to a host. (See Chapter 4 for diagrams of insect mouthparts.)

17. A classic yet stimulating activity to do with a class is to develop an understanding of the conditions needed to grow bacteria successfully. Some variables you might wish to test are temperature, light, and food media. To test the effects of temperature on the growth of bacteria, prepare a nutrient agar medium. Inoculate four petri dishes containing food media with a harmless bacteria, such as *bacillus subtilis* (the bacteria found in sour milk). This microorganism may be purchased from a biological supply house or secured from your own stock of sour milk. Once you have inoculated each petri dish with a culture of the bacteria, place each dish at a different temperature: one dish in the refrigerator at 4–8° C, two dishes at room temperature of the classroom (20–25° C), and one in a very hot area, such as in an incubator, if available, or on a stove. Check the temperature each day with a thermometer, and observe the rate of development that is visible.

18. Do the same type of experiment as in Activity 17, but this time expose two of the four petri dishes with the bacterial culture to strong light, keep one in a moderately light room, and one in the dark, such as in a closet. Where possible, keep the variable of temperature the same in each case. Observe the results.

19. You can vary this activity by using different types of food media in each petri dish to observe if one food is better for growth than another. Prepare a stock of chicken broth, vegetable broth, and some other broth of your choosing. Mix the broth with commercially available agar, and place in a petri dish. Inoculate as before with bacterial cultures, and set in an incubator at the same temperature and light source. Observe growth differences.

20. Another activity for students to undertake is the experiment that led Alexander Fleming to realize the concept of antibiotics. You grow two different bacteria in the same petri dish in order to show antibiosis or the suppression of growth of one bacteria by substances produced by the other bacteria. Inoculate a petri dish containing a nutrient agar medium with a suspension of *sarcina subflava* (which may be purchased at a biological supply house). Set it aside for a few hours. Now inoculate the petri dish with another bacterial culture, such as *bacillus subtilis,* by streaking the dish with this culture. Incubate the dish, and inspect after 24 hours. You should notice prominent cultures of *sarcina* over the plate, except where you streaked the *bacillus.* In those areas, you will note zones of inhibition or clear zones, showing that these bacteria have produced a chemical that appeared to inhibit the growth of *sarcina.*

21. An activity worth exploring is to have students examine under the microscope various prepared slides of disease-producing microbes. Students can draw and describe these microorganisms as compared to the coliform bacteria.

22. Once students have studied disease-producing organisms, ask students to look up in the library various diseases and to report to the class on their cause, how they are spread, symptoms, treatment, and any immunity that may be known. Some good diseases to discuss are herpes, tuberculosis, pneumonia, influenza, rabies, acquired immune deficiency syndrome (AIDS), and malaria. They may already have researched some diseases when working on Reproduction Page 64.

23. In planning laboratory activities using bacteria, be sure to refer to the section "Diversity in Microorganisms" in the student laboratory guide of the *yellow version* of the *BSCS—Biological Science: An Inquiry into Life* (Harcourt Brace). By using these activities, students can predict and develop hypotheses on the little-known environment of microbiology.

Activities in Oceanography

24. Another little-known environment interesting to explore, if available, is a salt marsh. By studying a salt marsh, you can understand the importance of this ecosystem and realize that it is the nursery of most fish that enter the oceans. We rely so much on this delicate environment, yet we do not realize its potential. A field trip might prove fruitful in exploring how it functions and the organisms associated with it.

25. An interesting way of introducing the study of oceanography is by reading some accounts from Jules Verne's *Twenty Thousand Leagues under the Sea,* which describes life-forms existing at the ocean bottom. Mention that Verne had a broad knowledge of the science of the 1800s and used his knowledge of the physical conditions existing at ocean depths to figure out what structure organisms would have to evolve in order to exist there. Describe some of the life-forms that have actually been found there, and discuss the insight and validity of many of Verne's predictions.

26. After reviewing various aspects of the ocean environment, have your students research organisms of the deep and encourage them to show the relationship between their structure or behavior and the abiotic and biotic factors affecting them.

27. Review adaptations of marine life dealing with pressure (the whale) and salinity (marine fish and reptiles) that were presented in Chapter 2.

28. In studying the ocean environment, you might take your class to a nearby pier in order to study the effects of light on organisms living near the pier. One way to study light in the marine environment is to find the limits of visibility using a Secchi disk. This device is a circular plate, usually 20 cm in diameter. The upper surface is divided into four equal quadrants, two of which are painted white, and two are painted black. The lower surface is painted black to eliminate the reflection of light from that side. Once you have secured such a disk, either from a biological supply house or from a bait and tackle shop, you are ready to undertake an interesting activity.

Have students lower the disk into the water by a graduated rope, which you calibrated in feet earlier. As students lower the disk on the rope, have them record at what depth the disk disappears from sight. Be sure the readings are done in the shade of the pier. Now have the students raise the disk and record the depth at which they first see the disk surfacing. The average of the two readings is the limit of visibility. Once this reading is found, ask the students questions on light and its depth in the ocean, such as why certain life-forms survive closer to the surface compared to those that dwell at the bottom.

29. Another activity focuses on organisms that have adapted to living at the bottom of the ocean. You may wish your students to become familiar with benthic organisms and ways of collecting such creatures in order to study the various adaptations they evolved over the millions of years of living at the bottom of the oceans. Two collecting devices that can be used are a biological dredge net and a Petersen grab. Both can be purchased from a biological supply house. If you have a limited budget, consider visiting a bait-and-tackle store, usually located near a beach community. These stores often carry equipment for use in studying the marine environment and usually are much cheaper than a supply house.

You can use the dredge and the grab off a pier or a boat. Sample the bottom of the marine environment using these two devices and place the samples in a pail of cool ocean water for the trip back to school. Be sure to label the pails as to the location and device used. Once back in the laboratory, students can examine specimens in each pail, using a hand lens or microscope, and identify and draw those organisms found at the bottom. You may wish to ask the class such questions as: How do benthic organisms breathe? How do they eat? How are they adapted to living at the bottom?

30. If a boat is available to you and your students, you can study the various types of plankton found in the marine environment. To collect plankton, purchase a plankton net or make one, using a nylon stocking, as illustrated in Fig. 9.1. The plankton net is towed by a boat in which several of the nets are attached to a

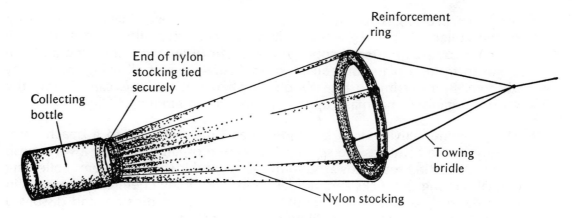

Fig. 9.1. Plankton net.

rope at different depths. As the boat moves along, the plankton are collected in the collecting bottle. See Fig. 9.2 on how to set up the net for collecting specimens.

31. Once you have collected various bottles containing plankton, you are now ready to study the samples in the laboratory. First, hold the collecting bottle containing the plankton samples up to the light, and examine the teams of living things that make up the plankton community. For more detailed study, students can view a sample of the plankton collected in a petri dish using a binocular microscope. Students will see the diversity of living things, including

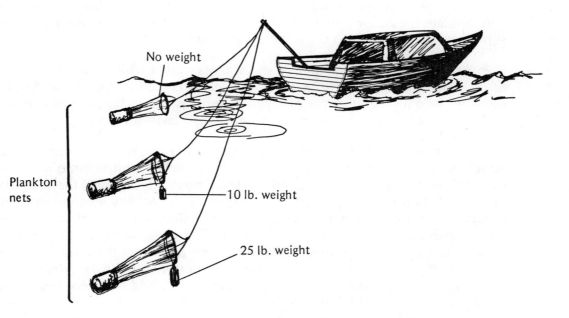

Fig. 9.2. How are plankton nets used?

predators, prey, eggs, larvae, and adults. For a closer examination, take a drop of the collected specimens, place it on a depression slide, and examine it under a compound microscope. Students can draw what they see and can begin to make a plankton collage of their drawings of all living things they observe. By referring to a textbook on plankton, students can identify the various organisms that make up this vast marine community.

32. Many marine activities can be undertaken on a field trip to a beach community. Some activities are seining for marine organisms using a wire mesh board; collecting seaweeds around the shore and identifying them; collecting animals among the rocks and in tidal pools; and doing chemical water tests in the area to determine the amount of salinity, carbon dioxide, and dissolved oxygen. These test kits are readily available from supply houses.

33. To illustrate currents present in the water off a seashore environment, use fluorescein dye, which is placed in the water at the tip of the shore. Students will notice how the currents move as they observe the pattern of the dye.

34. A worthwhile class project is to set up a saltwater aquarium. It is best to use only an all-glass tank (25 to 50 gal.) in which you place sand as a base or chips of pulverized shells secured from the seashore. To the glass tank, add an outside filter. It is recommended that you use the Dynaflo type of filter since it is quiet and long-lasting for the classroom situation. Do not buy commercially available salts to add to your aquarium. It is best to use seawater from a bay, which can be collected on a regular basis throughout the year during tidal changes. Be sure to have extra containers of seawater on hand to add as evaporation takes place. Keep the marine aquarium at room temperature. Use plant and animal specimens collected locally in your marine waters. Twice a week, cut up fish and throw into the tank. Do not feed daily, or you will contaminate the aquarium. It is recommended, if possible, that you raise brine shrimp for feeding various organisms in your tank.

35. If you wish to preserve any marine speciments caught while at a field site, use formaldehyde and seawater at a 1:9 ratio (9 parts seawater to 1 part formaldehyde). Add a small quantity of glycerin and a pinch of borax. You can now preserve your marine specimens for study in the classroom.

36. Seawater contains many dissolved substances that make it heavier than an equal volume of fresh water. Density is the mass per unit volume of a substance. You can find out the approximate salinity of seawater if the temperature and density of a sample are taken together. This activity involves students' using a thermometer, a hydrometer, and conversion tables. First have students secure water samples from different areas and at different depths. Fill the hydrometer jar with the sample. Place a clean hydrometer in the jar, being careful that it does not touch the sides or bottom of the jar. Record the temperature immediately. Note that all readings should be preceded by 1.0. Have students enter the data on Reproduction Page 65. Students will have to refer to a handbook of temperature/salinity conversions in order to determine density and temperature factors.

37. Using information presented in the Content Overview, discuss the newly discovered ecological communities existing along areas of the mid-oceanic ridge, particularly in the area of the Galapagos rift and the 21° north site west of Mexico. Stress that this system is based on chemical synthesis and contradicts the conventional idea that sunlight is always the main source of energy for life. Describe some of the life-forms found there and show how they have evolved adaptations suited to this environment (for example, clams that have blood-red meat rich in a hemoglobin possessing an especially high affinity for oxygen).

38. Have students read an account of this new ecological community described in "Incredible World of the Deep-Sea Oases," *National Geographic* (November 1979) or from other articles such as those listed at the end of the chapter.

39. Encourage students to read Dougal Robertson's *Survive the Savage Sea*, the story of how a family survived in the alien environment of the ocean surface for thirty-eight days needing food and fresh water. This is an excellent illustration of the basic needs and ingenuity of human beings and how we are not adapted to drink saltwater.

Activities of Outer Space

40. You might initiate a discussion on space travel by mentioning that some people have already signed to be passengers on the first commercial shuttle to the moon. Ask your students to make a list of all the items they would have to bring if they were making an expedition to the moon. Tell them to include and describe equipment, such as a space suit, they would need. After they have finished, desribe the conditions on the moon—one-sixth gravity, lack of air pressure, no water, etc.—and see if they thought of equipment to counteract the effects of this alien environment.

41. Have your class brainstorm the effects of zero gravity encountered during space travel. Use the information given in the Content Overview to complete their list. Ask what methods NASA and the Soviet space program used to overcome these effects.

42. Bring in a plastic punch bowl that looks like crystal. Put a small amount of water in it and ask a student to lift it. Most students will expend too much energy to lift it and react with an awkward motion. Discuss carrying packages up or down steps and misjudging the number of stairs. Such an experience— even thinking there is an extra step—is often unbalancing. Relate these experiences, where they misjudged the amount of energy needed, to the problems of astronauts walking on the moon with only one-sixth their normal weight.

43. Have your students work in groups to draw or build a cardboard model of a space station. Tell them that the ideal is to have their station as self-sufficient as possible whereby essential substances are recycled as they are in nature.

See how many groups think of using green plants to replace oxygen or solar cells to tap the limitless supply of solar energy.

44. Assign magazine articles such as A. Olberg's "Astro Medicine" (*Science Digest*) or A. Tonfexis's "The Hazards of Orbital Flight" (*Time*) that deal with the effects of space travel on humans, or A. Chaikin's "The Space Shuttle's Uncertain Environment" (*Sky and Telescope*), which discusses the contamination of the environment that envelops the space shuttle. Have students write reports on their readings.

45. An interesting aspect of space travel is the promise it extends to big business, luring commerce with highly efficient techniques for producing items, such as computer chips and various metals, or radar surveying and remote sensing of oil and valuable metals. Assign articles such as R. Jastrow's "Space Profits" (*Science Digest*), which discuss the economic rewards of space travel for industry.

46. You might capture your students' interest by discussing the existence of a space camp for children in Huntsville, Alabama, Space and Rocket Center (J. Kluger, "Space Camp," *Science Digest*) where students conduct simulated flights and try out devices used by astronauts in preparation for their missions.

47. Another fascinating article is D. Egge's "Cities of the Sun" (*Science Digest*), which discusses remodeling the solar system in order to build cities on other planets. Discuss the physical conditions that exist on other planets and elicit the effects such environments would have on people and how the effects could be overcome.

48. An activity to stimulate thinking about extraterrestrial life is to visit a planetarium and have students observe numerous stars with the potential for other solar systems, and planets within our own solar system that might receive sunlight, and have similar conditions for possible life-forms. Many planetariums have special shows on this theme.

49. Ask a biology professor from a local university to come and speak to your class on life in outer space. NASA has guest speakers available to discuss the effects of weightlessness and other factors of a vacuum environment on the physiology of the human body.

50. NASA has available color slides of satellites and other outer space technology, which may prove helpful in introducing your students to this new environment.

51. From the various readings, students might be innovative and build an "outer space tank" in which conditions of temperature, pressure, and lack of oxygen, can be designed into the tank. Now you can have students place selected plants and microscopic organisms in the experimental tank to see the effects it may have on the organisms. This simulated tank experiment can develop a special awareness in students about alien environments.

ASSESSING LEARNING EXPERIENCES

Several of the activities from this chapter can be used for evaluating student achievements. Among the Reproduction Pages there are questions posed to the students. The answer to these questions can be used to evaluate students' understanding of membrane technology and microorganisms.

Students' ability to master the skill of membrane technology can be assessed by directly observing the students handle the filtration system and successfully inoculate bacterial cultures.

The extent to which students have learned about the five-kingdom classification system can be measured by having them submit for evaluation the final products of the activity.

For an overall evaluation of students' ability to recognize the various aspects of little-known environments, including the oceans, outer space, and the world below the microscope, assign an in-class essay in which students can identify different types of microorganisms, describe the abiotic and biotic components of the salt marsh and ocean environments, and identify the physical and biological components of outer space.

RESOURCES FOR TEACHING

Books and Journal Articles

Ballard, Robert D. and Grassle, J., "Incredible World of the Deep-Sea Oases," *National Geographic* 156 (November 1979): 680. A fascinating account, in text and pictures, of the expeditions to the strange ecosystems located along the Galapagos rift and the 21° North sites.

BSCS, *Biological Science: An Inquiry into Life* (Yellow Version), Harcourt Brace. An excellent high-level secondary school text introducing biology to able students.

BSCS, *Student's Laboratory Guide* (Yellow Version), Harcourt Brace. The companion laboratory manual to the text.

BSCS, The Human Sciences Program, *Feeling Fit Module,* National Science Programs. One of twelve modules for intermediate grades that offers students a hands-on experience with health.

Chaikin, Andrew, "The Space Shuttle's Uncertain Environment," *Sky and Telescope* 64 (December 1982): 527. Discusses the problems of the immediate environment enveloping space craft due to natural phenomena and waste products of the shuttle.

Clark, W. B., *The Experimental Foundations of Modern Immunology,* 2d ed., Wiley. An updated book of the structures of the human immune system.

Edmond, John M. and Von Damm, D. "Hot Springs on the Ocean Floor," *Scientific American* 248 (April 1983): 78. A discussion of the communities found along submarine ridges, giving background information on plate tectonics and details on the origin of the chemical composition of the ocean.

Egge, David, "Cities of the Sun," *Science Digest* 90 (October 1982): 60. An imaginative account of three ways of remodeling the solar system so that no solar energy is wasted.

Hardy, Alister C., *The Open Sea: Its Natural History,* Houghton Mifflin. An excellent, well-written book covering all aspects of plankton.

Jastrow, Robert, "Space Profits," *Science Digest* 90 (March 1982): 12. A report on exciting new technologies—remote sensing, radar surveying, zero gravity production lines—that are luring big business into the space race.

Kluger, Jeffrey, "Space Camp," *Science Digest* 91 (February 1983): 76. Describes a space camp at Huntsville, Alabama, designed to allow children to experience simulated conditions of space travel.

McConnaughey, Bayard H., *Introduction to Marine Biology*, Mosby. A fine book describing the diverse biota of the marine environments.

Mandell, G. L., *Principles and Practices of Infectious Diseases*, Wiley. A two-volume set on understanding, diagnosing, and treating infectious diseases.

Margulis, Lynn, *Five Kingdoms: An Illustrated Guide to the Phyla of Life on Earth*, W. H. Freeman. An innovative treatment in which the traditional kingdoms are expanded based on structure and function.

Matthews, Samuel W., "New World of the Ocean," *National Geographic* 160 (December 1981): 792. A comprehensive presentation of the findings of thirty years of ocean exploration, detailing up-to-date facts on abiotic and biotic aspects.

Millipore Corp. Staff, *Experiments in Microbiology*, Millipore Corp. A laboratory guidebook developed by the technical staff presenting the skills of Millipore technology. An excellent experimental book for work on microorganisms in the environment.

Oberg, Alcestis, "Astro Medicine," *Science Digest* 89 (June 1981): 84. A detailed account of the effects of weightlessness during space travel and some of the means proposed to remedy the problems.

Robertson, Dougal, *Survive the Savage Sea*, Bantam Books. An incredible account of how a family survived being stranded in the middle of the ocean in a dinghy needing food and fresh water.

Singleton, P., *Introduction to Bacteria*, Wiley. A concise text on the latest theories and practices in the structure and function of bacteria.

Sussman, A. S. *Microbes: Their Growth, Nutrition and Interaction*, Heath. An excellent booklet on how to grow microbes and reasons for their patterns of development.

Tonfexis, Anastasia, "The Hazards of Orbital Flight," *Time*, February 8, 1983. A brief report on the effects of weightlessness experienced during the American and Soviet 1981 flights.

Verne, Jules, *Twenty Thousand Leagues under the Sea*. The classic tale of a sea captain's journey to the ocean depths in a submarine. Written before the submarine was invented.

Zottoli, Robert, *Introduction to Marine Environments*, Mosby Co. A fine paperback book describing the chemical and physical factors of the marine environments.

Films and Filmstrips

Membrane Filtration, (30 min.), Millipore Corp. A free-loan film with animated concepts on the use of the Millipore filter.

Unseen Enemies (30 min.), Shell Oil Co. An excellent film, free loan to schools, on the world of microbes, and some of the little-known diseases involved.

Virus (set of eight films, 29 min. each), Indiana University. A detailed account of research on the viruses. Technical.

Between the Tides (22 min.), Contemporary Films. A fine color film of plant and animal life at the intertidal zone.

Mysteries of the Deep (23 min.), Disney Productions. A well-made animated film showing marine life and the adverse conditions for survival.

Plankton and the Open Seas (19 min.), Encyclopedia Britannica. An illustrated film of life in the sea from surface to the deep.

NASA, various slides and photographs of outer-space phenomena, Washington, D.C.

10

Controversial Issues in Biology

INTRODUCTION

Many educators believe that in order to achieve the kind of active, reflective, politically, and scientifically aware citizens that a democracy requires, classroom instruction should not avoid full exploration of potentially controversial issues. Others, including some parents, teachers, and school administrators, disagree. This situation can be described as the controversy about controversy. Issues of science and society are often controversial. The decision to deal with them (or not deal with them) in the classroom must be carefully made by you.

In order to understand better this "controversy about controversy," we need to examine the definition of controversial issues, the arguments and counterarguments used to favor or oppose a controversial issue in the science curriculum, and the implications for the science teacher of the contemporary position favoring the inclusion of controversial materials in the student's school experience.

Controversial issues are easy to identify. Many agree that it is an issue for which society has not found a solution that can be universally or almost universally accepted. It is usually an issue of sufficient significance that each of the proposed ways of dealing with it is objectionable to some group in our society.

Before undertaking discussions and activities with your students on such issues in biology as evolution versus creation, test-tube babies, in vitro fertilization, abortion versus right to life, hunting of whales and seals, the snail darter versus the Tennessee Valley Authority (TVA), sex education, genetic engineering, or euthanasia, it is recommended that you read the Content Overview, which discusses selecting issues for consideration, as well as teaching strategies for controversial topics. Most of the Learning Activities discussed in this chapter will utilize aspects of value education, library research, and timely films that are recommended to get students involved in the issues.

The Resources section contains many books, updated articles, and relevant films on controversial issues mentioned in the Learning Experiences. Be sure to use this list when preparing for the various topics.

PERFORMANCE OBJECTIVES

As a result of the Learning Experiences in this chapter, students should be able to:

1. Identify controversial issues in biology.

2. Describe in detail the pros and cons of at least five controversial issues in biology.

3. Use the library as a research tool in gaining knowledge and understanding of a controversial issue.

4. Learn how to approach an emotional issue in an objective, open-minded manner so that truth, not a confirmation of one's opinion, is sought.

CONTENT OVERVIEW

Criteria on Issue Decisions

Given the limited classroom time and a variety of performance objectives, it is impossible to provide substantive instruction on all the issues that might be considered relevant and important to students.

You have to determine how to select issues for study. Students' interests and concerns play an important role. So do the background and interests of the teacher. Some possible criteria to consider in making your issue decision are the following:

1. Is the issue suitable for students of the maturity and background represented in the class?

2. Will the study of the issue help students achieve course objectives?

3. Is the issue one for which adequate study materials that present various points of view can be obtained?

4. Is the issue one that is important and likely to be of continuing significance?

5. Is the issue one that you are—or can be—adequately prepared to deal with fully and objectively?

6. Can you evaluate the students' outcomes related to the study of the controversial issue adequately?

7. Can the issue be appropriately considered within reasonable classroom time?

Once you have reviewed this list and can answer the questions posed, you are now ready to begin the teaching process of a controversial issue. It takes a different style and approach to teach such an issue; Chapter 1 offers some suggestions for an approach.

A good way to get a class started in controversial issues is to begin with a group process exercise in values education. Reproduction Page 66 might be one to use. Once students have a sense of what you mean by a value, you can begin a discussion using the various activities suggested in the Learning Experiences on one or several of the following issues:

1. Evolution versus creationism
2. In vitro fertilization
3. Abortion versus right to life
4. Right to death
5. Deep-freeze postponement of death
6. Euthanasia (painless death)
7. Genetic engineering
8. Captive breeding techniques
9. Snail darter versus TVA
10. Hunting of endangered species (blue whale)
11. Birth control
12. Herpes and promiscuity
13. AIDS and homosexuality
14. Food additives
15. Use of pesticides/PCBs
16. Acupuncture
17. Biofeedback
18. Drug abuse
19. Alcoholism as a disease
20. Teenage pregnancy
21. Moral and economic issues in organ transplants
22. When is a person legally "dead"?

LEARNING EXPERIENCES

Concepts in Values

1. A good beginning activity to have the class work on is one that develops the concept of a value as being either personal and/or societal in nature and incorporates the idea that choices made to enhance the quality of life are dependent on the values of an individual or group of individuals. Read Reproduction Page 66 with the class. Be sure that the students know what they are to do. When they have completed this exercise, repeat the procedure with

Reproduction Page 67. After completing this exercise, ask several students to place their list of ten people on the chalkboard and explain their reasons for their choices. From this list, categorize each according to the following value judgments:

a. immediate survival,

b. long-range survival,

c. culture and aesthetics

d. leadership and organization,

e. sexuality,

f. family and friendships,

g. chivalry

2. After discussing the values and groupings from Reproduction Page 66, have another group of students place their items, selected from Page 67, on the chalkboard. Discuss with the class the reasons for the items chosen. Group the items into the following major classes:

a. short-term survival,

b. long-term survival,

c. pleasure and entertainment,

d. value to society.

See if each student favors one type of value over another or if a balance is obtained.

3. A variation on the first activity that gets students involved and brings out many personal values and group interactions is to have them play out a decision-making activity on survival. You may want to have your students represent various occupations and life-styles by having them wear cards indicating various roles—for example, physician, married, housewife, mother of four; geologist, single. Tell them that they are on a large cabin cruiser that is sinking far off the coast and that they have only one lifeboat to carry survivors. Use tape to make a rowboat 3 or 4 feet long and 2½ to 3 feet wide on the floor. Give them an allotted time—about 20 minutes—to decide who shall go on the boat and another 15 minutes to fit everyone who is to survive inside the taped lifeboat. Instruct them that if anyone is standing on or outside the tape when the time is up, the entire boat will sink. During the decision-making portion of the activity, students are to respond to questions with answers appropriate to the roles they are playing.

After the activity is finished, ask students to discuss why they chose the people they did and to note how they interacted in this crisis situation.

Students may resort to standing or sitting on another's shoulders to fit everyone in the boat, so it is wise to have them remove their shoes. Since some students may resort to pushing others out of the boat, caution them to be careful in their treatment of others.

The time allotment and size of the boat should be adjusted to suit the number of those involved. Be sure the boat is too small to fit everyone.

4. A good activity to develop with the class is that of role playing. Select a controversial issue found in one of the scientific journals, and develop a simple script in which members of the class play a role. One could play a corporation president, one can play a banker, and so on. Have each student research in the library the issue at hand from the perspective of the role each is playing. For example, you might wish to undertake the controversial issue on abortion versus the right to life. Ask for volunteers to play a priest, a physician, a politician, a mother, a father, and anyone else deemed important who might be involved with this issue. Each can research the pros and cons of abortion, and present her or his view to the class in a play on the issue. The members of the class who are not directly involved in the role playing, can represent the press and ask questions of each of the participants. This technique is an excellent one to get all students involved.

Some issues that lend to role playing are: "The Right to Die—Who Decides?" (patient, relatives, doctor); "Should smoking be banned in public places?" (smokers, nonsmokers, doctor, tobacco company representative); "Should pesticides be used in agriculture?" (farmer, environmentalist, food industry representative, consumer). Prior to such an activity, assign roles and allow one period of library research on the topic, or you may discuss some reading material on the issue. An excellent book that discusses the right to die is R. Veatch's *Death, Dying and the Biological Revolution. The Feeling Fit Module* of the BSCS Human Sciences Program contains an excellent role-playing activity on the issue, as well as activities that deal with illegal drugs, stress and suicide, and death and disposal.

5. The following activity on life expectancy is an excellent way to give your students a better realization of the impact of modern medical advances and why we are having such problems with the aging and those being kept alive through the long-term use of life-support machines.

Have students visit a cemetery where people have been buried over the past 150 to 200 years. Ask them to choose 50 graves of people who died prior to 1900 and 50 graves of people who died after 1950. Tell them to record the name, year of birth, and year of death for each person. If students are not able—or inclined—to visit a cemetery, it is worth making the trip and recording the information yourself. (We found the results incredible!) When the data have been collected, have your students calculate the average life span of those who lived in the nineteenth century and compare it with the life span of those who died after 1950. Discuss some of the common causes of death in the nineteenth century.

Debate Topics and General Activities

6. Another fine activity is to have students debate an issue in class. You can debate whether unmarried teenagers should have free access to birth control counseling and devices without parental permission. You may use topics that

are less personal in nature such as the use of acupuncture in treating diseases; evolution versus creationism; the snail darter versus the TVA; the hunting of endangered species; the use of pesticides; moral issues in organ transplants, in vitro fertilization; or others. For such topics, give the debaters a sufficient amount of time to research the topic. You might appoint several "unbiased" students to judge the debate or ask the class which debaters gave the most convincing arguments. While both logical and emotional appeals are important in debates, have students distinguish between the two.

7. Debate the use of biofeedback in the treatment of diseases such as high blood pressure. To introduce the topic, review Activity 17 in Chapter 5, which deals with measuring blood pressure after various activities. After discussing how relaxation exercises can be used to lower blood pressure, have your students read about the Biobox, a device used to monitor tenseness, which is described in J. Barbarello's "What's Your Tenseness Level?"

8. An activity to stimulate a great deal of interest is to have students visit a grocery store, examine the labels on prepared foods, and make a list of all the chemical additives. Once such a list is generated, they can begin researching in the library whether the additives are necessary and safe, unnecessary but safe, or unnecessary and potentially harmful.

9. Ask students to explain the fallacies in each of the following statements:

    a. All synthetic food additives should be banned. We should all return to safe, nutritious natural foods.

    b. All foods are chemicals, so we should not worry about artificial chemical additives.

    c. Since all natural foods contain harmful chemicals, we should not be so concerned about synthetic food additives.

    d. Food additives are essential. Without them, we would suffer from malnutrition, food poisoning, and spoiled food.

10. To get students involved in a controversial issue sometimes is more difficult than having them research facts on the topic. One way of getting your class involved is to offer them a challenge! Ask them to find out what is meant by the GRAS list and the Delaney clause and to describe each. From this activity, students can become involved in the issue of cancer-causing substances found in our environment.

11. An excellent way to introduce students to the deceit as well as the dangers of drug abuse, including legal drugs, is to have them do a study of over-the-counter medications. First ask them to observe television commercials and written advertisements on one category of medications. A good area to choose is aspirin and aspirin substitutes. Have them list the claims made by various brand-name companies in these advertisements. Ask students which product they think is best. Now have them go to a pharmacy and look up and record the ingredients found in these products. Discuss the results and have them read related information found in Consumer Reports's *The Medicine Show.* You can have individuals investigate other products discussed in the

book. Be sure to have them note the price differences between brand-name and generic drugs.

12. Have your class visit a zoo. While in the zoo, ask the students to make a list of animals that might be considered endangered and the reasons for the endangerment. Once this is done and students have seen these species in captivity, develop the issue of captive breeding techniques—whether humans are tampering with nature.

13. The controversial topic of noise pollution in a community can offer an interesting activity. Borrow a sound pressure decibel meter from the physics teacher or nurse. Have your students make a community survey of sound pressure levels at different times of the day and at different locations. Plot the results on a map of your community. Correlate your findings with the standard chart on decibel levels and human hearing found in any text on noise or by the standard chart of the Environmental Protection Administration (EPA).

   Once you have determined that there is noise pollution in your community, you can have the class debate the rationale that we have always had noise and can get used to it.

14. One of the most fascinating areas of biological research today is on the functioning of the human brain. Controversies range from extrasensory powers of the brain and the degree to which our mental powers can control our bodies to whether differences in sex roles of males and females are caused by their different brain structures. Have students read and discuss several of the numerous articles that present such controversies.

   Have students test themselves to see if they are a left-brain or right-brain thinker. A. Munzert's *Test Your I.Q.* contains questions to determine if someone has left brain or right brain dominance and discusses attributes associated with each.

15. There are many problems in today's society that are dramatically affecting adolescents. Topics such as drug abuse (including alcohol and legal drugs) are controversial in nature because the abusers are satisfying certain needs and often do not see their use of drugs as abuse. It is also a difficult issue to discuss because of legal ramifications connected with drugs.

   Other topics such as teenage pregnancy, birth control, and sexually transmitted diseases must be treated delicately not only because of the sexual mores in society—affecting attitudes of students, parents, and administrators—but also because of the intimate nature of these topics.

   Another topic charged with emotion is suicide, but it is one of the leading causes of death in our adolescents and should be discussed.

   Because these problems are having such an impact on society and are so closely related to students, a great deal of time and money has been expended to produce high-quality films and filmstrips on these topics. While activities such as reading and role-playing can be used as good supplemental learning experiences, very few techniques have an ability equal to a film to involve, touch, and impress students and to stimulate discussion. For this reason, we have included in the Resources some of the best up-to-date films and filmstrips on these topics. After viewing and discussing a film pertaining to one of the topics, you might assign readings or have your students research the issue further.

16. After introducing the topic of sexually transmitted diseases, you may want to use Reproduction Page 68 to assist your students during such a research assignment. Have your class work in small groups to make up their own questions and to find answers. During this activity, it is advisable to have them choose the students with whom they will work since they will be less inhibited with their friends. Encourage each group to use all the avenues of information suggested, and assist them in obtaining a guest speaker from a health center in your area.

     Since a great deal of research on the causes, treatment, and hopeful cures of herpes and AIDS is currently being done, suggest using the most recent periodicals on these topics.

17. Have your students make posters, bulletin boards, showcases, or displays about sexually transmitted disease. Include the facts you think people should know about sexually transmitted diseases. Be sure to find out where students in your area can get checkups for these diseases.

18. Set up groups of three or four students to discuss this statement: "Curable or preventable diseases such as smallpox, poliomyelitis, and diphtheria have been nearly eliminated in the United States. Many sexually transmitted diseases such as syphilis and gonorrhea can be cured and prevented. Why, then, do they continue to exist in epidemic proportions?"

19. The most controversial issues are those that have only begun to affect our society but are destined to change every aspect of our outlook and life-style—for better or worse. Topics such as genetic engineering, deep-freeze postponement of death, cloning, and other modern techniques used in reproduction are innately interesting and require little motivation to stimulate discussion. For information on topics such as these, we suggest readings from *The Biological Time Bomb* (Taylor), *Bio-Revolution—DNA and the Ethics of Man-Made Life* (Hutton), and *Who Should Play God?* (Howard and Rifkin), to be followed by discussions.

20. In order to introduce a topic such as the deep-freeze postponement of death, you might explain what the term means, and ask students to list all the effects on society if such a technique were perfected. After discussing the effects your students listed, read some of the consequent problems described by Taylor in *The Biological Time Bomb* such as inheritance of property, loss of revenue from death duties, damage suits for reviving a "freezee" against his or her will, lack of funds for maintaining a frozen person, voting rights during the freeze, and the mental trauma of a "freezee" waking to an entirely different society. Could a criminal have himself or herself frozen to escape a court trial and incarceration?

21. Ask your students to list the techniques for reproducing human beings that they think will exist in the year 2050. Be sure to include possible techniques such as cloning, artificial inovulation, and artificial wombs. After discussing their impact on society, read several excerpts from *Who Should Play God?*

describing the inevitable racism against clones and the possible legislation already being discussed to protect their rights, or actual quotes from Chinese newspapers praising the prospect of artificial wombs that would allow women to continue working unheeded by pregnancies. After discussing possible techniques, ask your students which methods they think they would use.

ASSESSING LEARNING EXPERIENCES

Several of the activities from this chapter can be used for evaluating students' achievements. Those activities that involve library research on an issue can be written up and assessed in terms of their understanding of both the pros and cons of the issue.

Students' ability to understand an issue can also be measured through the oral presentations students make in debates on an issue or in role playing.

For an overall evaluation of students' ability to recognize the various aspects of controversial issues, assign an in-class essay in which students identify an issue, describe the pros and cons of the issue, and draw logical conclusions based on their findings.

RESOURCES FOR TEACHING

Books

Block, Zenal, *It's All on the Label,* Little, Brown. An excellent summary paperback book on food laws and additives.

Carson, Rachel, *Silent Spring,* Houghton Mifflin. Classic introduction to pesticides.

Consumer Reports Books, ed. *The Medicine Show,* Pantheon. A practical guide to everyday health problems and health products that exposes some of the deceitful techniques underlying advertisements of nonprescription drugs.

Eckholm, Erik P., *The Picture of Health,* Norton. Sponsored by Worldwatch Institute and the United Nations Committee on Health, it describes the causes and effects of undernutrition and poor sanitation.

Ehrenfeld, David, *Biological Conservation,* Holt, Rinehart and Winston. An excellent, readable book on conservation issues in America.

Guttmacher, Alan, *Birth Control and Love,* Bantam. Excellent description of birth control methods. A pioneer in the field.

Hardin, Garrett, *Birth Control,* Pegasus Press. A good historical summary of birth control.

Howard, Ted, and Jeremy Rifkin, *Who Should Play God?* Dell. Discusses existing and future techniques in the field of reproduction, from genetic engineering and test-tube babies to cloning and artificial wombs, and the implications of these techniques for society.

Huffaker, Carl, *Theory and Practice of Biological Control,* Academic Press. A definitive text on alternative uses of control.

Hutton, Richard, *BioRevolution—DNA and the Ethics of Man-Made Life,* Mentor. An excellent account of the background, controversy, possible benefits, and risks of genetic engineering.

Koblinsky, Roy, *Reproduction and Human Welfare: A Challenge to Research,* MIT Press. An excellent analysis of the existing methods and future research on fertility control.

Lerza, Catherine, ed., *Food for People, Not for Profit,* Ballantine. A source book on all dimensions of the food crisis.

Mellanby, K., *Ecological Effects of Pesticides,* Academic Press. A detailed treatment of the use of chemicals and implications on various environments.

Munzert, Alfred W., *Test Your I.Q.,* Monarch Press. An I.Q. test that contains questions to determine left-brain/right-brain dominance.

Richards, R. N., *Venereal Diseases and Their Avoidance,* Holt, Rinehart and Winston. A good source book on the topic with details on each disease.

Simon, Sidney B., *Values Clarification,* Hart Publishers. A fine book on the different strategies to use in understanding values and quality of life.

Stern, Edwin B., *Human Sex and Sexuality,* Wiley. Fine section on sexual diseases.

Taylor, Gordon Rattray, *The Biological Time Bomb,* Mentor. Provides a startling survey of the biological revolution, from genetic surgery and deep-freeze postponement of death to the outer limits of our future.

Veatch, Robert M., *Death, Dying and the Biological Revolution,* Yale University Press. A comprehensive, provocative confrontation with the legal, moral, and medical problems of death.

Verrett, J., *Eating May Be Hazardous to Your Health,* Simon and Schuster. Good overview of the potential dangers of food additives.

Whelan, Elizabeth, *Panic in the Pantry,* Atheneum. Advocates the use of food additives and case for eliminating the Delaney clause.

Journals

"Acupuncturists Point to New Uses," *Newsweek.* July 26, 1982, p. 10. Brief description of the technique and some of the controversies over the use of acupuncture.

Arehart-Treichel, Joan, "Duchenne Muscular Dystrophy: A Cure in Sight?" *Science News,* January 15, 1983, p. 42. Discusses research in attempting to identify the protein and gene responsible for the disorder, in order to find an effective treatment.

Asimov, Isaac, "Biotechnology: The Union of Genes and Genius," *Science Digest* 91 (March 1983): 64. An informative account of some of the research in genetic engineering that has already produced human insulin and interferon and in the future may provide energy, chemicals, food, and new mining techniques.

Barbarello, Jim, "What's Your Tenseness Level?" *Computers and Electronics* 21 (February 1983): 77. Explains some biofeedback techniques that can be used by connecting a Biobox to a color computer.

Begley, Sharon, et al., "The Big Bucks of Biology," *Newsweek,* April 5, 1982, 69. Presents the conflicts of interest between academic science and big business in the use of genetic technology.

Bishop, Jerry E., "Epidemic," *Discover* 3 (September 1982): 35. Discusses the grave disease, AIDS, its possible causes and effects, and how it is spreading from the homosexual community to the general population.

Clark, Matt et al., "When Doctors Play God," *Newsweek,* August 31, 1981, p. 48. Discusses the dilemma faced by relatives and medical professionals in deciding whether to help sustain life in newborns with major birth defects, those terminally ill or on life-support machines and others who are gravely ill.

Gould, Stephen Jay, "Enigmas of Evolution," *Newsweek,* March 29, 1982, p. 44. Describes some of the many controversies surrounding the theory of evolution and explains Gould's theory of punctuated equilibrium.

Kehrer, Daniel M., "Genes for Profit," *Science Digest* 90 (May 1982): 12. Recounts the speedy journey of interferon from its genetically engineered emergence in the lab to its billion-dollar promise in the investment world.

Langone, John, "Too Weary to Go On," *Discover* 2 (November 1981): 72. Discusses why so many children are committing suicide and what can be done to prevent it.

"Laser Beams Relieve Migraines." *Science Digest* 90 (August 1982): 94. Explains how laser beams are being used instead of needles in some forms of acupuncture treatment.

Marshall, Marilyn, "Teen-Age Suicides: Why Our Children Are Killing Themselves," *Ebony* 36 (September 1981): 36. Discusses the increase in teenage suicides and what can be done.

Weintraub, Pamela, "The Brain: His and Hers," *Discover* 2 (April 1981): 15. Theorizes that men and women may think differently because of differences in the structure of their brains.

Filmstrips

"The Innocent Addictions," 2 filmstrips, Sunburst. Exposes hidden dangers in junk food, over-the-counter drugs, diet supplements, and other substances that many consider harmless.

"How to Stop Smoking," 2 filmstrips, Sunburst. Directed at teenagers who want to stop smoking. Program presents six proved methods of quitting.

"Marijuana Bulletin: A Research Update," 1 filmstrip, Sunburst. Gives an objective roundup of physical and psychological studies; stresses new information on the effects of marijuana without using "scare tactics."

"Booze News," 1 filmstrip, Encore. This award-winning filmstrip uses reverse humor to depict the effects of alcohol.

"Smoking Clinic," 1 filmstrip, Encore. In this award-winning cartoon, a young person learns, through reverse humor, the absurdities behind cigarette advertising and the social pressures to smoke.

"Sexually Transmitted Disease: An Update," 3 filmstrips, Sunburst. Pulls no punches in this fact-filled, straight-forward explanation of sexually transmitted diseases.

"Herpie: The New VD around Town," 1 filmstrip, Sunburst. Teaches students the basic facts they need to know about the most frequently occurring venereal disease, genital herpes.

"Turning Off: Drugs and Peer Pressure," 2 filmstrips, Sunburst. Explores peer pressure as a motivating factor in why many teenagers become involved with drugs. Provides assertiveness techniques to cope with peer pressure.

"Four Pregnant Teenagers: Four Different Decisions," 4 filmstrips, Sunburst. Through poignant, true-to-life vignettes, this program forces students to weigh the emotional, ethical, and financial problems in the options available to pregnant teenagers.

"Teenage Birth Control: Why Doesn't It Work?" 2 filmstrips, Sunburst. Stresses that most teenage pregnancies occur because teenagers do not use birth control; gives insight into the emotional and psychological motivations for taking chances.

"Preventing Teen Suicide: You Can Help," 3 filmstrips, Sunburst. An in-depth analysis of a case of teen suicide that reveals some of the causes, warning signs, and ways of preventing suicide.

Films

"Addictions, Compulsions and Alternative Highs" (23 min.) Barr Films. An excellent new film that explores how and why people become addicted, how addictions ruin lives, and how to get "high" in healthy, positive ways.

"Richie" (31 min. edited version or 90 min.), Learning Corporation of America. The true story of a teenager whose deepening involvement with drugs, combined with family conflicts, lead eventually to a tragic death by his father's hand.

"Born Drunk: The Fetal Alcohol Syndrome" (10 min.) ABC Wide World of Learning. A moving film that describes the causes and effects of fetal alcohol syndrome and discusses how it might be prevented.

"How Do You Tell?" (13 min.) MTI Teleprograms. Geared to elementary grades, it is designed to help children say no to the use of drugs, alcohol, and tobacco and to use peer pressure to encourage others to say no.

"PCP—You Never Know" (15 min.), Churchill Films. Presents basic information on PCP (angel dust) and reveals the unique dangers of this drug.

APPENDIX A

Addresses of Producers of Resources

PUBLISHERS

Academic Press Inc.
111 Fifth Ave.
New York, NY 10003

Atheneum Press
597 Fifth Ave.
New York, NY 10017

Ballantine Books Inc.
Div. of Random House
201 East 50th St.
New York, NY 10022

Bantam Books Inc.
666 5th Ave.
New York, NY 10019

Basic Books Inc.
10 East 53d St.
New York, NY 10022

Boxwood Press
183 Ocean View Blvd.
Pacific Grove, CA 93950

Burgess Publishing Co.
7108 Ohms Lane
Minneapolis, MN 55435

Cornell University Press
124 Roberts Place
P.O. Box 250
Ithaca, NY 14850

Thomas Y. Crowell Co.
201 Park Ave. South
New York, NY 10003

Dell Publishing Co.
1 Dag Hammarskjold Plaza
New York, NY 10017

Discover
Time Life Building
Chicago, IL 60611

Doubleday and Company
501 Franklin Ave.
Garden City, NY 11530

Duxbury Press
Div. of Wadsworth Inc.
20 Providence St.
Statler Building
Boston, MA 02116

W. H. Freeman and Co.
660 Market St.
San Francisco, CA 94104

Harcourt Brace Jovanovich, Inc.
757 3d Ave.
New York, NY 10017

Harper and Row Publishers
49 East 53d St.
New York, NY 10016

Hart Graphics
P.O. Box 968
Austin, TX 78767

D. C. Heath Books
2700 North Richardt Ave.
Indianapolis, IN 46219

Holt, Rinehart and Winston
383 Madison Ave.
New York, NY 10017

Houghton Mifflin
1 Beacon St.
Boston, MA 02107

Little, Brown and Company
34 Beacon St.
Boston, MA 02106

McGraw-Hill Book Company
1221 Ave. of Americas
New York, NY 10020

David McKay Co, Inc.
2 Park Ave.
New York, NY 10016

Macmillan Publishers
Front & Brown Sts.
Riverside, NJ 08370

Mentor Books
c/o New American Library
1633 Broadway
New York, NY 10019

Millipore Corporation
Bedford, MA 01730

MIT Press
28 Carleton St.
Cambridge, MA 02142

Monarch Press
Div. of Simon and Schuster Inc.
1230 Ave. of Americas
New York, NY 10020

C. V. Mosby
Westline Industrial Dr.
St. Louis, MO 63141

National Association of Biology Teachers
11250 Roger Bacon Dr.
Reston, VA 22090

National Geographic Society
17th and M St., NW
Washington, DC 20036

National Kidney Foundation
2 Park Ave.
New York, NY 10009

National Kidney Foundation of
    Southern California
6820 La Tijera Blvd.
Suite 111
Los Angeles, CA 90045

National Science Programs
P.O. Box 41
West Wilson St.
Batavia, IL 60510

National Science Teachers Association
1742 Connecticut Ave., NW
Washington, DC 20009

New York Botanical Gardens
Bronx, NY 10458

W. W. Norton and Co, Inc.
500 Fifth Ave.
New York, NY 10010

D. Van Nostrand Co.
135 West 50th St.
New York, NY 10020

Oxford University Press
200 Madison Ave.
New York, NY 10016

Pantheon Books
Div. of Random House
201 East 50th St.
New York, NY 10022

Pegasus Press
735 Dolores
Stanford, CA 94305

Phi Delta Kappa, Inc.
P.O. Box 789
Bloomington, IN 47402

Plenum Publishing Corp.
233 Spring St.
New York, NY 10013

Prevention
c/o Rodale Press Inc.
33 East Minor St.
Emmaus, PA 18049

Raintree Press
P.O. Box 11799
Chicago, IL 60611

W. B. Saunders Publishers
West Washington Sq.
Philadelphia, PA 19105

Science Digest
c/o Hearst Corporation
224 West 57th St.
New York, NY 10019

Scientific American
See W. H. Freeman & Co.

Simon and Schuster Publishers
1230 Ave. of Americas
New York, NY 10020

Sky and Telescope Magazine
Sky Publishing Corporation
49 Bay State Rd.
Cambridge, MA 02238

Springer-Verlag, Inc.
175 Fifth Ave.
New York, NY 10010

Syracuse University
College of Forestry
Syracuse, NY

Time-Life Inc.
777 Duke St.
Alexandria, VA 22314

Time Magazine
Time & Life Bldg.
Rockefeller Center
New York, NY 10020

University of Chicago Press
5750 Ellis Ave.
Chicago, IL 60637

University of Washington Press
Seattle, WA 98105

J. Weston Walch Publishers
Portland, ME 04104

John Wiley and Sons
1 Wiley Dr.
Somerset, NJ 08873

World Book Encyclopedia, Inc.
P.O. Box 3564
Chicago, IL 60654

Yale University Press
302 Temple St.
New Haven, CT 06520

FILM DISTRIBUTORS

ABC Wide World of Learning
1330 Ave. of Americas
New York, NY 10019

AIBS
1401 Wilson Blvd.
Arlington, VA 22209

Appleton, Century & Croft
292 Madison Ave.
New York, NY 10016

Barr Films
P.O. Box 5667
Pasadena, CA 91304

Bell Telephone Co.
c/o New York Telephone Co.
140 West St.
New York, NY 10007
Distributed by:
Sterling Educational Films Inc.
241 East 34th St.
New York, NY 10016

Carolina Biological Supply House
2700 York Rd.
Burlington, NC 27215

Churchill Films
662 North Robertson Blvd.
Los Angeles, CA 90069

Contemporary Films
c/o Films Inc.
733 Greenbay Rd.
Wilmette, IL 60091

Coronet Films
5823 Santa Monica Blvd.
Hollywood, CA 90038

Disney Educational Materials
800 Sonora Ave.
Glendale, CA 91201

Ealing Film Loops
2225 Massachusetts Ave.
Cambridge, MA 02140

Encore Visual Education Inc.
1235 South Victory Blvd.
Burbank, CA 91502

Encyclopedia Britannica
Educational Corp.
180 East Post Rd.
White Plains, NY 10601

Film Associates, Eastern Region
Brookhaven, NY 11719

Guidance Association
Box 3000
Mt. Kisco, NY 10549

Indiana University
Audio Visual Center
Div. of University Extension
Bloomington, IN 47401

Learning Corporation of America
1350 Ave. of Americas
New York, NY 10019

McGraw-Hill Book Company
Text Film Dept.
1221 Ave. of Americas
New York, NY 10020

Millipore Corporation
Bedford, Mass. 01730

MIT Teleprograms Inc.
3710 Commercial Ave.
Northbrook, IL 60062

NASA Films/slides
Distributed by:
National Audio Visual Center
National Archives and Record Service
Washington, DC 20409

National Science Programs
P.O. Box 41
West Wilson St.
Batavia, IL 60510

Shell Film Library
5000 Park St. North
St. Petersburg, FL

Sterling Movies Inc.
Educational Film Division
241 East 34th St.
New York, NY 10016
or
309 West Jackson Blvd.
Chicago, IL 60606

Sunburst Communications
Room JR 5
39 Washington Ave.
Pleasantville, NY 10570

Syracuse University Film Rental Library
1455 East Colvin St.
Syracuse, NY 13210

Teaching Aids Inc.
P.O. Box 1798
Costa Mesa, CA 92626

APPENDIX **B**

Reproduction Pages

The pages that follow have been provided to facilitate the reproducing of exercises, field and laboratory techniques, and materials needed for activities suggested in the preceding pages. Each page is perforated to make removal from this book easier. Once removed, a page can be used in several ways:

1. *For projection with an opaque projector.* No further preparation is necessary if the page is to be used with an opaque projector. Simply insert it in the projector and the page can be viewed by the entire class.

2. *For projection with an overhead projector.* The Reproduction Page must be converted to a transparency for use on an overhead projector. Overlay the Reproduction Page with a blank transparency and run both of them through a copying machine.

3. *For duplication with a spirit duplicator.* A master can be made from the Reproduction Page by overlaying it with a special heat-sensitive spirit master and running both through a copying machine. The spirit master can then be used to reproduce 50 to 100 copies on paper.

HOW ANIMALS MAINTAIN SALT AND WATER BALANCE: THE FISH

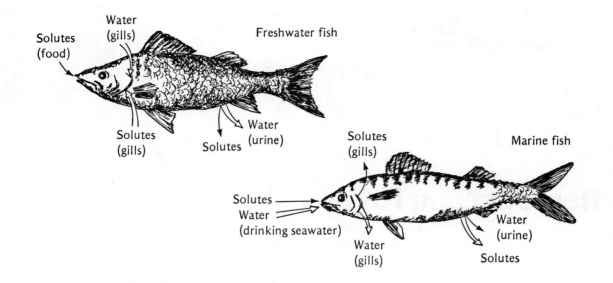

Water Balance in Humans and Kangaroo Rats

Gains	Humans (%)	Kangaroo Rats (%)
Drinking	48	0
Free water in food	40	10
Metabolic water	12	90
Losses		
Urine	60	25
Evaporation (lungs and skin)	34	70
Feces	6	5

Can you list the water-conserving, salt-excreting, or salt-absorbing mechanism present in each of these animals:

A Animal	B Adaptation
1. Turtle	1.
2. Marine fish	2.
3. Kangaroo rat	3.
4. Freshwater fish	4.
5. Marine bird	5.
6. Amphibians	6.

DETERMINING PARAMETERS OF pH TOLERANCE IN AN AMEBA

To Validate Experiment: Be sure to test each solution with a pH universal indicator to determine the actual pH. Also observe test amebas under the microscope to make sure they are living before placing them in a few drops of each solution.

Solution	Approximate pH	pH as Tested	Reaction Cyclosis Observed?
1. Lime juice	1.8–2.0		
2. Lemon juice	2.2–2.4		
3. Apple juice (freshly extracted)	2.9–3.3		
4. Vinegar	3.4		
5. Fresh rain	5.7–5.8		
6. Distilled water	6.8–7.0		
7. Drinking water	6.5–8.0		
8. Seawater	7.8–8.6		
9. Borax solution	9.2		
10. Milk of magnesia	10.2–10.6		
11. Ammonia water	11.1		

List the pH of solutions in which amebas showed evidence of life (cyclosis) starting with the lowest pH and continuing with the highest:

low _____ _____ _____ _____ _____ _____ _____ high

The tolerance range is between the lowest pH and the highest pH in which the ameba showed evidence of life.

Approximate Range: _____ to _____

TOLERANCE LEVELS DETERMINE SURVIVAL

Record the data as specifically as possible; for example:

	A	B	Result
Coleus	Sunlight 6 hours strong sunlight	Shade 0 hours sunlight	A. B.

In the last column, describe the effect on the test plant as compared to the control plant.

Organism	(A) Variable	(B) Control	Result
1. Elodea leaves	Cold water (refrigerate): _____ C.	Room temperature water: _____ C.	A. B.
2. Coleus	Shade: _____ hrs. light	Sunlight: _____ hrs. light	A. B.
3. Philodendron	Salt water, ___% salt, _____ ml salt water	Fresh water, no salt: _____ ml water	A. B.
4. Cactus (small)	Overwatering (½ cup per day)	Normal watering (½ cup per week)	A. B.
5. Sprouting carrot	_____ ml salt water: ___% salt	_____ ml fresh water: no salt	A. B.
6. Grass seed	Add lime: Amount _____	No addition	A. B.
7. Grass seed	Add acid fertilizer: Amount _____	No addition	A. B.

CAFETERIA LUNCH EVALUATION STUDENT INTERVIEW FORM

Select ten students—preferably five boys and five girls—who are eating the school lunch in the cafeteria. Ask each the two questions below. Try to write the answers in as few words as possible. (Use the letters of answers where possible.)

Boy ☐ or Girl ☐ (check one)	1. Which parts of the meal did you not eat?		2. Why did you not eat some of the food?
	Food Not Eaten	Food Group	(a) looks bad (b) tastes bad (c) smells bad (d) too full (e) other?

1.

2.

3.

4.

5.

6.

7.

8.

9.

10.

Which food groups were not eaten by students interviewed? (Place tally for each group.)

1. Meat _____

2. Vegetables and fruit _____

3. Cereal and bread _____

4. Dairy _____

5. Other foods _____

How many answers did you get for each of these five choices?

(a) Looks bad _____

(b) Tastes bad _____

(c) Smells bad _____

(d) Too full _____

(e) Other _____

ESTIMATING POPULATION SIZE

It is almost impossible to estimate populations of animals based on direct counts since it is too difficult to control the movements of an entire population. Thus we use a statistical method to estimate a given population.

The mark recapture method is based on trapping animals, marking and releasing them, waiting a short period of time, and then recapturing sample individuals. In this way, a known number of marked animals are released in the original area. After an interval of time, a population sample is taken. An estimate of the total population is then calculated from the ratio of marked to unmarked animals, as follows:

$$\frac{P_1}{M_1} = \frac{P_2}{M_2}$$

or

$$P_1 = \frac{P_2}{M_2} \times M_1$$

where

P_1 = total population,
P_2 = total number collected the second time,
M_1 = total number marked animals,
M_2 = number of marked animals caught the second time.

Exercise 1: Suppose 250 grasshoppers were marked and released, and 280 were captured the second time, of which 35 were marked. How many grasshoppers are estimated to be at the collection site?

Exercise 2: Suppose 39 rabbits were caught, marked, and released. After one week, you trapped 15 rabbits that were marked and 19 that were unmarked. What is the estimated size of the population of rabbits?

QUADRAT METHOD FOR ESTIMATING POPULATION DENSITY

A quadrat is a study area, usually a square or a rectangle, used to determine the frequency with which species of plants and animals are found in a given area. Quadrats may be any size, but usually a quadrat sample is approximately 10 percent of the total area being studied. Thus, if you are studying a meadow that is 100 square meters, the quadrat should be 10 square meters. Probably it would be better to have five randomly selected 2 square meter plots for the given area. Why?

Procedure

1. Cut 4 pieces of string or rope of lengths that will enable you to sample 10 percent of your area.
2. Tie each string to a stake with a strong knot. Be sure to allow about 2 inches in your total length for the knot.
3. Select an area to be studied. Determine its approximate size and throw a coin in the air at random. Where it lands will be considered the center of the quadrat.
4. Stake out the selected area by placing the stakes in the four corners you determined.
5. Examine the flora and fauna found within the quadrat, recording your data using the following chart:

Quadrat Number	Name or Type of Plant	Name or Type of Animal	Number of Plants	Number of Animals
1.				
2.				
3.				
4.				
5.				

Calculations

Frequency (f):   The percentage of quadrats occupied by a given species.

$$f = \frac{\text{number of plots in which species occurs}}{\text{total number of plots}} \times 100.$$

Relative frequency (R_f):   A comparison of the frequency of occurrence of a species with the frequency of occurrence of all of the species.

$$R_f = \frac{\text{frequency of species}}{\text{total frequency of all species}} \times 100.$$

Abundance (A):   The comparison of the number of plants of a species with the total number of plants of all species in the study area.

$$A = \frac{\text{number of plants of certain species}}{\text{total number of plants in plots}} \times 100.$$

Density (D):   The number of plants of a certain species for a total area being sampled.

$$D = \frac{\text{number of plants of certain species}}{\text{total area sampled}}.$$

Exercise: If 25 quadrats, each 1 square meter, were studied and a total of 125 dandelions were counted, what would be the density of dandelions for the area?

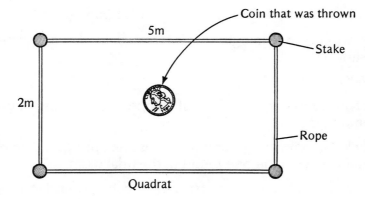

Illustration of a Quadrat

MARINE FIELD STUDY GUIDE: ECOLOGY OF A BEACH COMMUNITY

This trail guide of the beach community will cover the most significant biological aspects of the relationships between living things and their environment. It is suggested that you use the *trail guide map,* as well as the prepared guide questions, to make your biologic experience most successful.

A. *ON AN OPEN PATH* (if present in your location)

1. Identify the dominant plant population along the path.

2. Why can't you readily see animal life along the path?

3. What evidence of competition seems to exist in this area?

4. Why do you find soil in this area (the path) but not on the beach?

B. *THE TIDAL BASIN* (if present in your location)

5. What is meant by a tidal basin?

6. Collect a bottle of water from this area. This is to be kept for comparison and analysis in class.

7. What evidence of protective coloring is present in the area?

8. Identify and collect any organisms (plant or animal) present in the tidal basin.

9. What special adaptations are found on algae in the area?

10. What would be the three most critical factors found in the abiotic (physical) environment in this area?

11. Calculate the depth and area of the tidal basin.

12. Why would an ecologist be interested in the calculations made in question 11?

C. *THE SANDY BEACH AREA*

13. What evidence do you find of cooperation among organisms in this community?

14. Collect a sample of seawater from this area. Bring the sample to class for comparison with the one found in the tidal basin.

15. How would oil, similar to that released by grounded freighters, affect the ecology of the beach area?

16. Why would one find the densest population of organisms in the shallow water depths?

17. Why must plants in the tidal zone have firm anchorage mechanisms?

18. How would a deadly viral infection of the mussels in the area affect the ecological relationships in the area?

19. What evidence is present of symbiotic relationships in the area?

20. What is the dominant invertebrate of the area?

21. What stage in the ecological succession to beach-maple forest is indicated in the area?

22. What evidence of cooperation is seen within the community?

23. Using nets, collect organisms found within the water. Identify each.

24. How will each of the following affect the biotic environment of the area:
    a. Salinity?
    b. Sunlight?
    c. Food?
    d. Wind?
    e. Rain?

25. Why are blackfish commonly found around submerged rocks and vessels?*

26. What technique would an ecologist use to find out the density of the blackfish population invading the area?

27. Identify at least one organism found at a beach community from each of the following phyla:
    a. Mollusk
    b. Coelenterate
    c. Arthropoda
    d. Worm
    e. Chordate

Group Problem Analysis

1. Stake out ten square feet on the beach or picnic area. Investigate the area very closely for life. Collect specimens as you find them. Identify.

2. Make a stratification chart of a given area. Include all organisms.

3. Describe a food chain in a marine community. Name all organisms in it.

4. Devise a system for calculating the number of organisms making up a specific population in a given area.

5. Estimate the approximate density of the plant population or animal populations on rock surfaces.

---

*Blackfish are commonly found in the Atlantic Ocean community around New York City. You may use a species common to your area.

6. Explain the ecological significance of each of the following:

    a. If the beach began to be invaded by rocks and debris and eventually filled in.

    b. If a forest invaded the area in succession.

    c. If erosion continues to wash away the beach area.

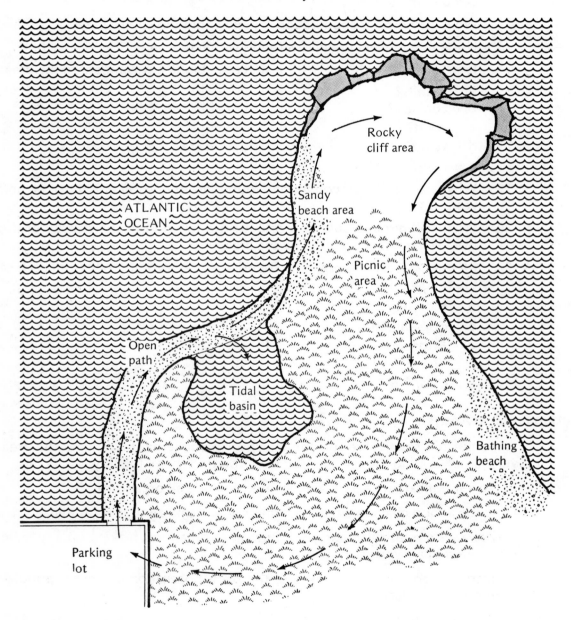

Aerial map of the Orchard Beach Area, Bronx, New York. Each teacher will have to prepare a map for the specific beach visited.

A BIOLOGICAL KEY TO MAJOR PLANTS AND ANIMALS

Simplified Key of the Major Groups of Plants

1.
  a. Plants without true roots, stems, or leaves 2
  b. Plants with true roots, stems, and leaves 10

2.
  a. Usually without leaf-like structures 3
  b. With small leaf-like structures, usually land plants .... BRYOPHYTA (mosses)

3.
  a. Very small, single-celled or colony of cells. Usually surrounded by slime or gelatinous layers outside ....SCHIZOPHYTA...................4
  b. Single-celled or many-celled, chlorophyll in plastids, usually no slime outside cell 5

4.
  a. No chlorophyll .... class—SCHIZOMYCETES (bacteria)
  b. With chlorophyll plus a blue pigment, occasionally a red pigment present, which masks the green and blue pigments .. class—SCHIZOPHYCEAE (blue-green algae)

5.
  a. Without chlorophyll, consists of minute branching filaments .... EUMYCOPHYTA (fungi)
  b. With chlorophyll, but chlorophyll may be hidden by other pigments 6

6.
  a. Green in color, chlorophyll .... CHLOROPHYTA (green algae)
  b. Chlorophyll masked by other pigments 7

7.
  a. Single-celled 8
  b. Many-celled (large sea weed) 9

8.
  a. No flagella, cell wall in 2 halves, one half fits over the other to form a box .... CHRYSOPHYTA (diatoms)
  b. With 2 flagella .... PYRROPHYTA (dinoflagellates)

9.
  a. Chlorophyll masked by brown pigment .... PHAEOPHYTA (brown algae)
  b. Chlorophyll masked by red pigment .... RHODOPHYTA (red algae)

10.
  a. Reproduce by spores, without seeds ....class—FILICINAE (fern)
  b. Reproduce by seeds 11

11.
  a. Seeds produced in cones, leaves needle-like ....class—GYMNOSPERMAE
  b. Seeds developed from flowers .... class—ANGIOSPERMAE (flowering plants) 12

12.
  a. Leaves usually parallel veined—flower parts in threes .... subclass—MONOCOTYLEDONAE
  b. Leaves usually net veined; flower parts in fours or fives .... subclass—DICOTYLEDONAE

For a more detailed key to specific names of plants, refer to specific keys of monocotyledons or dicotyledons; woody plants and shrubs, and so on.

References

1. Meunschner, W.C. *Key to Woody Plants* (Cornell University Press), 1950.
2. Gleason, H.A. *Plants in the Vicinity of New York* (Museum Publ.), 1947.
3. Bailey, L.H. *Hortus* (Macmillan), 1935.
4. Golden Book Series on Plants, Ferns, Flowers, etc.

Simplified Key of the Major Groups of Animals

1. a. Single cell or colony of cells without specialized body tissue .... PROTOZOA
   b. Many cells arranged in tissues 2
2. a. Radially symmetrical 3
   b. Bilaterally symmetrical, tubular digestive tract with mouth and anus present 4
3. a. Body soft and usually sac-like or umbrella-like; digestive tract with one opening .... COELENTERATA
   b. Hard body wall, spiny, body usually divided into five or multiples of five. Digestive tract with mouth and anus .... ECHINODERMATA
4. a. Never possess paired appendages, nonsegmented 5
   b. Paired appendages frequently present, segmentation present but may not be too clear 7
5. a. Body flat or ribbon like .... PLATYHELMINTHES (flatworms)
   b. Body not flat 6
6. a. Body elongated, cylindrical, pointed .... NEMATODA (roundworms)
   b. Body has flattened or branched muscular foot, a mantle; many possess a shell .... MOLLUSCA
7. a. No skeleton; appendages, if present, are nonjointed; body soft, segments quite similar .... ANNELIDA (segmented worms)
   b. Skeleton present, usually possess paired, jointed appendages 8
8. a. Skeleton internal, usually possess two pairs of jointed appendages, dorsal nerve cord .... CHORDATA 12
   b. Skeleton external, possess three or more pairs of appendages, ventral nerve cord .... ARTHROPODA 9
9. a. Segments similar, more than 10 pairs of legs .... class—MYRIAPODA
   b. Segments dissimilar 10
10. a. Without antennae, head and thorax united, usually 4 pairs of walking legs .... class—ARACHNIDA
    b. With antennae 11
11. a. One pair antennae, three pairs of walking legs, usually with wings, three part body .... class—INSECTA (HEXAPODA)
    b. Two pairs antennae, five to seven pairs of walking legs, wings absent .... class—CRUSTACEA
12. a. Without vertebral column, possess notochord .... subphylum—PROTOCHORDATA
    b. Vertebral column, brain case, has 2 pairs of appendages supported by internal skeleton .... subphylum—VERTEBRATA 13
13. a. Gills present at some time in life 14
    b. Never possess functional gills, lungs present 15
14. a. Possess gills during entire life, body covered with scales .... class—PISCES
    b. Posses gills during early life, lungs as adults, skin smooth, moist; legs present .... class—AMPHIBIA
15. a. Skin dry, scaly, does not have hair or feathers .... class—REPTILIA
    b. Skin covered with hair or feathers 16
16. a. Feathers present, lay eggs .... class—AVES
    b. Skin hairy, mammary glands present .... class—MAMMALIA

For more detailed, specific keys, consult a key in the library for that class.

Simplified Key to the Principal Orders of Insects

I. Phylum—Arthropoda .... Class—Insecta (Hexapoda)
   1. a. Wingless insects.. 2
       b. Winged insects.. 19
   2. a. Sedentary insects, incapable of locomotion; body scale-like, gall-like, or grub-like and covered with waxy secretion .... HOMOPTERA
       b. Not sedentary, with distinct head and jointed legs 3
   3. a. Mouthparts adapted for biting and chewing 4
       b. Mouthparts adapted for piercing or sucking 13
   4. a. Mouthparts apparently retracted with the head so that their apices are only visible; or they are exposed and body covered with scales 5
       b. Mouthparts fully exposed and body not clothed with scales 6
   5. a. Abdomen composed of not more than 6 segments; usually provided with a spring near the caudal end; first abdominal segment with a forked appendage on ventral surface .... COLLEMBOLA
       b. Abdomen composed of 10 or 11 segments; the abdomen may terminate in long caudal appendage or body may be covered with scales .... THYSANURA
   6. a. Abdomen terminated by a pair of movable forcep-like appendages................. DERMAPTERA
       b. Abdomen not as described above 7
   7. a. Head prolonged into a trunk-like beak, the mouthparts located at the tip of the trunk .... MECOPTERA
       b. Head not prolonged into a trunk-like beak 8
   8. a. Small, louse-like insects, usually flattened, soft or leathery 9
       b. Not louse-like in form; not flattened; exoskeleton well differentiated 10
   9. a. Antennae of not more than 5 segments; parasites of birds and mammals........... MALLOPHAGA
       b. Antennae of more than 5 segments; never parasitic.............. CORRODENTIA
  10. a. Abdomen sharply constricted at base........................... HYMENOPTERA
       b. Abdomen not sharply constricted at base, broadly joined to thorax 11
  11. a. Tarsi 3 jointed; first joint of front tarsi greatly enlarged ....EMBIIDINA
       b. Tarsi 2 jointed; first joint of front tarsi not enlarged ....ZORAPTERA
       c. Tarsi 3 to 5 jointed; first joint of front tarsi not enlarged 12
  12. a. Social insects living in colonies, usually pale in color and blind .... ISOPTERA
       b. Not social insects living in colonies, not pale in color, legs fitted for leaping or jumping..ORTHOPTERA
  13. a. Mouthparts consisting of a proboscis coiled up beneath the head; body more or less covered with long hairs or scales .... LEPIDOPTERA
       b. Mouthparts not as described above; body not covered with hairs or scales 14
  14. a. Body strongly compressed; legs nearly always long and fitted for running and jumping... SIPHONAPTERA
       b. Body not strongly compressed; legs fitted for running but not for jumping 15
  15. a. Mouthparts consisting of jointed beak within which are the piercing stylets..... 16
       b. Mouthparts consisting of an unjointed fleshy or horny beak or beak may be absent 17
  16. a. Beak apparently arising from the anterior end of head................ HEMIPTERA
       b. Beak apparently arising from the posterior end of the head between the coxae of the front legs... HOMOPTERA

17. a. Tarsi with apical joint terminating in a bladder-like enlargement; well-defined claws absent; mouthparts forming a triangular or cone shape, unjointed beak .... THYSANOPTERA
     b. Tarsi not as described above; with well-defined claws 18
18. a. Antennae located in pits not visible from the dorsal surface; tarsi with 2 claws .... DIPTERA
     b. Antennae exposed, not in pits, clearly visible from the dorsal surface; tarsi with a single claw .... ANOPLURA
19. a. With only two wings 20
     b. With four wings 22
20. a. Abdomen with long caudal filaments; mouthparts are vestigial 21
     b. Abdomen lacking caudal filaments; mouthparts are generally well developed for piercing, lapping, or sucking .... DIPTERA
21. a. Halteres absent; wings with many veins and cross-veins .... EPHEMERIDA
     b. Halteres present; wings with only a single forked vein .... HOMOPTERA
22. a. Fore and hind wings not alike in texture; fore wings thick, leathery, horny, and the hind wings membranous 40
     b. Fore and hind wings similar in texture, usually membranous 23
23. a. Wings entirely or for the most part covered with scales; mouthparts consist of a coiled tube beneath head and formed for sucking .... LEPIDOPTERA
     b. Wings not clothed in scales, transparent or clothed with hairs; mouthparts not as described above 24
24. a. Wings long and narrow with only one or two veins or none; last joint of tarsus bladder-like .... THYSANOPTERA
     b. Wings not as described above; last joint of tarsus not bladder-like 25
25. a. Mouthparts enclosed in a jointed beak and fitted for piercing and sucking; beak arises from the rear of head, almost between the front coxae ...... HOMOPTERA
     b. Mouthparts not forming a jointed beak; not located on the rear of the head 26
26. a. Wings with many longitudinal veins and cross-veins, appearing net veined (12 or more cross-veins) 27
     b. Wings with fewer longitudinal veins, not yet veined or they may be veinless (less than 12 cross-veins) 34
27. a. Tarsi with less than 5 segments 28
     b. Tarsi with 5 segments 32
28. a. Antennae short, setiform 29
     b. Antennae not short, not setiform 30
29. a. Front and hind wing of about equal size or the hind wings larger; front wings with a nodus; tarsi 3-jointed .... ODONATA
     b. Front wings much larger than the hind wings; nodus absent; tarsi 4-jointed .... EPHEMERIDA
30. a. Tarsi 4-jointed; wings of equal size .... ISOPTERA
     b. Tarsi 2- or 3-jointed; wings usually not of the same size 31
31. a. Hind wings smaller than the front wings; venation specific .... CORRODENTIA
     b. Hind wings as large or larger than front wings; venation not as above ....
         .... PLECOPTERA
32. a. Abdomen with long filiform, many joining caudal filaments .... EPHEMERIDA
     b. Abdomen without long filiform, many jointed caudal filament 33

33. a. Head prolonged, trunk-like with mandibulate mouthparts at the tip .... MECOPTERA
    b. Head not prolonged, trunk-like; mouthparts normal .... NEUROPTERA
34. a. First joint of front tarsi greatly swollen or enlarged .... EMBIIDINA
    b. First joint of front tarsi not enlarged 35
35. a. Tarsi 2- or 3-jointed 36
    b. Tarsi 4- or 5-jointed 38
36. a. Hind wings equal to or larger than the front wings .... PLECOPTERA
    b. Hind wings smaller than the fore wings 37
37. a. Minute insects, less than 3 mm in length; short cerci present; rare ... ZORAPTERA
    b. Larger insects; cerci absent; not rare ....CORRODENTIA
38. a. Abdomen with long, many-jointed filiform, caudal filaments ....
       .... EPHEMERIDA
    b. Abdomen with long, many-jointed caudal filaments 39
39. a. Front wings larger than hind wings; without hairs; clear and membranous; hind wings with but few veins ....HYMENOPTERA
    b. Front wings not larger than hind wings; front wings usually with long hairs and not transparent; hind wings with normal venation, not much reduced ....
       .... TRICHOPTERA
40. a. Fore wings reduced to slender club-shaped appendages; small insects ....
       .... STREPSIPTERA
    b. Front wings thickened at base, membranous at tip, generally overlapping; mouthparts enclosed in a jointed beak, fitted for piercing and sucking ..... HEMIPTERA
    c. Front wings of same texture throughout....................................41
41. a. Front wings horny or leathery, veinless covers for hind wings.................42
    b. Front wings parchment-like with a network of veins 43
42. a. Front wings short, never covering abdomen; abdomen terminates in pair of forcep-like, movable appendages .... DERMAPTERA
    b. Front wings usually cover abdomen, abdomen never terminates in a pair of movable forcep appendages ....COLEOPTERA
43. a. Hind wings folded fan-like beneath front wings; mouthparts formed for biting and chewing .... ORTHOPTERA
    b. Hind wings not folded; mouthparts enclosed in a jointed beak, formed for piercing and sucking 44
44. a. Beak-like mouthparts arise from front part of head .... HEMIPTERA
    b. Beak-like mouthparts arise from rear of head from almost between the front coxae ....HOMOPTERA

A GENERALIZED ECOSYSTEM MODEL

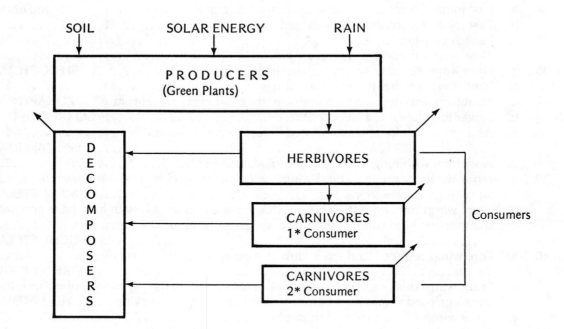

Problems

1. If in the above ecosystem model, the herbivores were more abundant and thus represented as a larger box than the producers, what do you think might happen to the system?

2. If the decomposers were eight times larger in proportion to all other levels in the model, what would you assume was happening to the system?

3. Draw a model, using the above, to represent a salt marsh ecosystem. Be sure the model is in proportion to each level.

ENERGY FLOW DIAGRAM

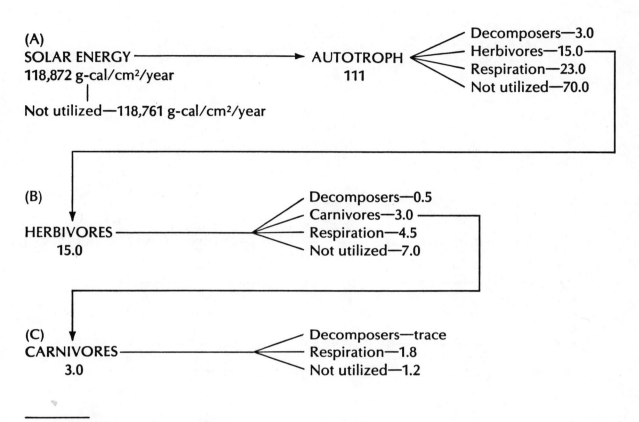

Note: Each number in the diagram is expressed in units of g-cal/cm²/year.

Problems

1. What is meant by *respiration* and *not utilized* in the above diagram?

2. Compare the percentages of energy for respiration among the producer, herbivore, and carnivore. Which accounts for the most use? Why?

3. From the diagram, which is considered more energy efficient: Corn? Grasshopper? Robin? Human? Why?

ENERGY FLOW IN A GENERALIZED ECOSYSTEM

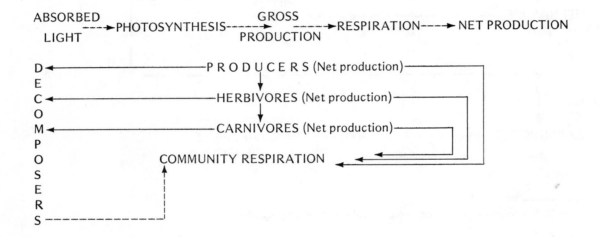

A BIOTIC PYRAMID

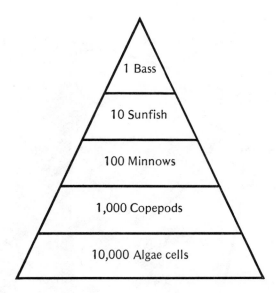

1 Bass

10 Sunfish

100 Minnows

1,000 Copepods

10,000 Algae cells

Questions

1. How does the pyramid shape fit in to the flow of energy within an ecosystem?

2. Why does the number of individuals at each trophic level decrease as you move from the base to the top of the pyramid?

3. Which level is considered the producer level?

4. Why can only one bass survive within this system?

5. Draw a biotic pyramid for your school yard, identifying the main or dominant organism at each trophic level.

BIOGEOCHEMICAL CYCLES

Carbon Cycle

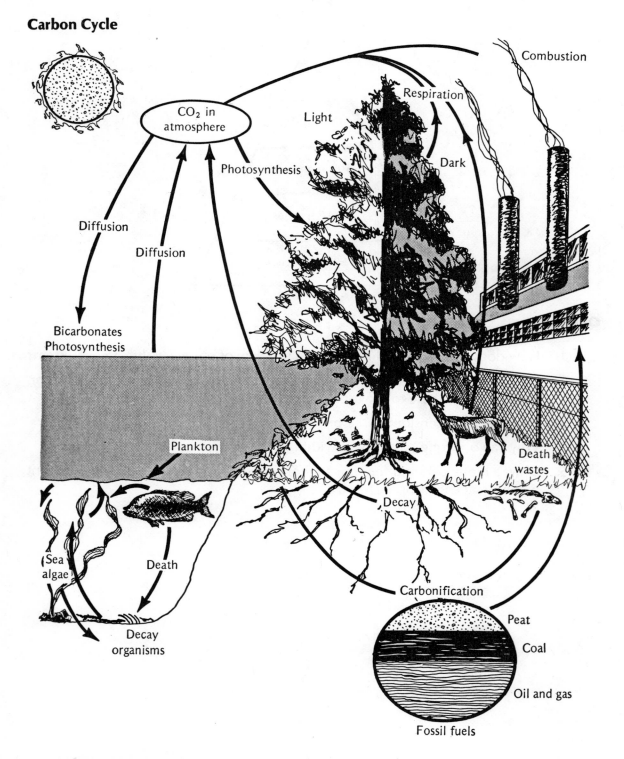

Phosphorus Cycle

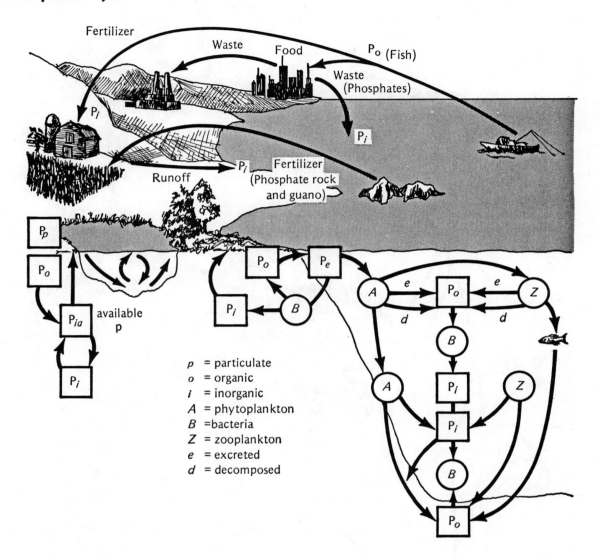

p = particulate
o = organic
i = inorganic
A = phytoplankton
B = bacteria
Z = zooplankton
e = excreted
d = decomposed

Nitrogen Cycle

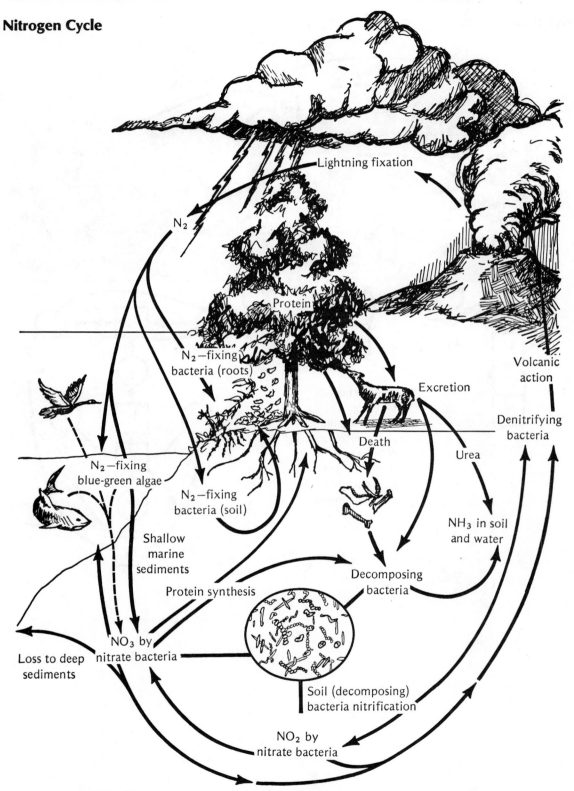

Lightning fixation

N_2

Protein

Volcanic action

N_2–fixing bacteria (roots)

Excretion

N_2–fixing blue-green algae

Denitrifying bacteria

Death

N_2–fixing bacteria (soil)

Urea

NH_3 in soil and water

Shallow marine sediments

Protein synthesis

Decomposing bacteria

NO_3 by nitrate bacteria

Loss to deep sediments

Soil (decomposing) bacteria nitrification

NO_2 by nitrate bacteria

Hydrologic Cycle

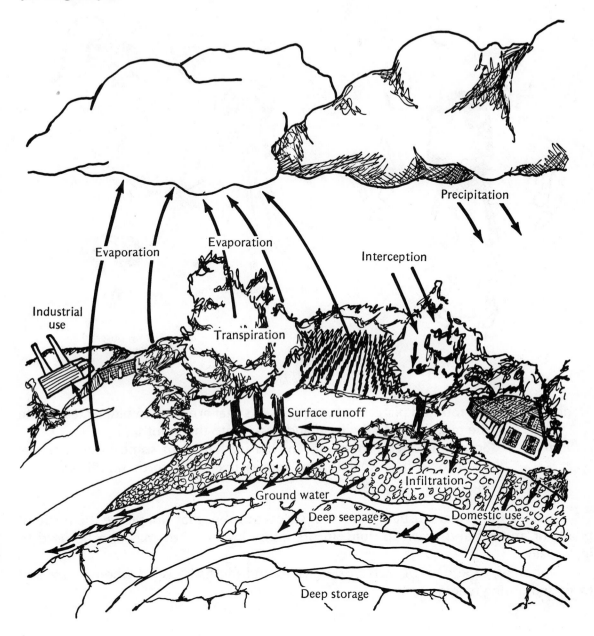

Precipitation

Evaporation

Evaporation

Interception

Industrial use

Transpiration

Surface runoff

Infiltration

Ground water

Deep seepage

Domestic use

Deep storage

INSECT MOUTHPARTS

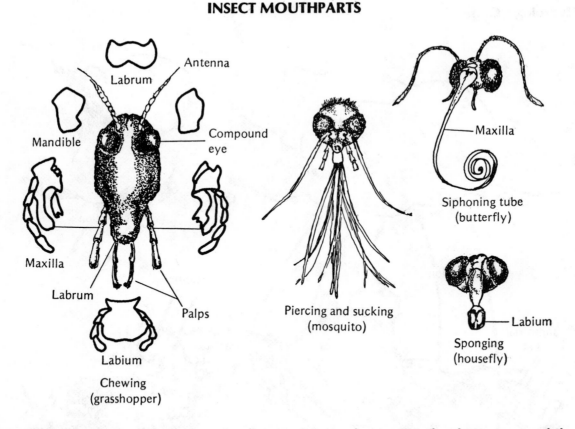

Chewing
(grasshopper)

Piercing and sucking
(mosquito)

Siphoning tube
(butterfly)

Sponging
(housefly)

Mandibles	are toothed plates in chewing insects that are used to bite or tear while the maxillae hold the food and pass it into the mouth.
Labium	acts as a tongue to sponge or lap up liquid. In some insects, as the honeybee, it is flexible and moves back and forth rapidly to draw up liquid.

Sucking mouthparts usually consist of stylets or tubes that can pierce the tissue of plants or animals and draw up fluid. In predatory insects, they may also be used to inject saliva.

Siphoning tube or proboscis of butterflies and moths is coiled when at rest and extended during feeding.

HERBIVORES VERSUS CARNIVORES

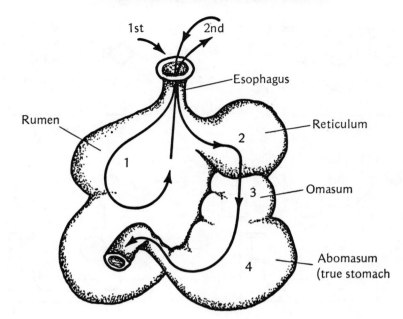

Four chambered stomach of a ruminant. The first time a cow swallows grass, the grass goes to the rumen, where bacteria begin to digest the cellulose. The grass is then returned to the cow's mouth in the form of cud where it is chewed thoroughly. On the second swallowing, the grass passes through the rumen, reticulum, and omasum to the abomasum for complete digestion.

Herbivore	Carnivore
1. *Teeth:* Strong, broad molars for grinding; suppressed canines. Rodents have sharp incisors for cutting.	1. *Teeth:* Well-developed, sharp canines for piercing and tearing; less-developed and fewer molars.
2. *Limbs:* Adapted for speed (such as hooves) to escape predators.	2. *Limbs:* Powerful and clawed for killing.
3. *Digestive tract:* Large and long; usually contains cecum (fermentation chamber where microflora digest cellulose).	3. *Digestive tract:* Shorter with very small cecum or none at all.
4. *Feeding habit:* Eats continuously.	4. *Feeding habit:* Eats separate meals.

ENZYME ACTION

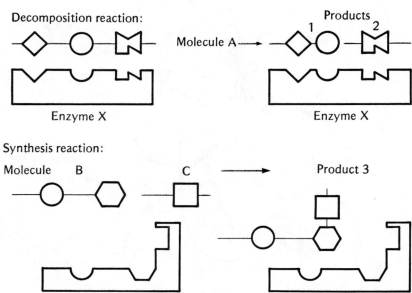

Decomposition reaction:

Molecule A →

Products
1   2

Enzyme X   Enzyme X

Synthesis reaction:

Molecule   B   C   →   Product 3

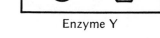

Enzyme Y   Enzyme Y

pH of Various Body Fluids (Human)

Fluid	pH Range
Gastric juice	1.2–3.0
Urine	5.0–7.8
Saliva	6.35–6.85
Blood	7.35–7.45
Semen	7.35–7.50
Cerebrospinal fluid	7.4
Pancreatic juice	7.1–8.2
Bile	7.6–8.6

Optimal Range for Enzyme Activity

Enzyme	pH Range
Pepsin	1.5–2.5
Castor bean lipase	5
Malt amylase	5.2
Salivary amylase	6.7–6.8
Pancreatic lipase	7
Most cellular enzymes	7–7.6
Trypsin	8–11

pH Values of Some Common Liquids

Liquid	pH Range
Lemon juice	2.2–2.4
Grapefruit juice	3.0
Cider	2.8–3.3
Pineapple juice	3.5
Tomato juice	4.2
Clam chowder	5.7
Milk	6.6–6.9
Pure (distilled) water	7.0
Eggs	7.6–8.0
Milk of magnesia	10.0–11.0
Limewater	12.3

CHEMICAL DIGESTION IN THE ARTIFICIAL STOMACH

Write your observations in the chart below describing the condition of each of the foods listed at each of the times, for example, beef jerky after 30 minutes is "discolored and partly broken down." Then fill in the reaction column, as indicated. In the conclusions, state which foods are digested in the stomach and what factors influence digestion.

FOOD SAMPLES

Reaction:
(a) partially digested
(b) fully digested
(c) undigested

		Hard-Boiled Egg White	Beef Jerky	Hard Bread	Fresh Fruit	Raw Vegetable
Artificial Stomach	After 15 min.					
	After 30 min.					
	After 1 hr.					
	After 24 hr.					
Control I pepsin alone	After 15 min.					
	After 30 min.					
	After 1 hr.					
	After 24 hr.					
Control II Hcl alone	After 15 min.					
	After 30 min.					
	After 1 hr.					
	After 24 hr.					

Conclusions

TEST FOR ASCORBIC ACID

Problem 1

1. First let us get acquainted with a chemical called 2, 6 dichlorophenolindophenol, which is used to test for vitamin C. To simplify matters, let us call it *indophenol*. Pour about 10 drops of indophenol into a test tube and add to it a small amount of ascorbic acid. What happened?

2. Prepare four test tubes as follows:

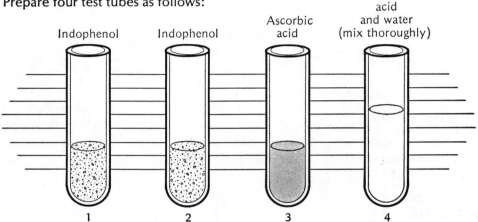

Indophenol   Indophenol   Ascorbic acid   Ascorbic acid and water (mix thoroughly)

1   2   3   4

Mix the contents of Tube 4 thoroughly.

To Test Tube 1, add, drop by drop, some of the contents of Test Tube 3. Shake Test Tube 1 after each drop and count the number of drops necessary to bleach the indophenol. How many drops did you have to use?

In a similar manner, test the diluted ascorbic acid (Test Tube 4) against the indophenol in Test Tube 2. How many drops did you have to use?

3. Summarize your results by completing the following statement below: The greater the concentration of ascorbic acid, the _____ the number of drops needed to bleach the indophenol.

Problem 2

There are two juices on your table. Which one contains more ascorbic acid?

1. What did you do to find out?

2. What results did you obtain?

3. What is your answer to the problem?

Problem 3

Some people add bicarbonate of soda when they cook vegetables. Use one of the juices to determine whether bicarbonate of soda has an effect on the ascorbic acid content.

1. What did you do to find out?

2. What results did you obtain?

3. What is your conclusion about the effect of bicarbonate of soda in cooking vegetables?

A DEMONSTRATION SHOWING CARBON DIOXIDE IN THE AIR AND IN THE BODY

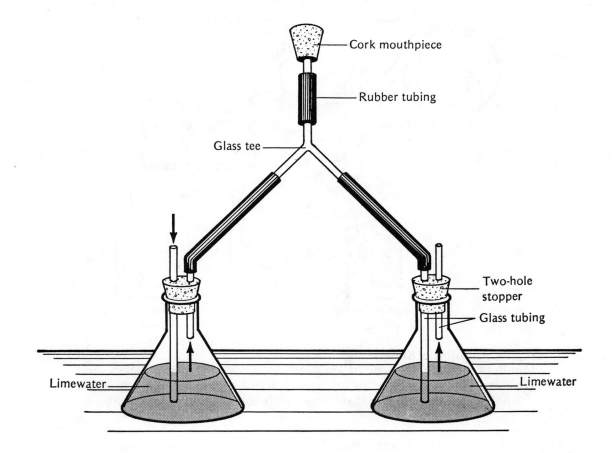

Variation in Respired Air

	Inspired Air (Vol. %)	Expired Air (Vol. %)	Alveolar Air (Vol. %)
Oxygen	20.96	16.0	14.0
Carbon dioxide	0.04	4.0	5.5
Nitrogen	79.00	80.0	80.5

ARTIFICIAL KIDNEY

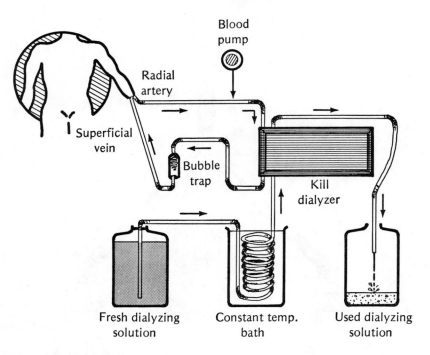

Fig. 20   Artificial Kidney
Monitors indicate changes in pressure, temperature, concentration, and possible leaks. An air detector not only indicates if air enters the system but also has an automatic device that clamps the blood line returning to the body.

The chief function of the kidney is to help maintain homeostatic conditions in the blood. This is accomplished by the removal of waste materials and excessive amounts of substances such as water and salts.

The artificial kidney accomplishes this goal in the following manner: Blood flows through semipermeable membranes, which have very small holes that allow waste materials, electrolytes, and fluids to diffuse through but are too small to allow red and white blood cells and proteins to cross the membrane. Substances always diffuse from a higher to a lower concentration. Therefore, the diffusion of substances is controlled by establishing precise concentrations of substances in the dialyzing solution and by adjusting these concentrations to suit specific needs.

A. COUNTING THE NUMBER OF STOMATES ON PLANT LEAVES

Using an optical compound microscope on low power, observe and count the number of stomates found on both the lower and upper surfaces of the plants listed below. Be sure to count only the number per premeasured square millimeter.

Plant Type	Number of Stomates per Square Millimeter		Predicted Type of Environment
	Upper Surface	Lower Surface	
Norway maple tree			
Red begonia plant			
Rubber plant			
Lily			
Lilac			
Tomato			
Bean			
Pumpkin			
Sunflower			
Pine			
Corn			
Cabbage			

Example of results: Norway maple tree: 440 stomates per square millimeter on lower surface only.

B. COUNTING THE NUMBER OF STOMATES ON PLANT LEAVES

Compare your findings with the data below. See how close your observations are to the approximate numbers listed.

Red begonia plant:	40 stomates per square millimeter on lower surface only.
Rubber plant:	145 stomates per square millimeter on lower surface only.
Lily:	62 stomates per square millimeter on lower surface only.
Lilac:	330 stomates per square millimeter on lower surface only.

	Upper Surface	*Lower Surface*
Tomato	12	130
Bean	40	281
Pumpkin	28	269
Sunflower	175	325
Pine	50	71
Corn	94	158
Cabbage	219	301

PATHWAY OF THE BLOOD*

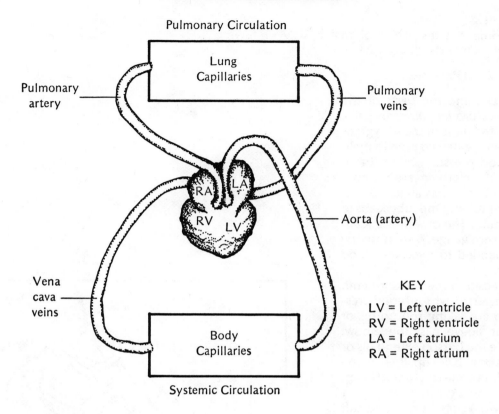

Pulmonary Circulation

Lung Capillaries

Pulmonary artery

Pulmonary veins

Aorta (artery)

Vena cava veins

KEY

LV = Left ventricle
RV = Right ventricle
LA = Left atrium
RA = Right atrium

Body Capillaries

Systemic Circulation

1. Place red-colored arrows in all structures on the diagram to represent the direction of flow of oxygenated blood and blue-colored arrows for deoxygenated blood.

2. Trace a drop of blood from the right atrium to the aorta.

3. Trace a drop of blood from the lungs to the vena cava veins.

4. Describe the route of a drop of blood from the right arm to the left leg by listing all the structures, in order, that the blood must flow through.

---

*A simplified diagram indicating main circulatory routes. Not all blood vessels shown.

BLOOD PRESSURE

MATERIALS
Sphygmomanometer (SFIG moh mah NAHM uh tur)
Stethoscope (STETH uh skohp)

What Is Blood Pressure

1. *Examine the parts of the blood pressure kit.* Work in pairs. Examine the parts of the sphygmomanometer, a device used to measure blood pressure. Note that it consists of a cloth-covered rubber cuff with two things attached to it by rubber tubes. One tube leads to a hand bulb. The other tube leads to a pressure gauge. A stethoscope is also needed to measure blood pressure.

2. *Position the pressure cuff.* Have the person whose blood pressure you are taking roll up his or her right sleeve past the elbow. Also have the person extend his or her right arm, palm up. Be sure the arm is at the same level as the heart, whether the person is sitting or lying down. Wrap the deflated cuff evenly and snugly around the upper arm, so that the lower edge of the cuff is about an inch above the elbow. Start wrapping the cuff by locating the large artery near the hollow of the elbow (as indicated by the dot in the diagram). This artery can be found by feeling for the pulse of the artery. Point the arrow in the cuff that says "right arm" to the artery. Wrap the cuff until the self-sticking tape holds the cuff securely.

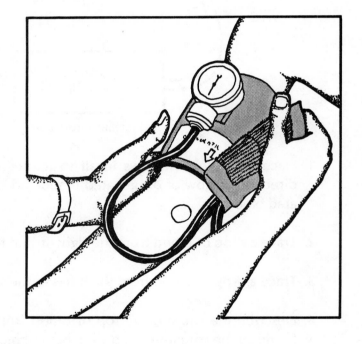

3. *Inflate the cuff.* Feel the pulse of the artery with your fingertips. Turn the valve on the bulb clockwise until it is closed. Squeeze the bulb and inflate the cuff until you can no longer feel the pulse. Keep your fingertips on the artery and deflate the cuff by turning the valve on the bulb counterclockwise. Watch the gauge as you do this. Note the point at which you once again feel the pulse in the artery. Allow the cuff to deflate completely. Wait 30 seconds. Repeat this procedure. Close the valve and inflate the cuff until you reach the point on the gauge that you noted before. Continue to inflate the cuff an additional 30 millimeters (30 mm). *Caution: Do not inflate the cuff beyond 30 mm above the pressure at which you felt the first pulse beat. Do not allow the cuff to stay inflated for more than 30 seconds.*

4. *Slowly deflate the cuff.* Place the flat side of the stethoscope evenly and firmly over the artery. Slowly open the valve on the bulb by turning it counterclockwise. Practice doing this until you can get the pressure to drop 2 mm to 4 mm (one to two marks on gauge) with each heartbeat. This usually means a drop of one to two marks on the gauge every second. This rate of deflation is important for an accurate reading. Remember, the pressure of the cuff has shut off all blood flow to the arm. *Do not leave it fully inflated any longer than absolutely necessary.*

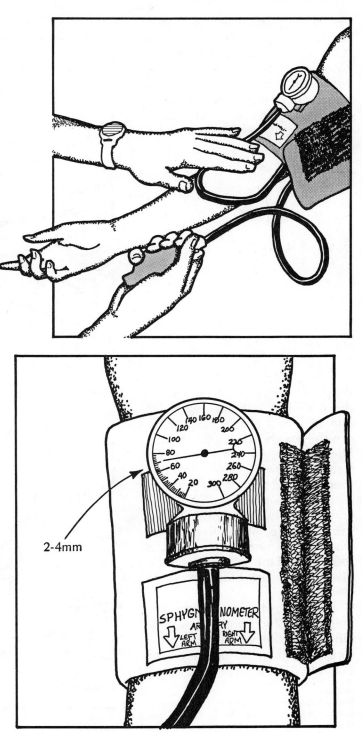

5. *Systolic pressure.* Listen carefully as you open the valve (turn counterclockwise) and let blood return to the arm. As soon as you clearly hear faint rhythmic tapping or thumping sounds, note the reading on the gauge. This is the systolic (upper) blood pressure reading.

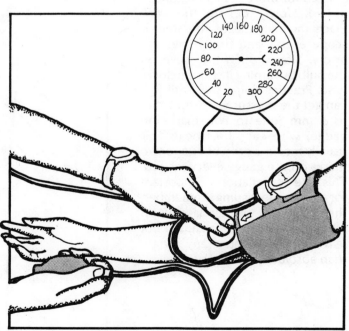

6. *Diastolic pressure.* Allow the pressure to continue to drop at the same rate as before—about 2 mm to 4 mm per second. Listen carefully with your stethoscope. The sounds you hear with the stethoscope will change. The first sharp tapping sounds will soften to blowing or swishing sounds. Listen very carefully. Watch the falling gauge needle. At the exact point when you can *no longer hear the sounds,* read the gauge. This is the diastolic (lower) blood pressure reading.

7. Record your readings immediately. Blood pressure is written as a fraction with systolic pressure over diastolic pressure—for example, 115/70.

Reproduced with permission of the National Science Products, Inc. BSCS, *Feeling Fit,* Human Science Program.

A SIMPLIFIED VERSION OF FEEDBACK EXAMPLES

Below are several examples of hormonal feedback that are crucial to the life cycles of the organisms. Review each and see if you can complete C and D.

A. *Sexual cycle in female dog*
Stimulus (male dog) ⟶ senses ⟶ sense organs ⟶
thalamus ⟶ hypothalamus ⟶ pituitary gland ⟶
GTH (gonadotropin hormone) ⟶ ovary ⟶ estrogen + progesterone ⟶
Response: estrus

B. *Egg incubation of birds*
Stimulus (eggs in a nest) ⟶ senses ⟶ thalamus ⟶
hypothalamus ⟶ pituitary gland ⟶ LTH (luteotropic hormone)
+ LH (luteinizing hormone) ⟶
loss of feathers (a patch formed) ⟶ sensitive to eggs ⟶
CNS (central nervous system) ⟶ *Response:* incubate

C. *Feeding response in pigeons*
S (stimulus) (young) ⟶ sense ⟶ thalamus ⟶
____?____ ⟶ ____?____ ⟶ LTH ⟶ enlarge crop ⟶
CNS ⟶ R (response): feed young

D. *Male sexuality in humans*
S (female) ⟶ _____?_____ ⟶ _____?_____ ⟶ thalamus
_____?_____ ⟶ _____?_____ ⟶ GTH ⟶
_____?_____ ⟶ testosterone ⟶ *Response:* _____?_____

THE POCKET GARDEN

By constructing a pocket garden and exposing it to changing stimuli, you can observe various tropisms found in radish seedlings.

Tropisms

A plant may react to stimuli. These reactions are usually very slow. Such slow reactions are called *tropisms.* A tropism can also be described according to the direction of the stimulus. If the organism grows toward the stimulus it is a positive tropism. If the growth is away from the stimulus, it is a negative tropism. *Geotropism* is a response to gravity; *hydrotropism,* to water; *phototropism,* to light, and so forth.

Procedure

Set up two pocket gardens—one for experimentation and one to be used as a control—in the following manner.

A. Prepare your garden by soaking a blotter or paper towel and placing it in a petri dish.

B. Scatter soaked radish seeds evenly onto the moist blotter and cover it with the inverted top of the petri dish.

C. Secure the petri dish with adhesive tape. Mark one point on the top of the petri dish with a red *x* or with a piece of tape. Note the location of the marker each time you change the position of your garden. Stand the petri dish on its edge.

D. Observe both gardens as the seedlings grow. Note the position of the roots and stems. Make a drawing showing the position of the roots and stems in both gardens.

Drawings of Plant Responses

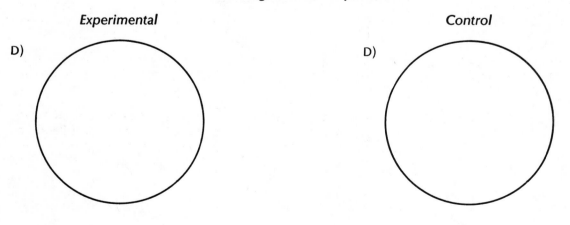

Experimental   Control

D)   D)

E. Now invert one petri dish (the experimental garden) so that the roots are pointing upward and the stems down. Observe the direction of growth of the roots and stems each day for the next three to five days. Compare the experimental garden with the control. Again, draw a diagram showing the positions of roots and stems in both gardens. (See page 202.)

   1. In which direction are the stems growing?

   2. Does gravity affect the growth of the roots; how?

   3. Is there unequal growth in the sides of the stems and roots as they respond to gravity?

   4. Do the stems show a positive or negative geotropism?

   5. Which tropism do the roots demonstrate?

F. After stems develop, lay your garden (experimental) flat on a table and cover half of it with a dark piece of construction paper. Place the dish in a location where the uncovered half is exposed to light. After a day, note the direction of stems and roots in relation to the light. Complete the table at the end of this reproduction page.

G. You may want to expand your investigation by placing your garden in a dark place and comparing the growth of plants in the experimental garden with those of the control garden.

If you want to test the radish seedlings' reaction to water, open the petri dish, remove the blotter, and place a piece of wet blotter on one side. Lay the petri dish flat on a table and during the next few days note the growth of the roots toward the water. What tropism does this show?

Drawings of Plant Responses

Experimental   *Control*

E) 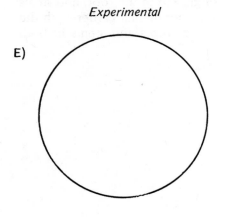   E)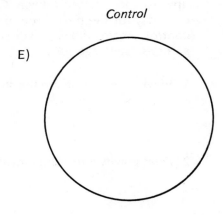

TABLE

Date	Time	Part of Plant	Stimulus	Response	Tropism
		Root	gravity		
		Stem	gravity		
		Root	light		
		Stem	light		

TROPISMS AND TAXES

Complete the chart below by filling in the spaces.

Organism	Stimuli	Response	Positive/Negative Tropism/Taxis
1. Bean plant root	_____	moves downward	+ geotropism
2. Snail	_____	moves away	− chemotaxis
3. Cockroach	walls	_____	+ thigmotaxis
4. Geranium plant leaves	light	_____	+ phototropism
5. Euglena	light	_____	_____
6. Grape leaves	light	_____	_____
7. Earthworm	vinegar	moves away	_____
*8. _____	_____	_____	_____
*9. _____	_____	_____	_____
*10. _____	_____	_____	_____

———————

*Try to fill in these blanks with animal and plant stimuli and/or responses you have observed. Then see if your classmates can fill in the tropism/taxis.

DIAGRAMS OF THE HUMAN BRAIN

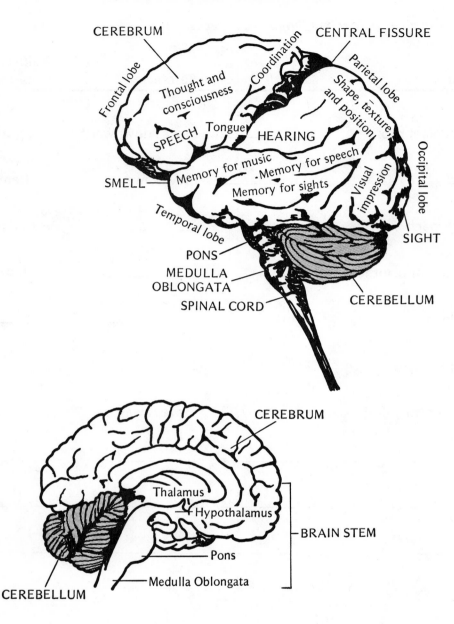

DIAGRAMS SHOWING THE HUMAN SENSE ORGANS

A. The Eye

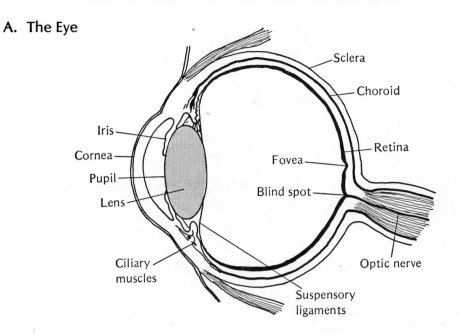

B. The Ear

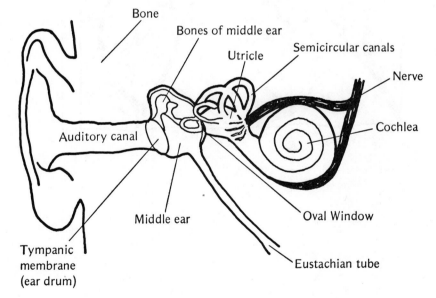

C. The Skin

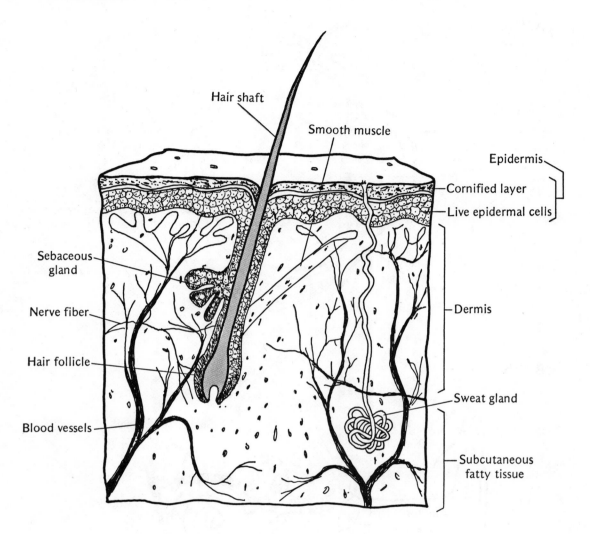

D. The Tongue, with taste receptors and taste buds

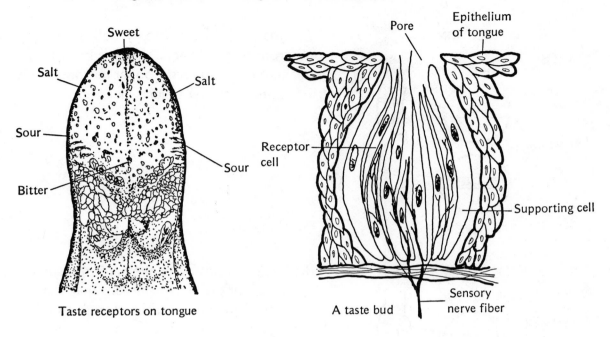

Taste receptors on tongue

A taste bud

E. The Nose, showing olfactory sense and receptor cells

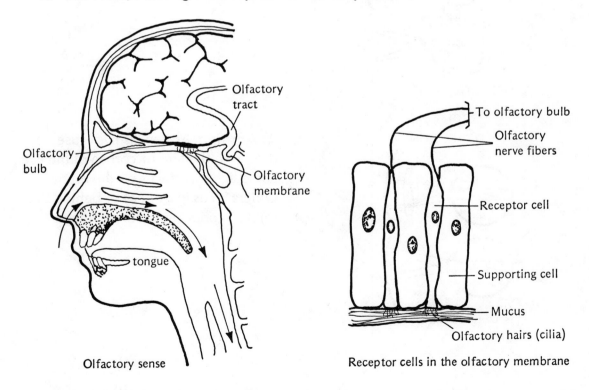

Olfactory sense

Receptor cells in the olfactory membrane

Copyright © 1985 by Allyn and Bacon, Inc. Reproduction of this material is restricted to use with *A Guidebook for Teaching Biology,* by Harold J. McKenna and Marge Hand.

DEFECTS OF THE EYE

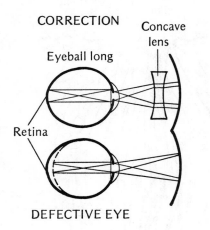

CORRECTION

Concave lens

Eyeball long

Retina

DEFECTIVE EYE

A. *Nearsightedness.* The eyeball is too long from front to back. The lens brings light rays into focus too far in front of the retina to see far objects clearly.

Convex lens

CORRECTION

Eyeball short

DEFECTIVE EYE

B. *Farsightedness.* The eyeball is too short from front to back. The lens may not bend light rays sharply enough to fall on the retina and focus near objects clearly.

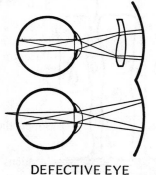

CORRECTION

DEFECTIVE EYE

C. *Astigmatism.* Astigmatism is caused by defects in the lens or cornea of the eye. Some light rays focus on the retina. Others focus in front of or behind the retina, producing a blurred image.

OPTICAL ILLUSIONS

1. Which is larger, line A or line B?

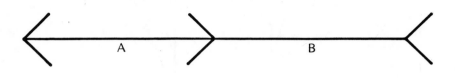

2. Are the diagonal lines parallel?

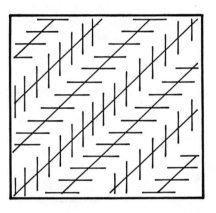

3. Which circle, A or B, is larger?

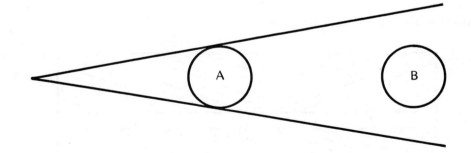

4. Is this figure a perfect square?

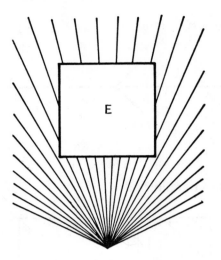

5. Which of the two lines, C or D, above the horizontal ones is a continuation of the line AB?

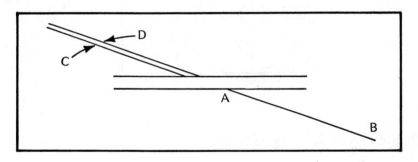

6. Are the horizontal lines parallel?

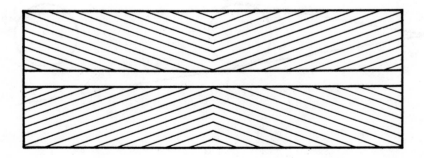

7. Which lamppost, A or B, is larger?

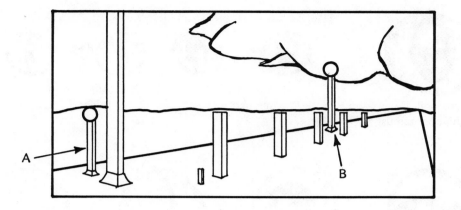

8. Do you see odd-shaped black spots, or do you see some letters of the alphabet?

PUPIL SHAPES OF ANIMAL EYES

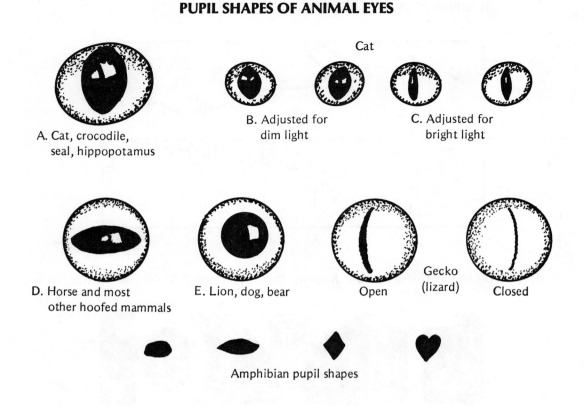

A. Cat, crocodile,
   seal, hippopotamus

Cat

B. Adjusted for
   dim light

C. Adjusted for
   bright light

D. Horse and most
   other hoofed mammals

E. Lion, dog, bear

Open

Gecko
(lizard)

Closed

Amphibian pupil shapes

In the table below, list an animal with the pupil shape from the diagrams above, and give an example of a type of behavior to which this visual adaptation is suited.

Animal	Pupil Shape	Behavior
Cat	Vertical slit	Jumps up and down

EYE POSITIONS

A. Hawk

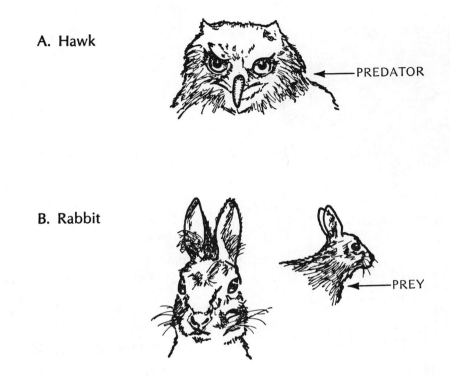

— PREDATOR

B. Rabbit

— PREY

Eye positions of vertebrates: As a rule, the eyes of predators are set in the front of the head, and the eyes of their prey are on the sides of the head. Generally, the closer the eyes are in the front of the head, the smaller the angle of vision. For example, humans see through about a 150° angular vision, a cat 200°, and a horse 215°. The horse has almost complete periscopy, enabling it to view almost all around without moving its head.

SIMPLE AND COMPOUND EYES

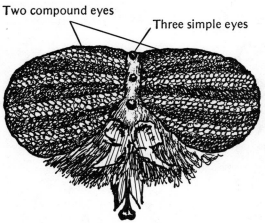

Two compound eyes

Three simple eyes

Compound eye, for distant vision
Simple eye, for seeing objects nearby

A. Eyes of a housefly

B. Mosaic pattern of facets

Approximate
NUMBER OF FACETS IN COMMON INSECTS

ants — 50
housefly — 4,000
dragonfly — 20,000
hawkmoth — 27,000

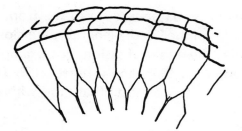

C. *Cross-section of compound eye.* Each facet is composed of a lens behind which there is a cone, a rod, nerve fibrils, and a basal membrane. This membrane perceives the image and transmits it to the brain. The cones and rods are surrounded by a pigment that prevents light rays from passing into the next facet.

PHEROMONES

The sense of smell plays an extremely important role in societies of insects since odorous chemicals, termed *pheromones*, have a great influence in controlling the growth, nutrition, sexual activity, and protection of these colonies.

Pheromones differ from hormones in that they are secreted externally and affect other animals, while hormones are secreted into the bloodstream and affect only the individual itself.

Types of Pheromones

1. *Primer-effect pheromones*, which seem to act on the endocrine system of the receiver, triggering a chain of physiological reactions that change its growth and behavior. (The pheromones regulating the caste system are this type.)

2. *Releaser-effect pheromones*, which produce a more or less immediate and reversible change in the behavior of the recipient. These seem to act on the central nervous system of the receiver. Most pheromones—as attractants, alarm signals, repellents—are of this type.

WAYS IN WHICH PHEROMONES HELP CONTROL INSECT SOCIETIES

1. *Assembling scent:* A simple attractant that signals the insects of a colony to gather. Sometimes it is very specific as in the female khapra beetle, which attracts only unmated males while immobilizing nearby females.

2. *Sex attractant:* Usually found in the females to attract males while acting as an aphrodisiac at close range. These pheromones are the most effective. Minute traces of the female sawfly sex attractant attracted 500 to 1,000 males over 200-foot distances.

3. *Regulator of caste systems in colonies:* The queen in insect colonies usually secretes a chemical that prevents larvae from developing into full-grown females or new queens. In tests on termites, if the queen—and therefore the pheromone—was removed, several larvae developed into new queens within ten days.

4. *Territorial markings:* Male bumblebees dab vegetation with scent spots to mark off their territory.

5. *Repellents:* Secretions that keep a uniform spacing between insects of a colony when there is a large population.

6. *Odor trails:* On finding a particle too large to carry, an individual fire ant returns nestward while laying down minute traces of secretion in broken streaks. This trail acts as an attractant. When the secretion is blown into the nest, it draws ants toward its source. Usually the pheromone will attract only the species of insect that secreted it.

7. *Alarm signal:* When secreted, ants react by excited zig-zag motion, aggressively running toward the stimulus. Most other insects react by fleeing. Some alarm signals are also defense repellents and even weapons of attack. The bombardier beetle when attacked by predators instantly aims the chemical spray at the seized limb of the enemy. This discharge will repel nearly all of its common predators.

DATA LOG ON FLOWERS IN YOUR COMMUNITY

Flower Parts

Date	Number of Petals	Color	Number of Stamens	Number of Pistils	Where Found	Name of Plant

Adaptations for survival: List below those adaptations you find on the plants you are observing. Examples are thorns on stems and leaves to keep away predators and colors to attract insects for pollination.

Plant	Adaptive Structures	Possible Function

STRUCTURE OF TYPICAL FLOWER

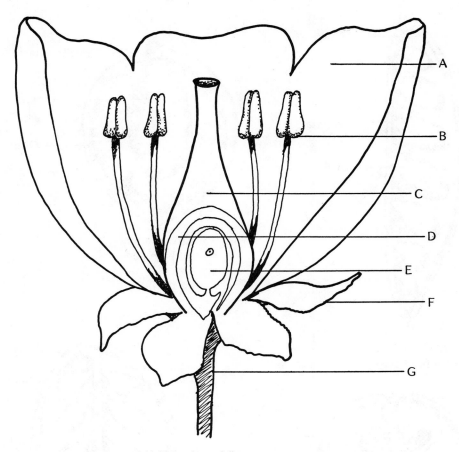

Half section of flower

1. Identify the flower parts A–G by placing the name of the structure next to the letter.

2. Explain the function of each flower part.

3. Explain various methods of pollination.

4. What is the difference between pollination and fertilization?

5. If this flower was found on an apple tree, which part would become the fruit we eat? Which part would become the seeds?

STRUCTURE OF THE OVARY

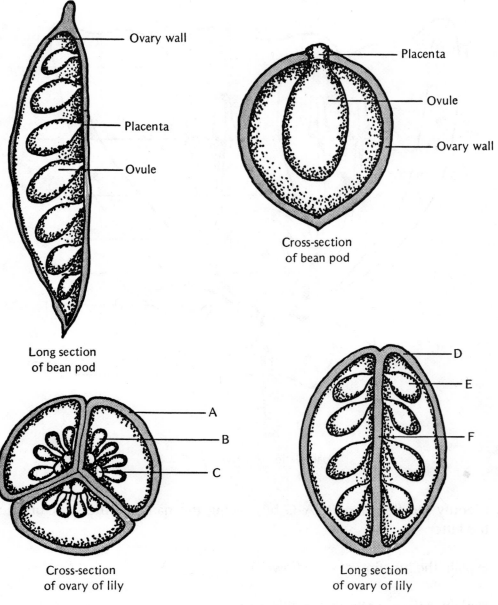

Ovary wall

Placenta

Ovule

Long section
of bean pod

Placenta

Ovule

Ovary wall

Cross-section
of bean pod

A

B

C

Cross-section
of ovary of lily

D

E

F

Long section
of ovary of lily

1. What is the difference between a fruit and an ovary? A seed and an ovule?

2. Using the diagram of the bean pod, complete the structure list of the lily by identifying the structures represented by the letters.

REPRODUCTIVE CYCLE OF FLOWERING PLANT: CRITICAL STAGES

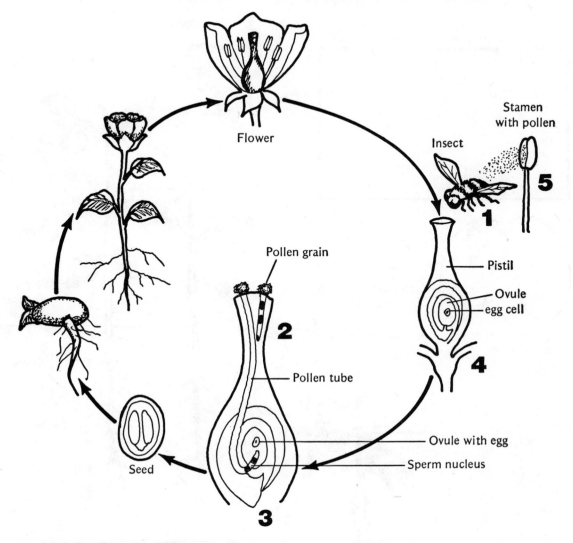

1. Explain what would happen if:

    a. Pollen does not land on the top of the pistil?

    b. A pollen tube did not grow down the neck of the pistil?

    c. The sperm nucleus did not enter the ovule?

    d. Insecticides were used on the flower, and no insects were found?

STRUCTURE AND GERMINATION OF SEEDS

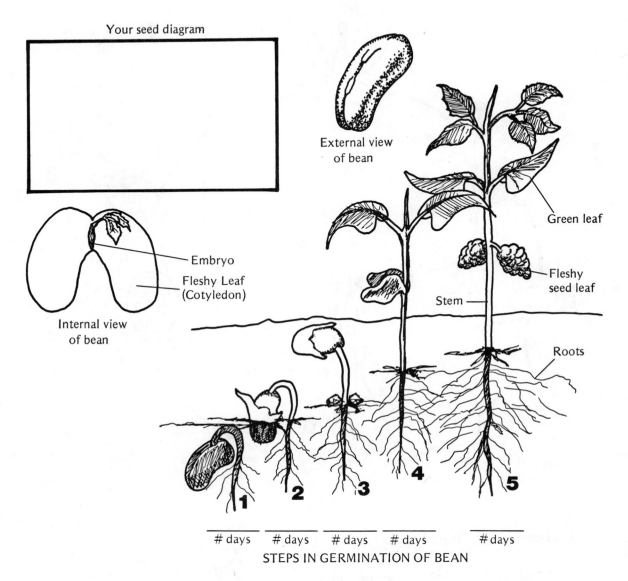

Your seed diagram

External view of bean

Embryo

Fleshy Leaf (Cotyledon)

Internal view of bean

Green leaf

Fleshy seed leaf

Stem

Roots

1   2   3   4   5

___ # days   ___ # days   ___ # days   ___ # days   ___ # days

STEPS IN GERMINATION OF BEAN

1. Dissect a soaked bean seed to uncover the embryo. Identify the embryonic leaves, stem, and root. Place your drawing of a seed that you dissected in the box at the upper left corner of the above diagram.

2. Each day dig up a planted bean seed from your container and record how many days were needed to match the diagrams numbered in "Steps in Germination of Bean."

REPRODUCTIVE ORGANS OF THE FROG

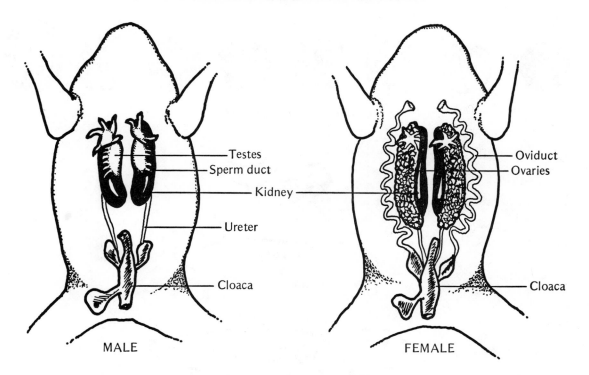

MALE   FEMALE

1. How can you identify the sex of a frog without dissecting it?

2. Uncover in your dissection all of the structures identified in the above diagram.

3. Where are sperm and egg cells produced? Stored?

4. Where do sperm and egg cells unite?

5. Where do embryo frogs develop?

6. From what structure do sperm and egg cells leave the frog? What other function does this structure have?

STAGES IN THE DEVELOPMENT OF THE FROG

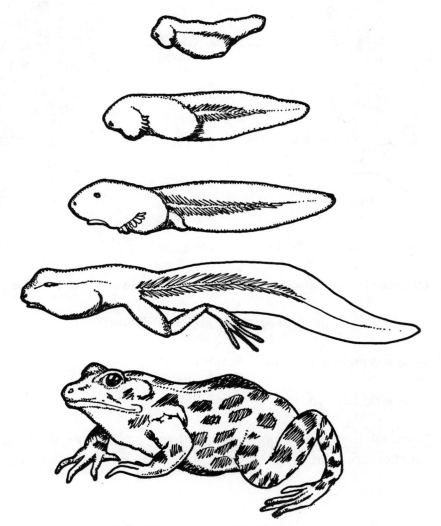

Fertilized egg becomes a tadpole

Tadpole becomes an adult frog

THE FROG'S REPRODUCTIVE CYCLE

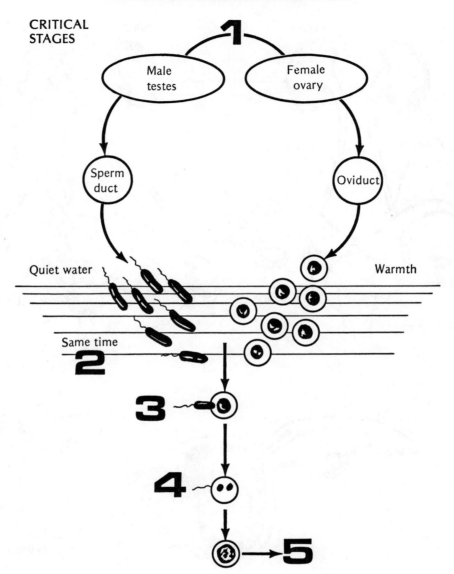

1. Which numbered stage illustrates fertilization?

2. What do you think Stage 5 represents?

3. What would happen if the water was not quiet or calm? Cold?

4. Why must frogs reproduce only in the water and not on the dry land?

THE REPRODUCTIVE ORGANS OF MAMMALS

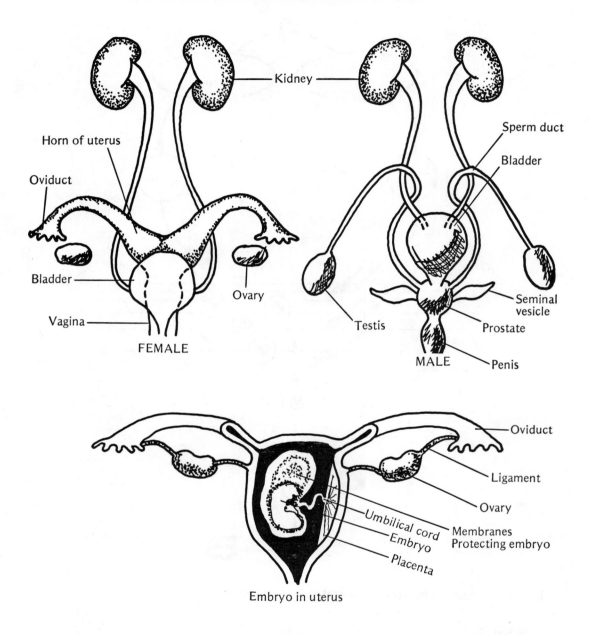

Kidney

Horn of uterus

Oviduct

Sperm duct

Bladder

Bladder

Ovary

Vagina

Testis

Seminal vesicle

Prostate

FEMALE

MALE

Penis

Oviduct

Ligament

Ovary

Umbilical cord

Embryo

Placenta

Membranes
Protecting embryo

Embryo in uterus

THE FEMALE HUMAN REPRODUCTIVE ORGANS

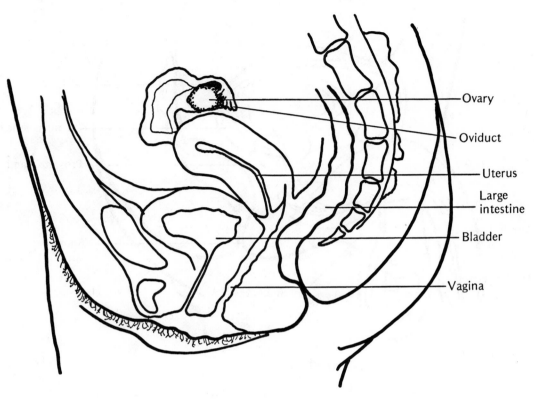

- Ovary
- Oviduct
- Uterus
- Large intestine
- Bladder
- Vagina

MEDIAN SECTION

THE MALE HUMAN REPRODUCTIVE ORGANS

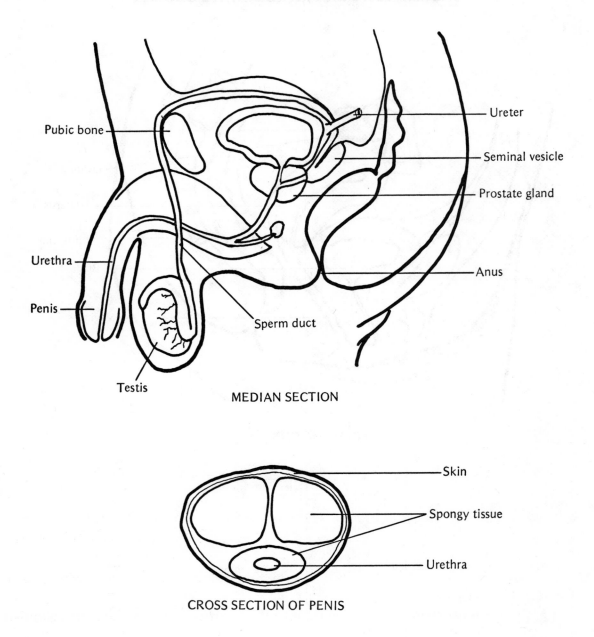

Pubic bone

Urethra

Penis

Testis

Ureter

Seminal vesicle

Prostate gland

Anus

Sperm duct

MEDIAN SECTION

Skin

Spongy tissue

Urethra

CROSS SECTION OF PENIS

THE HUMAN REPRODUCTIVE CYCLE

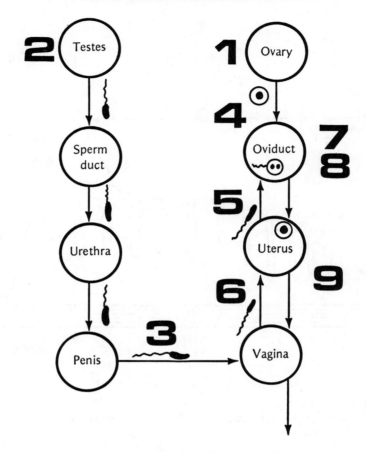

Critical Stages

1. Produces ovum or eggs.
2. Produces sperm (male gamete).
3. Sperm in seminal fluid must be ejaculated into the female through the vagina.
4. An egg is released into the oviduct, where it can meet sperm cells.
5. Sperm cells can remain alive for 2 or more days until one can meet with an egg and fertilize it.
6. Sperm must swim up the vagina into the uterus to the oviducts or Fallopian tubes, in order to fertilize an egg.
7. Sperm must be able to pass through the membrane of the ovum.
8. Only one sperm must enter one egg, where the two nuclei unite, forming a zygote.
9. The developing zygote becomes an embryo, being fixed to the wall of the uterus (womb), where it grows for approximately 281 days.

THE HUMAN MENSTRUAL CYCLE

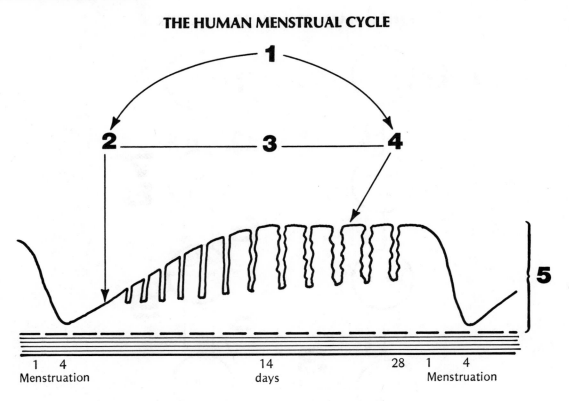

DIAGRAM OF MENSTRUAL CYCLE

1. Pituitary
2. Ovary—special cells that permit development of human egg cells
3. Ovulation
4. Yellow body—special cells—ovary—after ovulation
5. Lining of uterus

1. Explain the series of events in the menstrual cycle.

2. What is menstruation?

3. How is the lining of the uterus changed approximately every 28 days?

4. What causes the timing sequence of the reproductive cycle in the human female?

5. What seems to be the significance of menstruation?

6. What is the difference between menstruation and the estrous cycle?

EARLY DEVELOPMENT OF HUMAN EMBRYO

Sperm cell

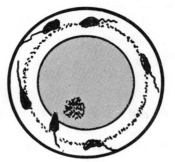

Egg cell—fertilization

Fertilized egg

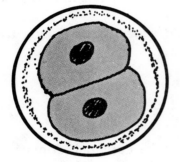

Two-celled embryo

Ball of cells

Hollow ball of cells

Embryo 5 weeks

PUNNETT SQUARES AND PREDICTIONS

If we know the genetic makeup of two parents with respect to a certain trait, we can determine in advance what type of offspring they can produce. Biologists have devised an easy tool, the *Punnett square,* to make such predictions.

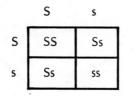

Over the two boxes on top, we put the *kind* of gametes the male or father can form.

Along the side boxes we put the *kind* of eggs the female or mother can produce.

By filling in each box, we can see the kind of zygotes (offspring) these parents might produce.

When you use the Punnett square method to solve a problem, it is important to set up a proper key as illustrated in the sample problem below:

Question: What are the possible offspring one could expect from mating two hybrid curly-tailed pigs?

Key

1. *Trait:* tail shape in pigs.

2. *Contrasting characteristics:* Let C represent the gene for curly tail (dominant). Let c represent the gene for straight tail (recessive).

3. *Cross between:* Two hybrid curly-tailed parents.

4. *Punnett square*

	C	c
C	CC	Cc
c	Cc	cc

5. *Analysis of results*

   a. *Phenotype ratio:* 3:1 (3 is the number of curly-tailed offspring and 1 is the number that will have straight tails)

   b. *Genotype ratio:* 1:2:1   1 is the number of pure dominant(s),
   2 is the number of hybrids,
   1 is the number of pure recessive(s).

Instead of using a ratio, we can express the phenotype in percentages, as follows: 75% curly and 25% straight. The genotype percentages would be 25% homozygous dominant, 50% heterozygous curly, and 25% homozygous recessive.

Problem: Show the results of the cross between a gray squirrel (pure) and a brown squirrel (recessive) using this method. *Note:* Traits considered dominant are usually represented by a capital letter; lowercase letters represent the recessive trait. (For example, Tt: T = tall, t = short).

The following are expected ratios of offspring from crossing parents with various genotypes for curly tails.

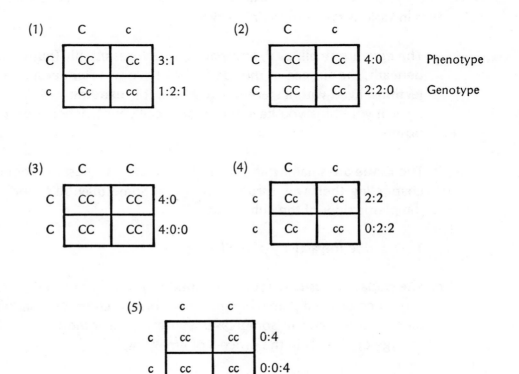

LIFE CYCLE OF THE DROSOPHILA

Aims

To familiarize ourselves with the life cycle of the common fruit fly, *Drosophila melanogaster,* and to learn the techniques involved in mating and raising fruit flies.

Procedures and Observations

A. *Life cycle:* Your teacher will distribute *culture vials* that contain numerous flies in various stages of their life cycle.

   a. The *eggs* are small, oval, transparent structures usually found on, or slightly beneath, the surface of the food. They have two slender antenna-like projections. Even with a stereomicroscope, it is extremely difficult to find the eggs. If you think you have found one, call your teacher over to verify your observation.

   b. The *larvae* are small, white, worm-like creatures. Most of them can be seen channeling their way through the food. Some may be found crawling up the plastic sides of the culture vial.

   1. *Describe the activity of the larvae.*

   c. The *pupas* are usually found attached to the side of the culture vial. They vary in color from pale white to a dark brown color. The darker pupas are more mature, and in some cases you can find some with adults ready to emerge or already in the process of emerging.

   d. The *adults* are easily observable flying about the culture vial.

   2. *From your observations, in which two stages of its metamorphosis is the fruit fly most active?*

   3. *What type of insect metamorphosis is found in the fruit fly?*

B. *Preparing a culture vial:* Your teacher will demonstrate the correct method for preparing a culture vial:

a. Take a clean culture vial and add 1 *level* cup of instant drosophila medium.

b. Using another cup of the same size, add 1 level cup of water.

c. Add a pinch of dry, activated yeast.

d. Insert a piece of nylon netting.

e. Cork the top with foam rubber stopper and plastic cap.

C. *Introducing males and females into your new culture vial:* In order to start a new population in the culture vial you have made, you must introduce 3 males and 3 females. This involves two problems: (1) identifying males and females, and (2) transferring flies from one culture vial to the next without losing them.

a. *Transferring flies:* Your teacher will demonstrate the correct way to etherize your flies. You should work in pairs, with one person handling the culture vial and the other person working the etherizer.

4. *Describe the technique you used to keep the adult flies at the bottom of the vial while you removed the top and replaced it with the etherizer.*

5. *Describe some of the difficulties you had in getting the adults unconscious.*

6. *How can you overcome these difficulties next time?*

7. *How will you know if you have overetherized and killed the flies?*

8. *Why should the room be well ventilated and without any flame or spark of any kind during this step of the lab?*

b. *Identifying the sexes:* Draw two circles on the piece of filter paper provided and label one male and the other female. Dump all the unconscious fruit flies on the filter paper with all the males in the appropriate circle and all the females in the female circle.

9. *Why do we use a soft camel hair brush in moving the unconscious flies?*

Although there are several differences in the two sexes, the following will be most helpful during this exercise:

- The male is slightly smaller than the female.

- The abdomen of the male is rounded; the female abdomen is more pointed.

- When looking at the dorsal tip of the abdomen, you will see that the male has a thick black band at the tip that is not found on the female.

All of these observations are best made using a hand lens or stereomicroscope.

10. *What structure is found on the front legs of the male that is missing from the female?*

Once you feel that you have successfully located 3 males and 3 females, call your teacher over to verify your observation. Now lay the culture vial you prepared previously on its side and remove the top. Gently, using the brush, move the 3 males and the 3 females and place them in the culture vial. Replace the gauze top. Keep the vial on its side until the flies awaken.

11. *Why should the vial be kept on its side until the flies awake?*

12. *If the females you just introduced started laying eggs today, how long would it be before these eggs emerge from their pupa as adults?*

Conclusions and Discussions

1. List six reasons why the fruit fly is an excellent organism to use in genetics experiments.

2. When a new female emerges from her pupal stage, she does not mate immediately. How long before she mates?

3. Why is this time interval important if you want to use this female in a genetics experiment?

4. In fruit flies, there are two contrasting characteristics with reference to the trait of wing length. An individual either has long wings (normal) or short wings (vestigial). Can you devise an experiment to show if Mendel's principle of dominance occurs with respect to the trait of wing length in fruit flies?

DOMINANCE AND SEGREGATION IN DROSOPHILA

Aim

To verify Mendel's principles of dominance and segregation by crossing two strains of drosophila.

Procedure and Observations

A. *First laboratory period:* Your teacher will provide you with two culture vials. The first will contain a pure culture of flies that possess a mutant condition known as *vestigial* wing.

   1. *Draw a diagram of one of these flies showing the shape and size of the wing.*

   The second culture vial will contain a pure culture of flies with normal wings that are long. These are often called the "wild strain."
   Prepare a new culture vial just as you did in the previous lab. Etherize the flies in the vestigial vial and isolate 3 males with vestigial wing. Place these males in your new culture vial, remembering to keep the vial on its side until the flies awaken. Now etherize all the flies in the wild culture and isolate 3 *virgin* females with long wings. Introduce these 3 females into the vial with the 3 vestigial males. Make sure you label the vial as your teacher indicates.

   2. *Explain how you can be sure that any females obtained from the vial culture must be virgins.*

   3. *Why is it wise to add at least 3 flies of each sex?*

B. *Second Laboratory Period:* One week after the first lab period, etherize the adults in your culture vial and remove them to the morgue.

   4. *After you have removed the adults, observe the vial. Is there any evidence that the flies successfully mated?*

   5. *Why do we remove the original parents from the vial?*

C. *Third Laboratory Period:* 10 to 12 days after the first laboratory period, the vial should contain newly emerged members of the first generation (F_1).
   Prepare a new culture vial. Etherize the members of the F_1 generation and place 3 long-wing males along with 3 long-wing females in the new vial. Label this vial and set it aside for the next laboratory period. Place all the remaining flies of the F_1 generation back in the etherizer. Overetherize these flies. When you are sure they are dead (check the wing position to determine this), dump the flies on a piece of filter paper. Using the chart below, count the number of flies in each category.

	Male	Female
Long wing		
Vestigial wing		

When you fill in the table, make sure you include the 6 flies that you put in the new culture vial.

6. On the basis of your observation of the F_1 generation, describe the phenotypes with respect to wing length that you obtained.

7. Which characteristic seemed to disappear in the first generation?

8. If the original parents were pure (homozygous) for their traits, what can you predict about all the individuals of the F_1 generation?

D. *Fourth Laboratory Period:* A week after the third laboratory period, remove the F_1 parents from the culture vial.

E. *Fifth Laboratory Period:* 10 to 12 days after the third lab period, the vial should contain newly emerged members of the second filial generation (F_2). Over-etherize these flies and record their phenotypes in the chart below:

F_2 results	Male (number of flies)	Female (number of flies)
Long wing		
Vestigial wing		

Conclusions and Discussion

1. Assuming that the original parents in this experiment had the following genetic makeup with respect to wing length, LL and ll, show the Punnett square that predicts the kind of offspring they should have.

2. How do your actual results in the F_1 generation compare with this Punnett square?

3. Why can you conclude that the long-wing condition is a dominant characteristic?

4. Using a Punnett square, show the results you would expect to get from mating the members of the F_1 generation.

5. What percentage of the offspring in the F_2 generation of *your* experiment had short wings?

6. How does this compare with the expected results predicted by the Punnett square?

7. Which of Mendel's principles is indicated by: (a) your F_1 generation and (b) your F_2 generation.

PROBABILITY AND GENETICS

Aim

To determine the role chance plays in genetic ratios.

Procedures and Observations

Your teacher will supply you with a pair of dice. You will observe that each die has 3 *even* numbered surfaces (2, 4, 6) and 3 *odd* numbered surfaces (1, 3, 5)

1. *If you roll one die, what is the chance that an odd-numbered surface will come face up? An even-numbered surface?*

    Let us suppose that each die represents a parent that is hybrid for a particular trait. The odd-numbered surfaces represent the dominant allele, and the even-numbered surfaces represent the contrasting recessive allele. In a sense, rolling the dice would be like mating two hybrids, and each result would be a new zygote. Just as chance determines which gamete will take part in fertilization, it will also determine which surface of the die will come face up, an odd or an even.

2. *If you roll both dice together, what are the three possible combinations of odd- and even-numbered surfaces you can get?*

3. *If the dice were rolled a great many times, can you predict the ratio that would occur between those three possible combinations?*

Roll the dice 20 times and record the results in the table below:

Odd–Odd (OO)	Odd–Even (OE)	Even–Even (EE)

4. *Compute the ratio of OO:OE:EE after 20 trials. Convert this into percentages.*

5. *How does this ratio compare with your prediction in Question 3?*

Continue rolling the dice until you have 100 trials.

6. *Compute the ratio and the percentage on the basis of 100 trials.*

7. *Which ratio comes closer to your prediction: the one based on 20 trials or 100 trials?*

Your teacher will record the results for the entire class on the chalkboard.

8. *Of the three sets of results (20 trials, 100 trials, and the entire class), why would you expect the results of the whole class to come closest to your prediction in Question 3?*

Conclusions and Discussion

1. Two hybrid black guinea pigs were mated and only 3 offspring were obtained. How can you explain the fact that all 3 were white when the Punnett square predicts that 3 out of 4 offspring should be black?

2. A coin was flipped 9 times, and each time it landed heads up. What is the probability that it will be heads on the tenth toss? Explain.

3. Two coins were tossed simultaneously. What percentage of the tosses should wind up both heads, both tails, one head and one tail?

4. Explain how chance makes it possible for two brown-eyed parents to have four children, all with blue eyes.

MEIOSIS AND MENDEL'S PRINCIPLE OF SEGREGATION

When Mendel cross-pollinated two hybrid tall pea plants, a certain percentage (25 percent) of the offspring grew into short pea plants. The recessive trait that appeared to be hidden in the hybrid parent separated into gametes during meiosis and recombined at fertilization. The diagrams below illustrate this process:

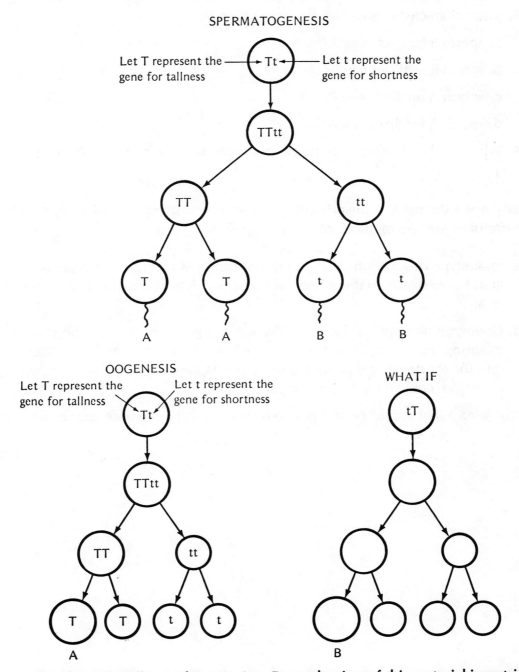

Answer the following questions referring to the diagrams on page 239:

1. Place the correct sequence of genes on the diagram on page 239 in which the circles are left blank.

2. What is the name given to the three smaller circles presented in the diagram?

3. What characteristics would the zygote have if:

   a. sperm B fertilizes egg A?

   b. sperm B fertilizes egg B?

   c. sperm A fertilizes egg B?

   d. sperm A fertilizes egg A?

4. What are the chances of getting a sperm cell with the gene for shortness (t)?

When we discuss the offspring that result from mating two parents, geneticists find it useful to use two methods of describing them.

a. *Phenotype description* describes the offspring as it actually appears by looking at it. For example, in the zygote where sperm A fertilizes egg A, the phenotype is tall.

b. *Genotype description* describes the kind of genes present in the cells of the offspring. For example, in the zygote where there is one gene for tallness and one for shortness, the phenotype of this offspring would be tall; however, the genotype would be hybrid or heterozygous.

Problem: What would be the genotype for the zygote where sperm A fertilizes egg A?

HOW IS EYE COLOR INHERITED IN FRUIT FLIES?

Your teacher will provide you with a pure culture of red-eyed drosophila and a pure culture of white-eyed drosophila.

Procedure

1. Describe the genetic makeup of the parents you will experimentally mate to demonstrate eye color inheritance.

2. How does the company that sold these pure cultures know that they are pure or homozygous for their particular characteristic?
   The females that you will use in your experimental mating must be virgin.

3. How can we know whether the females have not already mated with the wrong male genotypes?

Prepare a culture vial and introduce 3 males and 3 females of the genotype you have chosen. Place the vial in a safe place at room temperature for one week.

After 1 week, remove the 6 parents from the experimental vial. Restopper the vial, and put it in a safe place for another week.

4. Why are the original parents removed from the vials after 1 week?

At the end of 2 weeks, etherize all the offspring in the experimental vial and categorize them in the chart below. (List numbers for each characteristic.)

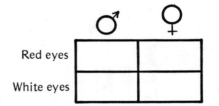

Conclusions

1. What conclusions can you arrive at on the basis of your class's results? Explain fully.

2. Using an appropriate key, show the Punnett square for your experimental mating.

3. How do your actual percentages compare with the percentages predicted by the Punnett square? How do you explain these deviations between the expected results and the actual results?

4. Were there any offspring genotypes that your Punnett square did not predict?

5. How do you account for any exceptions listed in Question 4?

6. What parents would have to be mated in order to get females with white eyes? Show all possibilities, assuming that the laws of chance operate.

HEMOPHILIA: QUEEN VICTORIA'S PEDIGREE CHART

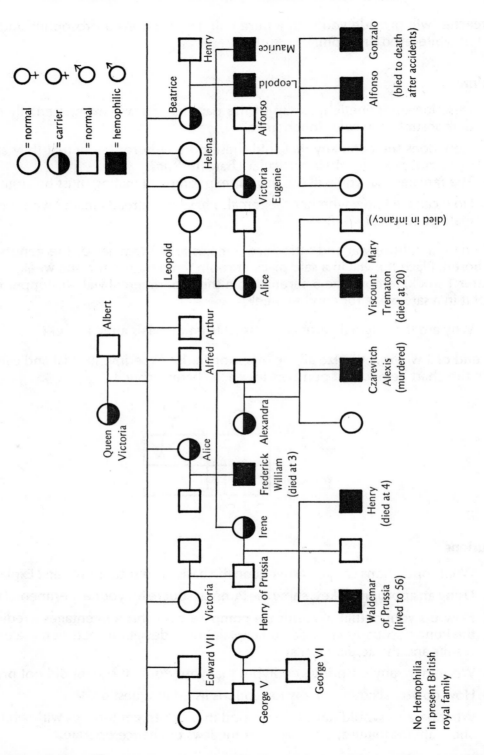

EXPERIMENT 1: PNEUMOCOCCUS TRANSFORMATION

Facts

    a. Pneumococcus bacteria with capsules can cause pneumonia in humans.

    b. Pneumococcus bacteria without capsules are harmless to humans because the white blood cells can engulf them.

 Capsule    No capsule

Question 1. What relationship seems to exist between the two types of bacteria and our phagocyte defense mechanism?

Facts

    a. When pneumococcus bacteria with capsules reproduce by mitotic fission, the daughter cells also produce capsules.

Question 2. What does this suggest about the appearance of capsules?

Facts

    a. The experiment diagramed below was carried out with the results indicated.

       1. In test tube 1, pneumococcus bacteria *without capsules* were grown on an agar slant.

       2. In the second phase of the experiment (diagram 2), a drop of solution containing *dead* pneumococci *with capsules* was added.

       3. A week later, the original test tube was studied again, and it was found that there were some colonies of *living* pneumococcus bacteria *with capsules.*

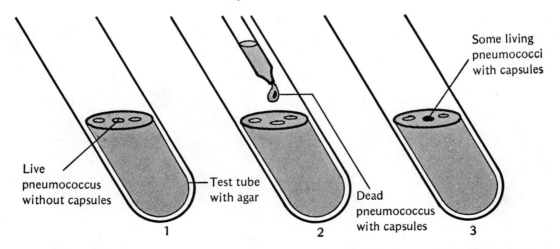

Question 3.   What conclusion can be drawn from this experiment?

Question 4.   How would you go about finding out which part of the pneumococcus cell carried the information for the formation of capsules?

     Avery, MacLeod, and McCarty had a hunch that the transforming principle was DNA. They took some DNA from dead pneumococcus bacteria with capsules and placed it in contact with living pneumococcus that did not form capsules. The DNA entered the bacterial cell and became part of that cell's hereditary material. The transformed cell and all its offspring formed capsules, thereby showing that the gene for capsule formation was actually in the form of DNA.

EXPERIMENT 2: BACTERIOPHAGE REPRODUCTION

Certain viruses, called *bacteriophages,* infect and destroy bacteria. A bacteriophage virus is composed of a central core of DNA surrounded by a protein shell.

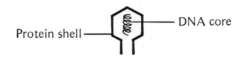

Protein shell ——— DNA core

Evidence indicates the virus somehow assumes command of the bacterial ribosomes and directs the production of virus protein and DNA rather than bacterial protein and DNA. Eventually the bacterial cell ruptures, releasing new viruses. The diagram below illustrates the process.

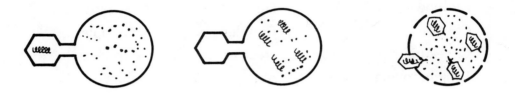

Question: How would you go about determining whether it was the DNA core or the protein shell that entered the bacteria and directed the production of more viruses?

Protein shell labelled with_____

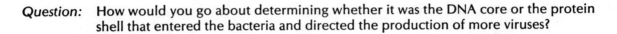

DNA labelled with_____

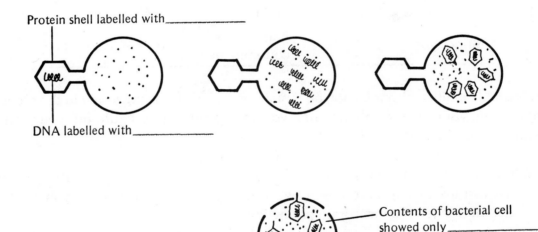

Contents of bacterial cell showed only_____

The experiment we have just outlined was originally carried out by Dr. Hershey and Dr. Chase, and it was shown that the viral DNA enters the bacteria cell, further proof that genetic information is somehow coded in the form of DNA.

CHARACTERISTIC TRAITS IN MY FAMILY

Procedure: The chart below lists several human traits. Also indicated are the dominant and recessive contrasting characteristics for each trait.

Trait	Dominant Characteristic	Recessive Characteristic
Color of iris	Nonblue	Blue
Color vision	Normal	Color blind
Hair texture (incomplete dominance)	Curly Wavy	Straight
Ear lobe	Free	Attached
Cheeks	Dimples	No dimples
Cheek pigment	Freckles	No freckles
Tongue rolling	Ability	Inability
Tasting PTC	Ability	Inability
Middigital hair	Hair	No hair
Thumb folding	Left over right	Right over left
Handedness	Right	Left
Blood type	A and B are codominant	O

Fill in the table entitled "Your Genotype" using the key of alleles suggested in the second column. From your parents' phenotypes, you should be able to figure out your genotype for most of the traits listed above.

1. If both of your parents show the dominant phenotype for a particular trait, we will assume that you are homozygous dominant for that trait. Why might this assumption lead to inaccurate predictions later on?

2. If you have the dominant characteristic for a particular trait, and both your parents also have the dominant characteristic, what would the existence of a brother or sister with the recessive characteristic tell you about the genotype of your parents?

Your Genotype

Trait	Alleles	Your Phenotype	Mother's Phenotype	Father's Phenotype	Your Genotype
Color of iris	B – brown b – blue				
Color vision	X^N – normal X^C – color blind				
Hair texture	C – curly c – straight				
Ear lobe	F – free f – attached				
Cheeks	D – dimples d – no dimples				
Freckles	F – freckles f – no freckles				
Tongue rolling	A – ability a – inability				
Taste PTC	T – taster t – non-taster				
Middigital hair	H – hair h – no hair				
Thumb folding	L – left over right l – right over left				
Handedness	R – right r – left				
Blood type	I^A – type A I^B – type B i – Type 0				

Once you have completed "Your Genotype," we will supply you with a mate chosen at random from the other members of your class. The both of you should fill in the table entitled "Your Future Children." Make sure you show each Punnett square and analyze the offspring using percentages.

3. What is the difference between "expected results" and "observed results"? In other words, why are the offspring we predict using Punnett squares often different from the actual offspring?

4. Which one of your Punnett squares (if any) would illustrate Mendel's principle of dominance?

5. In what way does the inheritance of color vision differ from the other traits on the lists?

6. In what way is the inheritance of blood types different from the other traits listed?

7. Select one trait for which you have the most reliable information with respect to your grandparents and construct a keyed pedigree chart using your maternal and paternal grandparents as the first (P) generation. If you have a small family, you might also include aunts, uncles, and cousins.

Example

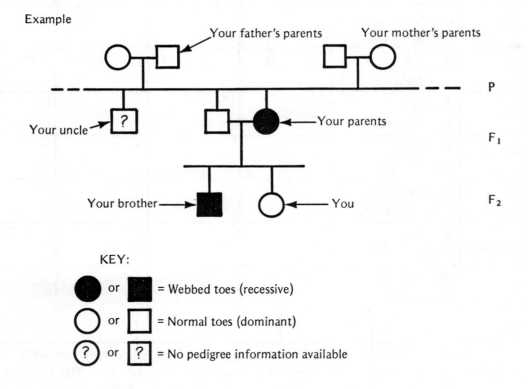

Your Future Children

Trait	Your Genotype	Mate's Genotype	Punnett Square	Analysis of Punnett Square
Color of iris				
Color vision				
Hair texture				
Ear lobe				
Dimples				
Freckles				
Tongue rolling				
Taste PTC				
Middigital hair				
Thumb folding				
Handedness				
Blood type				

PLANT AND ANIMAL BREEDING

Plant and animal breeders use modern genetic principles to obtain:

1. Increased quantity: Bigger corn, larger cattle, more milk.

2. Increased quality: Sweeter apples, leaner meat.

3. Immunity to disease: Cattle free from Texas fever, wheat immune to rust (fungus infection).

4. New varieties: Hornless cattle, seedless fruits, nectarine.

Methods Used by Breeders

1. *Artificial selection:* From each generation we select parents having the good traits we desire, and we breed only these parents. For example, race horses are selected on the basis of speed, and cattle selected for breeding are those with the highest milk yield.

2. *Hybridization:* The breeder mates two parents, each of which has a desired trait. He or she hopes that the offspring (the hybrid) will inherit both desired traits. Examples: the mule results from mating a female horse and a male donkey; Texas Brahman cow results from mating a Texas shorthorn (good-quality meat) and a Brahman (immune to Texas fever); zebroid (zebra and horse); tiglon (tiger and lion).

3. *Inbreeding:* The mating or crossing of two offspring (animal or plant) having the same parents. A bull and a cow from the same parents may both have the good trait we desire. By mating this brother and sister, we will have a much better chance of getting the desired trait again in their offspring. Generations of inbreeding produces highly pure individuals for the desired trait.

4. *Vegetative propagation:* Reproducing asexually by grafting, cuttings, bulbs, and so forth. If a plant has a desired trait, we can be sure the offspring will receive the trait because they will be exactly like the parent. Examples are seedless oranges and seedless grapes.

5. *Use of mutations:* Mutations occur spontaneously. Most are recessive and disadvantageous; however, occasionally a good mutation occurs. If the breeder selects this mutant for breeding, he or she can obtain more by using inbreeding, vegetative propagation, or other methods. Examples of useful mutations are hornless cattle (a rare dominant mutation), nectarines, and seedless fruits.

Problem: Describe how you might breed a variety of corn that has large kernels and is sweet tasting.

A FIVE-KINGDOM CLASSIFICATION TREE

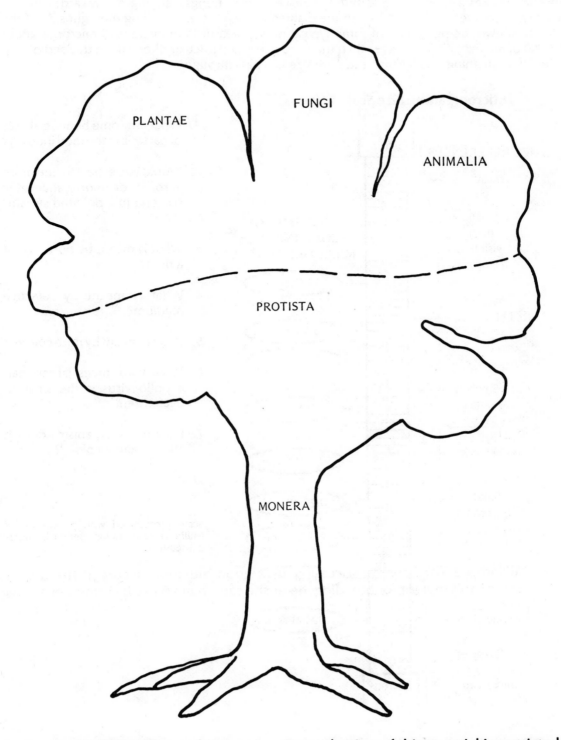

MICROORGANISM SIZE SCALE CHART

This chart makes a size scale of a number of very small things, ranging downward from the thickness of an average human hair to the diameter of a polio virus. Along the right side of the scale are shown the pore sizes of some typical filters, measured in microns (1 micron is about 1/25,000 of an inch). Things bigger than the pore size of a particular filter will be trapped on top of the filter; anything smaller than the pore size will pass through.

Microorganism Size Scale Chart

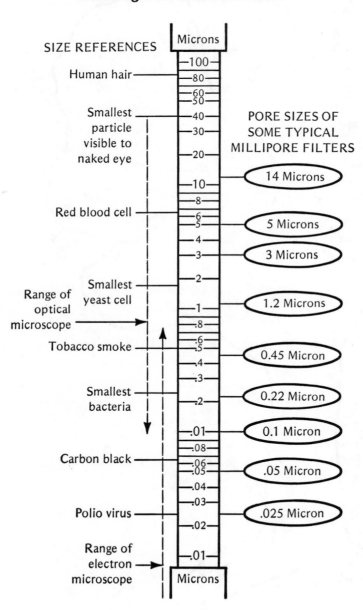

1. What are some beneficial uses of bacteria in the food industry?

2. Would you expect to find more *aerobic* or more *anaerobic* bacteria in a polluted stream? Why?

3. What is meant by *pore size* of a filter?

4. What is meant by *selective medium*?

5. What is meant by *pure culture*?

6. How many times larger than a polio virus is the smallest bacterium?

7. How many organisms does it take to start a colony?

Scale reproduced with permission of Millipore Corporation, Bedford, Massachusetts 01730.

MICROORGANISMS IN THE AIR

No *special* species of bacteria or other microorganisms inhabit the air . . . the kinds found there depend entirely on what particular sources are stirred up in the immediate vicinity. On a windy day, the air above a dusty field would contain the same types that are found in the soil. In places where many people congregate, microorganisms are often dispersed into the air by coughs, sneezes, or even vigorous talk. Usually, these are the normal bacteria found in the throat and mouth, but sometimes they are pathogenic. Transmission of disease from one person to another by coughing or sneezing is quite common, and is known as *droplet infection*. In a room containing a number of people, therefore, we'd expect to find airborne soil bacteria (from the dust), along with a number of other types coming from the people themselves. If the air in the room is undisturbed by any convection currents, the bacteria will slowly settle, and the air will become virtually sterile. Sweeping with a broom tends to disperse microorganisms into the air, while a vacuum cleaner of good design collects them along with the dirt and dust, and traps them in its tank. The following experiment demonstrates the presence of bacteria and molds in the air, and shows why the microbiologist must continually protect his experiments from airborne contamination.

1. Using a Millipore Filtration System, prepare four petri dishes with absorbent pads and Total Count (yellow) medium.

2. Place a Type HAWG filter on each pad, replace the petri dish covers, and mark each dish with your name, the experiment number, and date.

3. Label one of the dishes with the word CONTROL. In any scientific experiment, you must make as certain as possible that the results are not due to some factor you had ignored, or to an error. In this case, the "control" filter will indicate whether or not there is a flaw in the experiment, due perhaps to nonsterile filters, petri dishes, or medium or to a fault in aseptic technique.

4. Label dish No. 2, OUTSIDE AIR - 30 MIN.; No. 3, INSIDE AIR - 90 MIN.; and No. 4, DUST.

Reproduced with permission of Millipore Corporation, Bedford, Massachusetts 01730.

5. Place dish No. 2 outside in a convenient location, and remove the cover. After 30 minutes, replace the cover . . . unless there is snow on the ground, in which case leave the cover off for one hour and change the label accordingly. Snow reduces the opportunity for microorganisms to become airborne.

6. Place dish No. 3 in the classroom, and leave the cover off for 90 minutes.

7. Find some dry dust, and blow a little of it lightly over the surface of the filter in dish No. 4.

8. After completing the required exposure periods, incubate the closed petri dishes at normal room temperature. Examine them after 48 hours, one week, and two weeks.

Use a magnifying glass to see more detail. Bacterial colonies will show up as red dots, mostly round, but sometimes spreading out in a lopsided way. Yeast colonies will be characteristically grayish or greenish, slightly raised, and slightly oval. They grow fast, and will quickly take up more room than bacterial colonies of the same age . . . also, an individual yeast cell is a lot bigger than an individual bacterium. Mold has a stringy look, and in fact is made up of huge numbers of filaments (mycelium) having varied and elaborate structures. Mold colors can sometimes be quite vivid (there is one bright orange one that grows on sugar cane waste), but most of them are gray or green. All are fast growers, so in time your bacterial colonies could get totally buried under a combination of yeast and mold.

Questions for Review and Discussion

1. When would the chances of droplet infection inside a public building be greater: summer or winter? Why?

2. Do you think bacterial cells grow or multiply while suspended in the air? Why?

3. List ways to avoid contaminating a culture of bacteria when it is being transferred from one test tube to another with a loop.

BACTERIA AND THE HUMAN BODY

The human body has a number of highly effective defenses against serious bacterial invasion. On the simple structural level, the skin (if unbroken) is an impenetrable barrier to microorganisms. The thinner membranes, such as those around the eyes and in the nose and throat, are more easily penetrated by bacteria, but in a healthy person these areas are further protected by secretions . . . such as tears, sweat, and mucus . . . which themselves have a bacteriostatic or even bacteriocidal effect. Once these surface tissues are penetrated, still another line of defense is aroused, in the chemistry of body fluids such as blood serum, and the activity of specialized cells such as leukocytes (white blood cells) which energetically destroy bacteria.

The body plays continual host to a "normal flora" of bacteria, on the skin and in body secretions. The vast majority of these microorganisms are totally harmless, and in fact may play an active part in restraining the aggressions of the pathogenic types. However, when the body's tissues are penetrated, or its defense mechanisms are weakened by fatigue or an injury, the chance of pathogenic infection is increased. This is why such extreme precautions are taken during surgery, and in the care of people who are very ill, or very old, or very new.

This experiment is in two parts. The first demonstrates the existence of bacteria on our hands, by "culturing" a fingerprint. Though tough skin protects the hands themselves, these bacteria are easily transferred to more susceptible tissue or to food. Washing with soap and water does not kill bacteria, but does send a lot of them down the drain, where the few pathogenic ones among them have far less chance of doing any harm.

1. Using a Millipore Filtration System, prepare a petri dish with an absorbent pad saturated with Total Count medium, and using flamed forceps place a Type HAWG filter on top of the absorbent pad.

2. Press your thumb firmly on the wet filter.

3. Cover the petri dish, label it "BEFORE WASHING," and incubate at normal room temperature.

4. Prepare a second petri dish and test filter in the same manner, wash your hands thoroughly with soap and water, and dry them with a fresh paper towel. Then press your thumb firmly on this second test filter. Cover the petri dish, label it "AFTER WASHING," and incubate at normal room temperature or at 37°C if an incubator is available.

Reproduced with permission of Millipore Corporation, Bedford, Massachusetts 01730.

5. After 48 hours at room temperature or 24 hours at 37°C, examine both test filters. The difference between the numbers of colonies on the BEFORE and AFTER filters is a rough indication of how washing reduces the number of bacteria on your hands.

The second part of the experiment shows the existence of bacteria in our mouths. Something very much like this might be done by a doctor, to help him determine if a sore throat is due to dangerously pathogenic bacteria, or is just an aggravated symptom of a common cold.

1. Using procedures described by the teacher, prepare the following:

   a. Sterifil apparatus, with Type HAWG filter.

   b. Swinnex-25 Holder, with Type GS filter.

   c. One petri dish, with absorbent pad and Total Count medium.

2. Using a syringe, filter 20 ml of dechlorinated water through the Swinnex-25 into the Sterifil funnel. On filling the syringe, remember to remove the Swinnex before drawing up unfiltered water into the barrel.

3. Rub a sterile cotton swab against the inner surfaces of your mouth.

4. Swirl the swab in the sterile water. Be careful not to touch the test filter with the cotton tip of the swab, as this might rupture the filter.

5. Apply vacuum, and filter the sample through the test filter.

6. Using flamed forceps, transfer the test filter to the pad in the petri dish. Replace the cover, and culture at normal room temperature for 48 hours, or at 37°C for 24 hours.

7. Repeat the experiment, after using an ordinary mouthwash. The difference in number of colonies on the two test filters is a rough indication of mouthwash effectiveness in reducing bacteria in the mouth.

Questions

1. Why is a puncture wound more dangerous than an open cut?

2. What factors will alter or affect the natural balance of bacterial flora in your mouth?

BE A DISEASE DETECTIVE

Society's disease detective is an epidemiologist (ep uh dee mee AHL uh jist). An epidemiologist studies epidemics. Disease detectives investigate the causes of communicable diseases, the behavior of the disease, how the disease spreads, where it occurs, what form it takes, how to cure it, and how to prevent it.

Throughout history, epidemiologists have investigated such diseases as the plague, (playg), malaria, typhoid fever, polio, tetanus, diphtheria, and whooping cough. Today epidemics of these diseases are rare and epidemiologists are becoming more concerned with conditions such as stroke, cancer, heart disease, arthritis, loneliness, accidents, suicide, and venereal disease. The modern definition of epidemiology (ep uh dee mee AHL uh jee) has become broader with the addition of conditions like loneliness and accidents. However, a disease detective still looks for the causes of the condition, where it most often occurs, how it is spread, and how it can be prevented.

How are you at detective work? How would you go about stopping an epidemic that was affecting more and more people every day? What agencies could give you support? Who would you go to for help? If you are interested in learning about disease detective work, complete the following activity.

1. Work alone or with a classmate. Choose *one* of the following behaviors, conditions, or diseases to study.

   a. Coughing and shortness of breath due to smoking
   b. Problem drinking
   c. Cancer
   d. Heart disease
   e. Stroke
   f. Arthritis (ahr THRIGHT is)
   g. Accidents
   h. Suicide
   i. Syphilis (SIF uh lis)
   j. Obesity
   k. Ulcers
   l. Headaches
   m. Acne
   n. Colds
   o. Influenza
   p. Allergies
   q. Dental disease
   r. Gonorrhea (gahn uh REE uh)
   s. Tuberculosis (too bur kyuh LOH sis)
   t. AIDS
   u. Herpes

   Note: Pick one that has made the biggest impression on you. Choose the disease or condition that you believe should be eliminated first.

2. Use the "Be a Disease Detective: An Epidemiological Study" sheets to help you do an epidemiological study. Find the answers to as many of the questions as you can. Do not be overly concerned if you cannot answer all the questions. A

Reproduced with permission of National Science Programs, Inc. BSCS, *Feeling Fit*, Human Science Program.

disease detective puts as many clues as possible together to find an answer to the problem. Choose one or several of the following sources to help you find the necessary information.

a. Library resources: Encyclopedias and books on diseases, epidemiology, and personal health. Ask the librarian for help.

b. City or county health department: Call for an interview. Have a prepared list of questions.

c. School nurse.

d. Local city and county nurses, doctors, dentists, and other health workers.

e. Health science, health education, or public health department at a nearby university or college.

f. State department of health: Write a letter or make a phone call. Make sure you have studied the disease before you contact the department. Prepare five to ten questions to ask. Ask for any additional information about the disease they might send you.

g. Write to the Bureau of State Services, National Center of Disease Control, Atlanta, Georgia 30333. Study the condition or disease first so that you can ask intelligent questions.

h. Write to the National Institute of Health, 9000 Rockville Pike, Bethesda, Maryland 20014.

Review all of the data you have collected. Decide how you will proceed to control, prevent, and cure the epidemic. Use the Disease Prevention and Control Worksheets to help plan your attack.

This worksheet has three main parts: health educator, medical personnel, and community health worker.

If you were a health educator responsible for communicating general knowledge in the fields of health and disease, what would you do? Complete the "Health Educator" part of the worksheet.

If you were a doctor, nurse or therapist (medical personnel), what would you do? Complete the "Medical Personnel" part of the worksheet.

If you were a community health worker, a person working to improve health conditions in a particular community, what would you do? Complete the "Community Health Worker" part of the worksheet.

Communicate What You Learned

Write an article for your class health journal about what you learned, or get together with several students who have done this activity and discuss what they have learned. You might want to have an all-class discussion.

Name _____

Date _____

BE A DISEASE DETECTIVE:
AN EPIDEMIOLOGICAL STUDY — PAGE 1

Disease being studied: _____

   A. Condition or behavior: _____

   B. Signs and symptoms: _____

        _____

   C. Tissue or organ destruction due to disease or condition:

        _____

   D. Estimated number of cases in your community: _____ In the U.S. _____

   E. Locations in your community where disease is most prevalent:

        _____

   F. Months of year in which the condition or disease is most prevalent:

        Jan. _____ Feb. _____ Mar. _____ Apr. _____ May _____ June _____

        July _____ Aug. _____ Sept. _____ Oct. _____ Nov. _____ Dec. _____

   G. Age groups most often affected: _____

   H. Sex most often affected: (check one)   male _____ female _____

   I. Personality characteristics of the individuals who have such a condition:

        _____

        _____

   J. Race most often affected in: 1940 _____ 1980 _____

   K. Number of deaths/100,000 people/year in the U.S. _____

   L. Reported incidences of the condition or disease in the following decades:

        1900 _____ 1920 _____ 1930 _____ 1940 _____

        1950 _____ 1960 _____ 1970 _____ 1980 _____

   M. Organism, if any, that causes the disease or condition:

        Name: _____

        Description: _____ | Draw Picture:

Environmental factors (pollutants, noise, stress, water contaminants, (etc.) that contribute to condition or disease: _____

_____

How is the disease or condition transmitted? (peer pressure, insect, wind, heredity, kissing, etc.) _____

Incubation period (time organism or stress factor is acting on body before first symptoms appear): _____

Nutrition of individuals affected: (check)   Calorie: High _____ Low _____

Cholesterol: High _____ Low _____ Balanced _____ Not balanced _____

Diet: Meat _____ Vegetarian _____ Vitamins: Adequate _____ Inadequate _____

Physical fitness level of victims: (check)

_____ Excellent   (exercises regularly; low pulse rate and blood pressure; strong and flexible; high endurance)

_____ Good   (exercises regularly; moderate pulse rate, blood pressure, and endurance)

_____ Poor   (exercises occasionally; high blood pressure and pulse rate; not flexible; weak and low endurance)

Special health habits of victim (e.g., drinks liquor, cigarette smoker, race car driver):

_____

Vaccines available: _____

Cures available: _____

Preventive programs available: _____

_____

Other: _____

_____

Name _____

Date _____

DISEASE PREVENTION AND CONTROL WORKSHEET

Disease being studied: _____

Health Educator

A. *How* would you communicate about the disease?

_____

B. *What* would you communicate?

_____

C. Whom would you communicate to? (age, sex, race and special characteristics of audience to which the program is directed)

_____

Medical Personnel

A. What type of medical examination would be used?

_____

B. What drugs would be used? Why?

_____

C. What other therapies would be used?

_____

D. Other

_____

Community Health Worker

A. What should be done in my community?

_____

B. How could this work be financed? Whom do I contact? What governmental agencies can help?

_____

C. What community agencies (churches, free clinics, PTAs, etc.) can be contacted to help?

_____

D. Other

_____

WATER DENSITY MEASUREMENTS

Record your data from your samples of water obtained from the marine environment as follows:

Sample	Hydrometer Reading	Temperature	Correction Factor	Density 15°C	Salinity (ppt-o/oo)
1.					
2.					
3.					
4.					
5.					

Questions

1. What are the advantages and disadvantages of using the hydrometer for salinity measurements?

2. What other physical methods are used for measuring salinity?

3. What is the effect of barometric pressure on hydrometer readings?

4. What are the effects of dissolved gases on hydrometer readings and water density?

5. How do suspended particles affect water density?

6. How does a hydrometer work?

CASE STUDY ANALYSIS: A CRASH LANDING

You are on a jet plane with a large crew and passengers from all walks of life heading toward the Hawaiian Islands. All of a sudden, a fuel leak causes the plane to go out of control. The computer, which is navigating the ship, flashes an emergency signal for a crash landing. The entire crew readies for the crash even though no one knows where they will eventually land.

Here is a list of some of the people aboard the ship with you. Whom would you prefer to survive to ensure that you can survive the hardships ahead? Indicate your choices and rank them in order of preference from 1 to 10. (Assume that only 10 will survive the crash landing.)

A botanist	_____	A lawyer	_____	Women and children	_____
A zoologist	_____	A sexy model	_____	An engineer	_____
A geologist	_____	An artist	_____	A computer expert	_____
An astronomer	_____	A priest	_____	An actor	_____
A wrestler	_____	Your brother	_____	An author	_____
A physician	_____	A four-star general	_____	Your sister	_____
Your father	_____	A pianist	_____	Your best friend	_____
Your mother	_____	A farmer	_____	A carpenter	_____
A cripple	_____	An inventor	_____	A hunter	_____

CASE STUDY ANALYSIS: ITEMS NEEDED FOR SURVIVAL

Using the case in Reproduction Page 66, we find that in addition to people needed for survival, we also need some items that were taken on the trip. Rank in order of preference the items you would consider the most important for your survival. (#1 being most important)

Pots and pans	_____	Mink coat	_____
Portable television set	_____	Stocks and bonds	_____
Clothing	_____	Money and jewelry	_____
Musical instruments	_____	Electric saw	_____
Transistor radio	_____	Museum painting	_____
Bible	_____	Crucifix	_____
Fishing tackle	_____	Cigarette lighter	_____
Hunting knife	_____	Flashlight and batteries	_____
Rifle and shells	_____	Book of matches	_____
Deck of playing cards	_____	Vegetable seeds	_____
Ten bags of pretzels	_____	Rope and string	_____
Chess set	_____	Ten chickens and two roosters	_____
100 cartons of cigarettes	_____	Pair of cows and bull	_____
Book on survival	_____	Case of canned food	_____
Case of bottled water	_____	Case of beer	_____

SEXUALLY TRANSMITTED DISEASES: WHAT ARE YOUR QUESTIONS?

What additional information would you like to know about venereal disease, now called sexually transmitted disease (STD)? For example:

- What are some common types of sexually transmitted diseases?

- How common are sexually transmitted diseases in your community?

- What laws apply to people in your state who have this type of disease?

- How can you be tested for various types of sexually transmitted diseases?

- Why might people avoid getting treatment?

With a group of friends, make up a list of questions about VD or STD that you would like to have answered. Try to find answers to your questions by:

a. Reading books or magazine articles on venereal diseases that may be borrowed from your library.

b. Visiting the VD clinic in your community, hospital, or public health department.

c. Talking with a nurse or VD worker.

d. Inviting a person from the VD clinic in your area to visit your classroom. Have a question-and-answer period to find out more about venereal disease.

e. Calling a VD hotline.

APPENDIX **C**

Feedback Form

Your comments about this book will be very helpful to us in planning other books in the *Guidebook for Teaching* Series and in making revisions in *A Guidebook for Teaching Biology*. Please tear out the form that appears on the following page and use it to let us know your reactions to *A Guidebook for Teaching Biology*. The authors promise a personal reply. Mail the form to:

Longwood Division
Allyn and Bacon, Inc.
7 Wells Avenue
Newton, Massachusetts 02159

Your school: _____

Address: _____

City and State: _____

Date: _____

Longwood Division
Allyn and Bacon, Inc.
7 Wells Avenue
Newton, Massachusetts 02159

Dear Longwood Press:

My name is _____ and I wanted to tell you what
I thought of your book, *A Guidebook for Teaching Biology*. I liked certain things about
the book, including:

I do, however, feel that the book could be improved in the following ways:

There are some other things I wish the book had included, such as:

Here is something that happened in my class when I used an idea from your book:

Sincerely yours,

_____